POLITICAL AND SCIENTIFIC ARTICLES

POLITICAL AND SCIENTIFIC ARTICLES

VOLUME 3

Gerald McIsaac

ISBN: 978-1-957009-02-5 (hc)
ISBN: 978-1-957009-03-2 (sc)
ISBN: 978-1-957009-04-9 (e)

Library of Congress Control Number: 2021924323

TABLE OF CONTENTS

PREFACE

Since I first began to publish, various people have approached me to express their concern and confusion, as regards to "what I am" and "what I am trying to do". They are of the opinion that I should confine myself to either political or scientific articles, but not both.

To this, I can only respond that such a division is simply not possible. The political and scientific are tied together, and both are tied to the cultural and historic. They are all part of one huge body of civilized society, and as such, it is not possible to separate them. Further, capitalism has sunken its tentacles into every aspect of this society. As a result of this, all branches of society are contaminated.

I maintain that the capitalists must be challenged, and not just in the political arena. The fact is that they are deeply entrenched in all fields of culture and science. They must be allowed no peace.

This is class warfare, the working class against the capitalists, the proletariat against the bourgeois. It is just a matter of time, and very likely a short time, before the working class rises up in open rebellion. We had best be prepared.

After the revolution, the capitalists will be overthrown but not destroyed. By contrast, the existing state apparatus will be destroyed and replaced with a different state apparatus, set up to crush the desperate and determined resistance of the capitalists, as they seek to restore their "paradise lost". This new state apparatus is known as the Dictatorship Of the Proletariat. It is up to us, the Proletariat, to make sure that the Dictatorship is complete. No half measures. Shoddy work is simply not acceptable. The capitalists must be rooted out and crushed, wherever they are hiding. And rest assured, they are hiding out in all fields of culture and science.

While it is true that I am a member of the working class, a proletarian or "blue collar", as is the common expression, I consider that to be incidental. I work for wages but have a scientific background. As that is the case, I can testify to the fact that anyone who challenges a scientific theory is not allowed to earn a living, working in any field of science. As challenging scientific theories is my specialty, I speak from experience.

This has not stopped me from challenging scientific theories, as I am not terribly shy. It merely makes it more difficult, and in fact I love a challenge. For that reason I earn a living as an hourly employee, while working on my "little science project" in my spare time.

This is another way of saying that I am a working class intellectual, one of the few. I say that I am blazing the trail, or more accurately, blazing several trails, in the process of challenging any number of scientific theories. So you could say that I am a theoretical scientist. I say that I am doing that which needs to be done. As far as I am concerned, it is simply a matter of pointing out the obvious. In the process, I go wherever my research takes me.

The capitalists, the billionaires, the bourgeoisie, the current ruling class, has done more than just crush and exploit us. They have also robbed us of our heritage and our history. It is up to us to restore both.

As a great many working class people are now politically active, I have chosen to write these articles with them in mind. The popular term is followed by the scientific term. Repetition is deliberate. The goal is to raise the level of awareness of the working class. With proper training, the most advanced will be raised to the level of true Marxists.

We will know that we are getting our message through when the term Dictatorship Of the Proletariat is in common usage, among working class people.

CHAPTER 1

USE THE MAGNETIC FIELD OF THE EARTH TO GENERATE ELECTRICITY

It is common knowledge that our planet earth is nothing other than a giant magnet. This is indeed a good thing, as the magnetic field of the planet creates an electromagnetic shield against the radiation from the sun. Without this shield, massive doses of radiation would kill us, as well as almost all other life on the planet. At the same time, it frequently provides us with a magnificent spectacle, the aurora borealis, or northern lights.

It was the Chinese who first took advantage of this magnetic field, and learned to use it for their own purposes. They found that a small piece of metal, carefully balanced on a small stand, always pointed to one of the poles, either north or south. This very simple invention has gone down in history as one of the greatest of all time, making possible the navigation of vast oceans. The point is that an invention does not have to be extremely elaborate, in order to be very effective.

In other words, the magnetic field of the earth has been utilized to explore the planet, as well as a source of entertainment. It has yet to be used as a source of energy. It is the purpose of this article to rectify that little oversight, to use this energy source to its full potential. The use of the magnetic field of the earth as a source of electricity is considered to be the "Holy Grail" of inventions.

Of course, those who invented the compass had no way of knowing that they were taking advantage of the magnetic field of the earth. For that matter, it is doubtful that they cared in the slightest. Most people are more concerned with the fact that something works, as opposed to the reason it works. Countless people drive cars, without having any idea of the action going on under the hood. While there is perhaps no harm in this, it is my opinion that it is best to have some basic understanding of nature, including the electromagnetic force.

With that in mind, I can mention that most people are well aware of the magnetic force. Playing with magnets is great fun, and in fact my grandchildren have a great time with them. They especially love to pin their pictures and home work onto the metal refrigerator. Little do they know that while playing with magnets, they are also learning a great deal. At the same time, I have a great time playing with my grandchildren.

As they get older, they will learn, probably to their surprise, that magnetism and electricity are two sides of the same coin. That is the reason we refer to the force as electromagnetic. The flow of current through a wire, commonly referred to as juice, amounts to electricity, a very powerful force, one which essentially powers our world.

We now tend to take that power for granted, but without electricity we would be in a very sad state. That is quite well known, but that which is not so well known is that every flow of electricity creates a magnetic field at right angles to it, or perpendicular to it, to use the correct scientific term. It may help to think of electricity as going straight ahead, with the magnetic field going directly off to the side.

Granted, this is an over simplification, and for those who find this to be confusing, not to worry. It is not necessary to understand this, just as it is not necessary to understand the inner workings of a car. We can still drive a car without knowing everything that is happening under the hood. In much the same way, we can understand that electricity and magnetism are related, without knowing the precise details.

This may help to explain the reason that the turning of a magnet, within a wire, creates a current to flow within that wire, which we all know as electricity. It stands to reason that the biggest, strongest magnets, create the most power. This takes place in the biggest power plants, and the electricity thus generated provides the heat and light for countless homes. This is a good thing, make no mistake.

The trouble is that the easiest way to get these huge magnets moving is with the use of flowing water, which necessitates the building of dams, which results in the flooding of huge tracts of land. This is not such a good thing.

As for those who object that the same goal could be reached with the use of batteries, I can only respond that it is simply not practical. Batteries are only useful for creating a rather small voltage, for a rather short period of time, at a rather high price.

Yet there are alternative methods of generating electricity, which are less harmful to the environment. These are commonly referred to as "green" sources of energy, and include solar and wind power. In these methods, the solar panels absorb the heat from the sun as a means of generating electricity, while the wind turns huge mechanical arms. But then both of these methods are dependent upon the weather, which frequently has a mind of its own. The wind blows as it pleases, and the clouds block the sun as they please.

This stands in stark contrast to the magnetic field of the earth, which is absolutely stable. Now it is a matter of finding a way to utilize that energy source.

With that in mind, I will now approach the subject of that which is commonly referred to as "water witching". The expression is not mine, I do not like it, it is not at all accurate, but as it is deeply entrenched in the popular language, I have chosen to use the expression.

On that subject, I can state that there are a great many people who believe that underground reservoirs of water can be detected by simply holding two wands of willow, one in each hand, crossing the tops of the willow and walking around the surface of the ground. At the point where the water is closest to the surface, the tips of the willow will experience a considerable downward force. This is commonly referred to as water witching.

Of course, the people who believe this tend to be members of the public, common people, with a rather limited education. The people who have been blessed with a more extensive education tend to dismiss these beliefs as mere superstition. Sadly, this response is characteristic of the well educated. These same people also dismiss reports of UFOs, flying saucers, sasquatch, ogopogo, loch ness monster, dragons and leperchauns, as well as a great many other "legends and myths", as that is precisely the words they use. This shows the arrogance of these people, and must be overcome, as this is the only way we can possibly achieve any meaningful breakthrough in any field of science.

That being said, I must confess to previously sharing that same belief, if only because I could not think of any rational explanation for that phenomenon. The fact is that there are four fundamental forces in the world, which is gravity, electromagnetism, the strong nuclear force and the weak nuclear force. The current scientific belief that there is a fifth force, which they refer to as "dark energy", is utterly ridiculous.

Yet the people who engage in water witching swear there is a force there, and I believe them, if only because I have experienced this same force. We can rule out the two nuclear forces, as to assume this force is nuclear is ridiculous. We can also rule out the force of gravity, as the people holding those wands are quite capable of distinguishing between the pull of gravity on those wands, which is very weak, and the force they are experiencing at certain spots on the ground. That leaves the electromagnetic force, and as we have ruled out the other forces, this last possibility, which seems to be so extremely unlikely, must be the force responsible. After all, extremely unlikely is not the same as impossible.

With that in mind, it stands to reason that the person holding the two wands is creating a battery by means of touching together the tips of the two wands. This must be a rather weak battery, with the difference in potential between the two wands, which is to say the voltage, being rather small, but even a small voltage results in a flow of current. This current, or electricity, is a force which is not to be taken lightly. Almost everyone who has been "zapped", which is to say received an electrical shock, at one time or another, can testify to that fact.

All of the so called "water witchers" can testify to the fact that there is a force which can be generated by the simplest of all possible means, that of crossing two pieces of willow. This current flows and the magnetic field of the current interacts with the magnetic field of the earth, which is to say that there is an attraction which draws the willow down, and in fact this force is considerable and can be amplified. We now have the possibility of a great supply of cheap electricity.

Of course the scientists and electrical engineers refuse to even consider this possibility, so that leaves it up to the members of the public to prove that electricity can be produced in this manner. This will amount to a major scientific breakthrough, but will not require a great deal of money. In the current political climate, a scientific experiment which does not cost a great fortune is out of the question. The existing powers choose to believe that it is simply not possible. More accurately, they hope it is not possible. As incompetent fools, one and all, they live in mortal dread of being exposed.

That leaves it up to us, common people, members of the public, to do that which the scientists should be doing, but will not. I can only suggest, perhaps as part of a high school or even a middle school science project, that of buying a pizoelectric crystal and a simple volt meter. These items are very cheap and readily available, but can be considered to be the most expensive part of the experiment. Then it is a simple matter of walking around a yard with a willow in each hand until feeling a force acting upon the willow. Placing the willows, at the point where they cross, upon the pizoelectric crystal should create a voltage, which can be measured by the voltmeter.

It is to be recommended that someone who is familiar with water witching, a member of the public, be involved in this experiment. They can no doubt be very helpful and I highly recommend combining the wisdom and experience of common people with students who are interested in science.

Different things can be tried, as that is the basis of scientific discovery. One simple thing is to try peeling the willow, as well as wrapping copper wire around the willow at the point of intersection, soaking the willow in water, pouring water on the ground, etc. They may also try to use metal rods and varying the length of the willow and rods. It is doubtful that the use of dry willow will produce the same effect, but that can be part of the experiment. As well, it is doubtful that someone who is wearing rubber soled shoes or rubber gloves, will be able to achieve the same result, but this too can be part of the experiment.

After we prove that it is possible to generate electricity in such a simple manner, then it will be up to the engineers to design practical applications.

No doubt the kids taking part in this experiment will come up with ideas which will surprise us, as they always do. It is my opinion that the location of underground water is secondary to generating electricity, but there are many who may disagree with that statement. In my opinion, the main thing is to prove that the magnetic field of the earth can be used to generate electricity.

If nothing else, the people taking part in this experiment can expect to have a rip roaring good time.

CHAPTER 2

THE PARIS COMMUNE AND THE HEROIC COMMUNARDS

It has been just over a year since Trump was sworn into office and the anniversary of that day is now being considered as a day of mourning. The press is taking great delight in pointing out the lies and hypocrisy of this self proclaimed "great deal maker", a task which may be pleasant but is by no means challenging, as the man lies constantly. Then there is the not so little matter of his tweets, which reveal that this man, who is no less than a head of state, has the mentality of an adolescent. All self respecting Americans are ashamed and embarrassed by his behaviour.

That is one side of the coin, while the other side is that the revolutionary motion is continuing to grow. The class distinctions are becoming ever more sharp and clear. The battle lines are being drawn. On one side we have the working class, the proletariat, and on the other side we have the capitalists, the bourgeoisie. There is no middle ground. Most of the middle class people, the small business owners, the petty bourgeois, have been ruined, driven into bankruptcy, forced to join the ranks of the working class, the proletariat. People are either with us or they are against us. Very soon the class struggle will break out into open warfare and those who try to straddle the fence could well find themselves caught in the crossfire. As an indication of the strength of the revolutionary movement, we have only to consider the fact that the latest allegations of sexual improprieties of Trump, such as his alleged affair with a porn star, is being met with complete indifference by the members of the working class. It should be noted that these allegations are coming from one of the most prestigious publications in the country, one which has never been accused of any left leaning bias. The working class is no longer capable of being shocked by anything Trump is alleged to have done. Now there are people who think that the way out of this boondoggle is through the midterm elections, in that later on this year, each and every member of the House of Representatives and one third of the Senators will be seeking re-election. As Trump is a member of the Republican party and that same party has a majority in the Senate, these same well meaning people are of the opinion that electing members of a different party, most likely the Democratic Party or at least an Independent party, will strip Trump of his power. They would have us believe that peace and tranquility will reign. The age of Aquarius is right around the corner. Workers and capitalists will soon be exchanging hugs and kisses. Trump and the other members of his class will soon see the error of their ways and insist on becoming responsible, honourable, tax paying members of society, or at least paying their fair share. Fat chance! That is not about to happen, and anyone who thinks otherwise is a starry eyed optimist, about to receive a rude awakening. It is absolutely necessary to drive the point home to the working class that we are members of a class whose scientific term is proletariat and further, our interests are diametrically opposed to those of the class which is our antipode, the class opposite to ours, the capitalist class, the bourgeoisie. They, the capitalists, are the class of parasites which contribute nothing to society but leach off of us, the members of the working class, the proletarians. The harder they work us and the less they pay us, the higher their profit. It does not take a genius to figure out that our interests are diametrically opposed and in fact they are antagonistic. In short, we are in a constant state of war with the capitalists. Sometimes this war is concealed and sometimes this war breaks out into open battle. Any day now, we can expect this war to break out into open rebellion. The point must be driven home to members of the working class that we are all members of the same working class, a class of proletarians, and any and all differences are completely superficial. Our skin colour, religious beliefs, and ancestry are a matter of no importance. We all have the same class interests and the only way to achieve our goals is to unite against our common enemy, the capitalists, the bourgeoisie. The current leader of the capitalists, in the form of Trump, is merely a typical capitalist. He is by no means exceptional. On the contrary, he is an average, ordinary, garden variety, dime a dozen, run of the mill capitalist. The only difference between Trump the Clown and the other members of his class is that Trump is an entertainer. The Three Stooges were also entertainers, but the Stooges did a far better job. As far as Trump is concerned, the White House is merely another stage upon which he can perform. Just as all entertainers crave applause and praise, so too Trump longs for praise. The difference between Trump and the other capitalists is merely superficial. As members of the ruling class, most of them are too lazy to take any part in running the country. They merely allow the members of the working class to choose a particular member of the ruling class, a flunky, to go to the nations capital, in this case Washington, and misrepresent them. To remove Trump from office would not change anything. The capitalists would merely replace him with another figurehead. Capitalism has to be overthrown and replaced with socialism. The current form of government, which is the dictatorship of the bourgeoisie, can and must be replaced with the Dictatorship Of the Proletariat. The capitalists must first be overthrown and then crushed under the iron boot of the proletariat. This is the only way in which a socialist, workers revolution can possibly be successful. This is another way of saying that without a proper revolutionary theory, there can be no successful revolution. The fact of the matter is that no one wakes up one day and decides to take part in a revolution. No, the discontent of millions of people builds up, usually over a period of many years, and then frequently something rather minor, such as a burglary, may serve as a spark to ignite a major uprising. When this happens, countless people take to the streets and lash out at their enemies, or at least those who are perceived to be their enemies. In the excitement and the heat of the moment, mistakes are sometimes made. This is where a revolutionary theory comes into play. As long as the people who are taking part in the revolt are aware of themselves as a class, then they will know the importance of attacking their class enemies, the capitalists. They will also know the importance of being friendly with their friends. There is no more sure way of leading a revolution to failure than by giving your enemies a break and attacking your friends. Most working people are aware that the best way to kill a snake is to cut off its head. With that in mind, they should be reminded that the White House is the lair of the president and his boot licking belly crawlers. Capital Hill is home to the democratically elected politicians who are sent to Washington by the voters, and those politicians do a fine job of misrepresenting the very people who placed them in office. They can be found in the Senate and House of Representatives. The Pentagon is the vipers nest of the Joint Chiefs of Staff, where the finest military minds of the country plan all the wars, in which the working class is expected to fight and die. Then there is Wall Street, the financial headquarters of the capitalists, where the geniuses of money management plan their great robberies of the working class. Workers should also be reminded of the fact that the three richest men in America have more wealth than half the working people in the rest of the country, which is to say that these three capitalists have more wealth than two hundred million working people. These are the people and institutions which should be the primary target of the revolution. This awareness can only come from an outside source, as the working class is not aware of itself as a class. With that in mind, workers should be encouraged to read revolutionary literature by Marx and Engels such as The Communist Manifesto and Wage-Labor and Capital. As well, several books of Lenin are especially relevant, such as Imperialism, the Highest Stage of Capitalism, State and Revolution, and What Is To Be Done? This current revolutionary movement is distinctive in that it is world wide, with the headquarters in America and for possibly the first time in history, led by women. These women have every reason to be proud. They are following in the footsteps of other great revolutionary women. So in the spirit of international working class solidarity, it is perhaps best to examine the revolutionary history of our class, the proletariat. Before the industrial revolution of the early seventeen hundreds, which began in Great Britain, there was no working class, the proletariat. Of course people worked hard, but not as wage labourers. Many worked as peasants or as artisans, which is to say tradesman, but as there were no capitalists, there was no one to hire workers and pay them for their labor power. That all changed with the advent of the industrial revolution. The former burgers, or merchants of the middle ages, took advantage of the opportunities presented by this newly discovered source of wealth, invested their money in mills and factories, which is referred to as capital, and hired labourers to work their machines. Almost overnight, two new classes were created. The burghers became capitalists or bourgeois, and the people they hired became wage labourers or proletarians. Ever since then, the war has been raging, sometimes open and sometimes concealed, between the capitalists and the workers. For the purposes of this article, we are mainly focused on this class struggle which raged in the country of France, as in that country the conflict was very sharp and clear. It was the opinion of Marx and Engels that "France was the country where, more than any other, the class struggle was fought to a conclusion". So in this country we will begin our investigation, starting with the the creation of the new classes of capitalists and proletarians in the early seventeen hundreds. These new classes immediately came into conflict with the other existing classes, those which had been around for hundreds of years. The workers, or proletarians, were mainly drawn from the ranks of the peasantry and artisans. The burghers turned capitalists, or bourgeois, came into conflict with the nobility and the church, as at that time the nobility and church owned a great deal of land. As capitalism is incompatible with the feudal system, the war was immediately engaged. This resulted in a rather strange alliance of capitalists, workers, peasants and artisans against the nobility and landlords, those who were determined to uphold the old feudal system which had been in place for hundreds of years. It should be noted that at the time, it is very likely that no one was conscious of this alliance. The ever increasing wealth of this upstart capitalist class posed a threat to the nobility in particular, and eventually led to their defeat. It is worth mentioning that this was by no means the intention of the newly minted capitalists. On the contrary, their overriding ambition was to join the nobility. They tended to assume, rather reasonably, that the nobility would welcome some fresh blood, as well a massive infusion of capital. After all, the nobility was, at that time, becoming ever more strapped for cash, as well as deeply inbred. The capitalists could not possibly have been more mistaken. Impoverished or not, the nobility look upon the members of all other classes as contemptible, regardless of the amount of wealth we may have. As far as they are concerned, we are all commoners. Peasants, artisans, workers and capitalists, it makes no difference. This in no way changed the fact that times had changed. The industrial revolution had done more than create new classes. It had also changed conditions, which in turn led to new ideas, that of liberty, equality and fraternity. Just as the nobility was not about to embrace the new class of capitalists, so too it was not about to embrace these new ideas. On the contrary, they were determined to have nothing to do with this. As far as they were concerned, everything could stay as it had been for hundreds of years. The lesson here is that the nobility were typical in the sense that as the ruling class, they were determined that nothing would change. They wanted everything to stay precisely the way it was. The fact that conditions had changed did not impress them in the slightest. In much the same way, our current class of rulers, the capitalists, the bourgeoisie, are also determined that nothing should change. Just as the nobility of France had to be persuaded to part with their wealth and power, so too our current rulers, the capitalists, must also be persuaded to part with their wealth and power. As a result of this, forces came into play which were beyond the control of human understanding or intervention. At that time, no one knew just what was happening. The newly created classes came into conflict with the land owners and nobility, the old guard, so to speak, and the war was underway. In short, a revolutionary movement developed against the nobility and the church, both landlords, and in 1789, broke out into open revolt. The nobility were overthrown and many of them were killed, including the king and queen. Strangely enough, this did not result in the end of the French nobility. Many of the capitalists who took part in the revolution were not satisfied with overthrowing the nobility. They merely wanted to replace the nobility with themselves, to set themselves up as the new rulers. This too is typical of revolution, in that some of those who take part in a revolution will attempt to replace the old rulers with new rulers, themselves. This too we can expect in this, our current revolution. In the case of France, a certain young military commander who claimed to be of noble birth, by the name of Napoleon Bonaparte, decided to seize power and restore the nobility, and set himself up, not as king but as emperor. The difference is that the emperor is king of kings, so that once he crowned himself emperor, he appointed his relatives and friends as kings and queens of other countries. This lasted from 1804 to 1815, when he was overthrown. At that time, other nobles, those who were closely related to the previous king, who was executed in the revolution, took to the throne. In this case, King Louis Philippe ruled France until 1848, and as he was preoccupied with restoring the power of the monarchy, this meant a time of terrible reaction on his part, with all citizens deprived of ever more democratic rights. He and his closest advisors were preoccupied with squabbling among themselves and with curtailing the power of the ever more wealthy bourgeois. In the confusion, they forgot about the working class. This led to the revolution of 1848. This revolution was one of the greatest revolutions in the world, and in fact the world has still not seen anything quite like it, at least up until now. The revolution spread across Europe and the various governments were shaken but not toppled. The revolution was supremely powerful but not coordinated, as the working class of Europe was still unaware of itself as a class, with its own class interests, which transcended national borders. In addition, the working class was far outnumbered by the peasants and middle class, or petty bourgeois, who also had their own class demands. Then there was the bourgeoisie, which resented the power of the monarch, in the form of King Louis Philippe, and all of these classes came together in February of 1848 to force the abdication of the king. This led to the formation of the French Second Republic. This also led to the dissolution of the alliance of the workers, peasants, petty bourgeois and bourgeoisie. Aside from the poorest peasants, the French workers were on their own. The newly formed Second Republic wasted no time in attacking the workers, the same people who had helped place them in power. They had a real problem with the idea of guaranteed paid work for all citizens, and the right of workers to "combine in order to enjoy the legitimate benefits of their labor." This is another way of saying that the capitalists were dead set against trade unions, as they are now. They are well aware that there is strength in numbers. The workers of France did not take this lying down, and once again, as in February of 1848, the barricades were placed on the streets of Paris. This has gone down in history as the June Days Uprising. Of course, the capitalists, the bourgeoisie of France, took a dim view of these shenanigans. They decided that the workers needed to learn to respect their "natural superiors", to put those workers in their place. The French National Guard was called out and the rebellion in Paris was crushed with great brutality and considerable loss of life. Possibly ten thousand workers were either killed or wounded and thousands of others were banished to Algeria. Louis Napoleon, the nephew of the former emperor, came to power and reaction set in, as it always does after the successful suppression of all revolutions. It should be noted that Marx and Engels followed that revolution very closely, and were able to draw the lessons from that first great European uprising, even though it was not successful. Now we have a similar situation to that of 1848, in that a revolution in one country, in this case America, is spreading around the world. Very soon it will break out into open class warfare around the world. After the revolution of 1848 was crushed, the capitalists of Europe breathed a sigh of relief. They thought that their greatest nightmare, that of a working class uprising, was properly dealt with, and they could now get back to the serious business of making a profit. The workers had been taught a lesson they would never forget and had been put in their place, that of being servants of the capitalists. In this, the capitalists were completely mistaken. Within several years, the revolutionary motion of the working class picked up again. Once again, the workers were on the offensive, demanding better wages and working conditions, as well as more democratic rights. At the same time, the class of people who are known as the nobility were not about to accept their new lot in life. They refused to accept the fact that the common people had spoken up very loud and clearly in the revolution of 1789, had overthrown the nobility and killed a great many of them. They were convinced that they had been granted the divine right to rule and with their superior intellect, it was just a matter of seizing power and exercising that divine right. With that in mind, the nephew of the first emperor, Napoleon I, named Louis Napoleon III, came to power in 1852 and declared himself to be Emperor of the Second French Republic. He was determined to restore France to the former glory as had been enjoyed under his uncle. At least, that is what he thought. His rule as Emperor was that of the last rule of the nobility in the country of France. It mercifully came to an end in 1870, when France was defeated in the Franco-Prussian war and the emperor was deposed. We can learn from this the lesson that a class which has formerly been in power tends not to accept the fact that they have been overthrown. After the current revolution, after the capitalists, the bourgeoisie, have been overthrown, they will make every effort to return to power. We can expect their resistance to increase ten fold as try to regain their "paradise lost". They will stoop to any level, any subterfuge, to return to power, just as they did in the Soviet Union and China. We must not allow that to happen here, in America. We must learn from the mistakes of previous revolutions, just as Marx and Engels learned from those revolutions. Just as Louis Napoleon tried to restore the nobility to power and regain the respect and honour of bygone days, so too Trump the Clown is preaching "make America great again". He refuses to accept the fact that the American empire is in decline, on the verge of collapse. He is determined to restore it to its former state of "greatness". This brings us to the eve of the first socialist revolution in France, in the city of Paris. After the defeat of France in the Franco – Prussian War of 1870, Thiers became the new president and realized that the supremacy of the propertied classes, which was the large land owners and capitalists, was in constant danger as long as the workers of Paris were armed. Not only were they armed, but the workers were well armed, with a great deal of cannon. The workers formed a National Guard which was separate from the regular French army, and was well respected, if not feared. With that in mind, Theirs sent units of his regular army into Paris in the early hours of March 18, 1871, with orders to capture the cannons of the National Guard, which is to say the cannons belonging to the workers of Paris. Things did not go quite the way he had planned. The working women of Paris, or at least the wives of the workers of Paris, stumbled upon the army troops who were attempting to steal the cannon, surrounded them, and sounded the alarm. The soldiers were ordered to open fire upon the unarmed women but refused to do so. Instead, they went over to the side of the workers, to the Communards. This too is characteristic of revolution, in that as the revolutionary motion gains strength, those who are sent to crush the revolution tend to join the rebels instead. The day of March 18, 1871, is celebrated as the first workers government in history. Possibly after the successful completion of this, our current revolution, we will be honouring the memory of the heroic Paris Communards by celebrating the day of March 18 as a holiday. The workers of Paris immediately seized the city hall and hoisted the red flag of socialism over it. The revolution was truly under way. Thiers and his generals fled to Versailles, which was a palace ten miles or 16 kilometres from Paris, and his regular army and government officials joined him there. The workers of Paris then made the huge mistake of not attacking them immediately. Instead, the workers set about building a new society, starting with elections, and universal suffrage, if only for the men. The women were not allowed to vote and had no part in the decision making process, this despite the fact that they played a very important role in the commune. It is entirely possible that if the workers had listened to their wives, the outcome would have been far different. It was Marx who was following developments very closely from England, and advised the workers to march immediately on Versailles. At that time, the government of Thiers was at its weakest, and could easily have been overthrown if the workers had mobilized, possibly with their cannons and attacked. They did not. Marx was of the opinion that this magnanimous attitude of the Communards was one of the reasons for their defeat. For those who are not familiar with the meaning of the word "magnanimous", it means "generous or forgiving, especially towards a rival". Perhaps the Communards regarded the capitalists as their rivals, and decided to be generous. Such noble sentiments have no place in the class war, as the capitalists are not our rivals but our enemies, and implacable enemies at that. It is very likely that the women of the Commune sensed this, but then they were not in charge. This stands in sharp contrast to the revolution we are currently experiencing. The women of today are absolutely not content to sit back and remain passive, helping out as best they can, whether tending the wounded or running errands, as the women of the Paris Commune did. The fact that the Communards did not grant them the right to vote or take part in any decision making process was completely understandable in 1871, but now times have changed. A great many women are now members of the workforce, which is to say that they are proletarians, and are demanding equal rights. Not only that, but they are leading the revolutionary motion which is based in America but is spreading around the world. We can expect these women, our sisters and comrades, to not repeat the mistake the Communards made in being magnanimous, in being generous and forgiving towards our class enemies, the capitalists, the bourgeoisie. Women tend to be more practical than men, if only because they have more to lose. In the case of the Paris Commune of 1871, this failure on the part of the Communards to act immediately and decisively was a huge mistake. It allowed the Thiers government at Versailles to immediately regroup and go on the offensive. Perhaps the Communards felt that Thiers was no longer a threat, as he did not have sufficient troops to attack the Commune. While that may have been true, it was also true that Thiers knew precisely where to find those troops. At that time France had just fought, and lost, a war with Prussia, which is to say Germany. The Germans had captured a great many French soldiers and were quite fully prepared to lend a helping hand to a worthy cause. As far as the capitalists are concerned, there is no more worthy cause than crushing a working class uprising. So the Germans quite generously released one hundred thousand French prisoners, on condition that these prisoners be used to crush the Paris Commune. This is precisely what they did. The Communards fought a ferocious battle, but on May 28, 1871, after a week of fierce fighting, a mere two months after the birth of the first socialist workers republic, the workers were overcome and surrendered. There followed a massacre such as has not been seen since the time of the Romans. Defenceless men, women and children were shot down as fast as the breach loading rifles could be fired. As this method of slaughter was not fast enough, mitrailleuse were put to work, an early model, crank operated machine gun. Almost immediately, thirty thousand workers were slaughtered. The bodies were hastily thrown into a mass grave, even though some of them were still alive when buried. Many thousands of others were sent to prison. The workers of the world should be advised that this response is typical of all capitalists of the world, to be expected when workers stand up to them, to challenge their authority, to threaten their power and wealth. In 1871, the capitalists thought it best to teach the workers a lesson they would never forget. It is not too often that I agree with the capitalists, but this is one such occasion. I too think that this is a lesson the workers should never forget. With that in mind, and in view of the fact that the Statue of Liberty was a gift from France to the people of America, I can only suggest that the workers of North America take up a collection and send a gift to the workers of France, possibly in the form of a statue, in honour of the great sacrifice the workers of Paris made many years ago. A local artist can be asked to design an appropriate figure. The heroism of the Communards can be compared to the heroism of the three hundred Spartans of hundreds of years ago, those who stood at Thermopalae, against the whole army of invading Persians. Those men performed their duty, and died at their posts. Since that time, they have served as an inspiration for countless others. The Communards also did their duty, and serve as an inspiration for working people around the world. May their sacrifice never be forgotten. There are further parallels we can make between the revolution of Paris in 1871 and the revolution which is currently gathering strength around the world, and we can learn from this. In the Commune, there were various factions among the leaders. At that time, as now, the workers had spontaneously gravitated towards socialism and the leaders agreed on setting up a socialist society. They just could not agree on the best way to set up that society. Some of the leaders were anarchists, followers of Prondhon and Bakunin, while other were middle class, or petty bourgeois, reformists who thought capitalism could be patched up and made to work. Very few of them were followers of Marx. This lack of a correct scientific theory was one of the reasons the Commune was defeated. The battle of the workers, the Communards, against the capitalists, lacked focus, and they became complacent. We trust that with the working women leading the revolution, this feeling of complacency will never set in. We further trust that with working people being encouraged to read works of Marx and Lenin, they will learn the correct scientific revolutionary theories. The work of Marx, titled the Civil War in France, covers the Paris Commune. All other theories have been proven to be faulty. The point must be driven home to the working class that it is not enough to simply overthrow the capitalists, they must then be crushed under the iron boot of the proletariat. We must exercise Dictatorship over them, absolutely preclude any effort on their part to return to power, as they will most certainly try. The spontaneous nature of the current revolution is the biggest obstacle to its ultimate victory. It currently lacks focus and workers are thrashing around in much the same manner as a boxer who is blindfolded. To bring to workers the awareness of themselves as a class is equivalent to removing the blindfold from the boxer. Then with the theories of Marx and Lenin as our guide we can toss aside superficial differences such as skin colour, race, religion and background, and focus on defeating our common enemy, the capitalists, the bourgeoisie, and follow in the footsteps of the heroic Communards. We should add that in the Paris Commune there were a great many middle class people, or petty bourgeois, which is to say small business owners, shopkeepers. For the most part, they took part in the revolution until it was clear that it was doomed to failure. Then they ran for their lives, leaving the working class people to fight on alone. This is typical of middle class people, those who vacillate. It is only the working class, the proletarians, who are consistently revolutionary. In this revolution, we can expect similar behaviour on the part of the middle class. At present, there are very few political parties or organizations which are truly Marxist, although there is no shortage of groups who refer to themselves as Marxist or Marxist-Leninist or even Communist, where the word Communist is possibly a corruption of the word Communard. That is perfectly acceptable. That which is not acceptable is any revision of the revolutionary theories of Marx and Lenin.

There is one Marxist revolutionary theory which all revisionists find to be completely unacceptable, and that is the Dictatorship Of the Proletariat, or DOP. I have deliberately introduced the capital letters, as a means of stressing the importance of the theory. Such a Dictatorship is the worst nightmare of every capitalist. The idea of having the "tables turned", of having no democratic rights, of being unable to hide behind lawyers, with no court of appeal, of having to answer to the same working people who formerly worked for them, being forced to perform manual labor, for perhaps the first time in their lives—no wonder it terrifies them!

Yet that is the key to a successful revolution. After the working class, the proletariat, seizes political power, it will be necessary to crush the "desperate and determined resistance of the bourgeoisie, as it will be increased ten fold", according to Lenin. Hence the necessity of crushing them, under the iron boot of the proletariat.

For that reason, as a means of distinguishing the true Marxist Party from any and all revisionist parties, I can suggest that the name be that of the Communist Party, Dictatorship Of the Proletariat, or CP,DOP.

That is hardly the ideal solution, but there are no ideal solutions. Still, the problem has to be faced, as the members of the working class are bound to be confused when faced with so many groups who claim to be Marxist, but are in fact revisionist. As all phoney Marxist groups are dead set against that Dictatorship, as it is the worst nightmare of their lords and masters, the capitalists, it is safe to assume they will not have anything to do with that title.

After the revolution, after the existing state apparatus is destroyed and replaced with a new state apparatus, for the purpose of crushing the desperate and determined resistance of the capitalists, in the form of the Dictatorship Of the Proletariat, may I suggest allowing the capitalists to perform useful, productive work. As most have never worked a day in their lives, and have no practical skills, perhaps they can handle a job in the countryside. They may just be able to manage to work on a farm, shovelling manure and growing livestock such as horses, hogs and cattle. As well, they may be able to grow crops such as potatoes, turnips, and carrots. At the same time it may be best to not allow them access to any electronic devices, such as computers or cell phones, as they will use them to make contact with other members of their class and plot a return to power. They are not about to embrace their new life of productive members of society.

CHAPTER 3

TRUMP AND NORTH KOREA

Posted on December 12, 2017 by geraldmcisaac

The most recent development in the ongoing conflict between the American imperialists and Korea is the launch of a ballistic missile, by the Koreans, which is considered to be capable of reaching the continental United States. As a result of this, a great many people are deeply concerned about the possibility of war with Korea.

There is a good reason for this concern. If Trump and his closest advisors, imperialists one and all, have their way, America will soon be at war with Korea, and it is a war which America cannot possibly win.

As Lenin explained quite clearly in his excellent book, Imperialism, the Highest Stage of Capitalism, monopoly capitalism is capitalism at its highest, most rotten form. It is completely reactionary. By definition, a reactionary is someone who opposes any political or social reform. It is characteristic of such people that they take great pride in being classified as reactionary. They are typically against any social programs whatsoever, from food stamps to medical assistance, and are constantly trying to erode any such programs which do exist. As far as they are concerned, those who cannot support themselves, for whatever reason, are free to starve. The money thus saved can be better spent on more important things, such as the military, which can then do that which the military does best, which is to say, go to war.

The reactionaries are careful not to phrase it in quite that manner, as that would be honest and no one in his right mind has ever accused the reactionaries of being honest. They make a career of lying and very likely practice those lies in front of a mirror, trying their best to fake sincerity. As the con artists who coach them phrase it, "if you can fake sincerity, you got it made". So now the military is referred to as "defence", war is referred to as "peace", and outright lies are referred to as "alternative facts".

The White House frequently has press briefings, and at such events the press secretary of the president tries to "spin" reality to a more acceptable state of affairs. The current press secretary earns her pay, whatever that pay may be, and in fact she deserves a raise. Most people would not, or could not, degrade themselves to that extent, regardless of how much they were paid. The members of the press are agreed that the former press secretary was the worst, most ignorant individual they had ever seen, but that was before they met the current stooge. She makes her predecessor look downright polite by comparison.

She would have us believe that Trump is concerned only with peace, and further the three American aircraft carriers, along with their support warships, which are stationed in the waters off the coast of Korea, are there in the interests of peace. The two countries could go to war at any time, and as far as Trump and his flunkies are concerned, the sooner the better.

The first world war made it clear that the imperialists love war, and the loss of millions of people are a matter of complete indifference to them. At that time, the imperialists, mainly those of the British, French and German empires, were squabbling over a repartition of the world. The current war which is planned with Korea is for similar reasons. It irritates the imperialists when any country of the world refuses to submit to them, as they are able to control the policies of all countries by controlling their economies. By contrast, the country of Korea does not owe a dime to the International Monetary Fund, the IMF, the World Bank or any one else. They are completely independent, self sufficient. As a result of this, the imperialists cannot control their economy, and they cannot control the country.

At the moment, the country of Korea is divided into two parts, north and south. This is completely artificial, as it has a history spanning thousands of years. But recently, it was divided into the north, or the Democratic Peoples Republic of Korea, DPRK, and the south, which refers to itself as the Republic of Korea, ROK. The DPRK considers itself as the true government of Korea and considers the south as a mere puppet of the American imperialists, which is precisely what it is. For purposes of this article, I refer to the DPRK as Korea.

By contrast, the American imperialists consider the DPRK to be a "hermit kingdom" and the president, Kim Jong Un, to be a madman. Of course they have learned nothing from their defeat in Viet Nam, and are determined to repeat the experience. Korea is also a small country, but in contrast to Viet Nam of many years ago, Korea has a vast military, well trained, well equipped, and is fully prepared for war. Some of their military equipment may be obsolete, but for that reason, may well be superior to the more modern equipment of their enemies.

It should come as no surprise to anyone that there is no love between the two countries. The Koreans hate the American imperialists every bit as much as the American imperialists, led by Trump, hate the Koreans.

This hatred has a rather long history, going back to 1950, when the American imperialists instigated the war in Korea. Technically, the war was led by the United Nations, and a great many nations took part in that war, but it was the American imperialists who were behind it. In 1953 an armistice was signed, and it is commonly thought that the war ended at that time. It did not end, but entered a new phase.

In this new phase, the American troops remain stationed in the south, supposedly to protect the American puppet regime which calls itself the Republic of Korea. The north, or DPRK, is determined to liberate the southern part of the country from their American oppressors. They should not be under estimated, as they have been preparing for the outbreak of hostilities for over sixty years. They never lost sight of the fact that the country is still at a state of war.

Even the most conscientious American military planners, and such are few, are of the opinion that to go to war with Korea would be a disaster. They estimate that in such a war, each day twenty thousand American men would be either killed or wounded, even without the use of nuclear weapons. These same experts also estimate that the war will last only two weeks as they expect the army of the DPRK will break and run when confronted with the overwhelming American fire power. They acknowledge that in the first Korean war, this did not happen, but on the contrary, particularly at the battle of Chosen

Reservoir, it was the American troops who "bugged out", as is the popular expression for deserting their posts. They also touch on the possibility of China and Russia becoming involved, in the sense that those countries may take a dim view of having Americans on their doorstep. The leaders of those countries are supremely well aware that Korea borders their country and if the Americans conduct a successful invasion of Korea, then they will be blessed with some completely disagreeable neighbours. To forestall such a possibility, they, the Chinese and Russians, may join in the war against the Americans, just as the Chinese did in the first Korean war.

It should be noted that both countries used to be socialist but as the bourgeoisie of both countries have managed to restore capitalism, such is no longer the case. Further, both countries have embraced imperialism and are just as determined to rule the world as are the American imperialists. Needless to say, they now hate each other, which is characteristic of imperialists of competing countries, but may put aside their differences in order to deal with a common enemy, which is of course America. This is to say that if America goes to war with Korea, both China and Russia may go to war with America.

The thought processes of the American analysts, and here I am using the expression in its loosest possible sense, is that the possibility of certain responses to an invasion of Korea are too terrible to consider and are therefore dismissed out of hand. They choose to believe that the Korean army will desert their posts and run in a panic, when confronted with "overwhelming American fire power", even though the experience of the first Korean war showed that this was not the case. Then there was the war in Viet Nam which lasted over ten years, until the American invaders were finally defeated. In that war also the American firepower was overwhelming, so the Vietnamese merely adopted tactics of guerilla warfare, as was recommended by Chairman Mao. In such warfare, the enemy is not challenged at the point where he is strong, but at the place where he is weak. As the Vietnamese won the war, these tactics have been proven to be correct.

It should be noted that in the second world war, or the Great Patriotic War, as the then socialist Soviet Union referred to it, at the battle of Stalingrad, the soviet defenders worked out the proper defence to an enemy which had overwhelming air and artillery superiority. In that case, it was urban warfare, which is to say warfare in a city, the worst nightmare of every attacking general. The soviet troops defended every building and consistently stayed as close as possible to the enemy. As they phrased it, they "hugged" the enemy. The battle raged up close and personal. As a result of this, the Germans were reluctant to call for artillery and air support, as that would involve killing their own men.

For the sake of completeness, we should add that one reason for the overwhelming air and artillery superiority of the enemy was the decision of the soviet high command to deliberately send to the troops in Stalingrad just enough equipment to hold on, while at the same time building up a huge army in reserve, in preparation for a massive counter offensive. This worked, and the German army in Stalingrad was surrounded and captured, at great expense of course.

Such similar tactics were also used in Korea as well as Viet Nam, although in Viet Nam it was more frequently used in a jungle setting. They also used the tactic of attacking in the darkness, when American aircraft could not fly. The point is that overwhelming firepower can be dealt with and overcome. It does not necessarily lead to victory.

The military analysts are also concerned that the morale of the American military servicemen may soon be at the point where they may disobey a direct order to engage in combat. In this, their fears are well grounded. Such servicemen may well question the rationale of fighting and dying in a country half way around the world, against a country which minds its own business and could not possibly pose a threat to the peace and security of America. By contrast, the morale of their Korean counterparts is at an all time high, defending their homeland, determined not to submit to any imperialist. They are no more likely to bow down to the American imperialists than their Vietnamese counterparts of years ago.

We can compare this to the situation of Europe in 1941, in that Hitler and his fascist advisers were convinced that war with the then socialist Soviet Union would last a very short time, that they had only to "break in the door and the whole rotten structure will collapse". Of course, such was not the case and this led to the defeat of the fascists. The German fascists broke in the door and the whole of the Soviet state rose against them. The Soviet soldiers were fighting for their homeland and their morale was generally far superior to that of the invaders.

It is entirely possible that a war with Korea would be over in two weeks, but not for the reasons the American analysts consider. In contrast to the country of Viet Nam at the time of the American invasion, the country of Korea is fully prepared for war. They have been preparing for this war for over sixty years, knowing full well that it is just a matter of time. They never lost sight of the fact that the war did not end in 1953. Ever since that time, the Koreans have been building up their military. They do not advertise as it is no ones business but their own, but reports are that all teenage boys have to serve ten years in the military, followed by many years in the reserves. A great many girls also serve in the military. As a result of this, the Koreans have a standing army of over one million and a reserve army of perhaps eight million. Their morale is high, as all are consumed with a deep, passionate hatred of the imperialists. They are determined to never again be ruled by any imperialists.

It was Napoleon who once referred to artillery as the "god of war", and he was one of the greatest military leaders of all time. The Koreans very likely agree with this assessment as their artillery is second to none. I use the word artillery in the broader sense, in that I consider rocket launchers to be a form of artillery. The Koreans have a great many pieces of artillery of various calibers and as anyone who has ever survived an artillery barrage can testify, such a barrage can be devastating.

The bourgeois military analysts quite gleefully point to the fact that most of the equipment of the Koreans is obsolete, no match for the more modern equipment of the Americans. The Koreans have no intention of challenging the Americans at the point where they are strongest. To do so would be supremely stupid, and much as the bourgeois military planners prefer to think only the worst of their enemies, such is not the case.

As an example of obsolete military equipment being put to good use, we have only to refer to Viet Nam. In that case the Soviet Union sent world war two surplus military equipment to the Vietnamese to assist them in their war with the Americans. These included T34 tanks, as well as more modern tanks. The Vietnamese put these armoured vehicles to good use, as the Americans can testify. They especially loved the older model T34 tanks, as they were rugged, reliable, easy to operate and repair. They preferred them to the later model tanks.

This is not to say that the Vietnamese challenged the American armour directly. They did not. Their policy was to hit the enemy at the point at which he is weakest, and this they did supremely well, sometimes using obsolete vehicles which were in some ways superior to the more modern models.

In much the same way, the Koreans also have a very large air force, although many of those aircraft are considered to be obsolete. Such aircraft may not be any match for more modern American jets in air to air combat, called dog fights by the pilots, but then it is not likely that the Koreans plan to use them in this manner. It is far more likely that they plan to attack the enemy aircraft with surface to air missiles and anti aircraft guns. As for those who object that these latest stealth aircraft cannot be detected, are invisible to radar, and cannot be shot down by missiles, I can only respond that you are mistaken. Such stealth aircraft have been around for a great many years, and by now the military engineers have no doubt found ways to detect them, perhaps from their exhaust, which is red hot and visible in a different wavelength, perhaps ultraviolet.

They are also well aware that the weakness of all aircraft is that they need a base on which to land, and the bases of any and all aircraft are well within the reach of Korean missiles. These include islands such as Guam, as well as bases in Japan and Australia. The Koreans have already served notice that in the event of war with the Americans, these bases will be targeted.

The Korean navy is also quite impressive, although considered to be obsolete, and perhaps it is. For that reason, it may be superior to their American counterparts. They have no intention of challenging the American navy to direct combat as that would be suicide. The Korean submarines are rather small, at least compared to American models, but then they are not designed to cross vast oceans. They are designed to protect the homeland, which is the peninsula of Korea. For that reason, they are not about to wander far from their home base. Their torpedoes are very fast, accurate and powerful, far more so than the torpedoes of world war two. These same submarines also carry missiles which are equally effective.

All of the most modern equipment has one thing in common. They are all computer controlled. The Koreans have noticed this and have responded by training a great many very intelligent people in the field of high tech, specialists in the field of "hacking", to use the common expression. These specialist are referred to as Information Technology, or I.T. people, and they are experts at breaking into computers. The bourgeois intelligence experts consider them to be some of the finest in the world. It is entirely possible that they are quite capable of breaking into the American military computers, and may have done so already.

As for those who consider this to be impossible, as there are numerous "firewalls" protecting such computers, I can only draw the attention of the reader to the situation of world war two in which the German enigma code was considered to be unbreakable. The British mathematicians were of a different opinion and even without the use of modern computers, were able to "crack" the code. Of course, they did not advertise their great accomplishment, and it was not until many years after the war that this was made public. It is entirely possible that a similar situation could exist today, in which the Koreans may have already cracked the code of the American computers.

The difference now is that computers control vehicles, everything from trucks to aircraft to warships. Whoever controls the computers also controls the vehicles.

It is also a fact that a strong electro magnetic pulse is quite capable of destroying, or "frying" any and all computers. There are weapons which have been developed which are quite capable of doing just that. It is quite reasonable to assume that the Koreans have developed such weapons. If such a pulse was released at a modern aircraft, perhaps a stealth jet, then the pilot would immediately lose control of the aircraft.

It should be noted that the ultimate weapon for releasing a very strong electro magnetic pulse is a nuclear explosion. In such an event, all computers within the blast radius would be destroyed. The bourgeois analysts should be reminded that the Koreans have not developed nuclear weapons for decorative purposes, only to be admired when placed on display. They are to be used in time of war, and if used, will completely disable the most modern military equipment, as all such equipment is computer controlled. The same cannot be said of the "obsolete" equipment, which is very likely not computer controlled.

If nothing else, this reveals the whole process of thought of the imperialists, or to be more accurate, all their appalling imbecility, which is characteristic of all imperialists. First the military analysts state the facts correctly, and then they come to conclusions which are directly contradicted by the facts. They cannot do otherwise, as their job as military analysts is to justify the upcoming war which their masters have planned. By their masters I mean the monopoly capitalists, the imperialists, the bourgeoisie, the billionaires.

If Trump has his way, the war which he has planned with Korea will no doubt result in a great slaughter of Americans and Koreans, civilian as well as military. This is of no great concern to Trump or his cronies, as a war would be the excuse they need to call for the country to unite behind their president and forget all about the investigations that are currently being carried out. No doubt they consider this the ideal way to divert the revolutionary movement onto a path of defence of the fatherland.

The current situation could soon resemble the situation of Europe in 1914, at the beginning of the great slaughter of the first world war. At that time, the so called great powers entered into a war to divide and redivide the world. The monopoly capitalists, the bourgeoisie of each of those countries, were determined to secure an ever greater measure of colonies of the world and increase their wealth and power. The fact that this could, and did, result in the death and disfigurement of millions of people was of no consequence. The citizens of each country were called to "defend the fatherland" and the so called Marxists of each country joined the chorus in calling for the support of their own imperialists, their own bourgeoisie. In so doing, they betrayed their own working class, their own proletariat, and revealed themselves as traitors to the working class. Their reward for this baseless act of treachery was absolutely nothing, as the imperialists of all countries merely accept this as their due.

The only exception to this was the Bolshevik party of Russia, led by Lenin. They were the only Marxist party which stood on principle, preferring penal servitude in Siberia to craven submission to the imperialists.

Our current crop of rulers, our monopoly capitalists, our billionaires, our imperialists, our bourgeoisie, are supremely well aware of the revolutionary motion which is sweeping the world. They have numerous faults, but stupidity is not one of them. They are well aware that the working class has spontaneously gravitated to socialism and are demanding change. The working class is no longer content to be ruled in the old way and they, the monopoly capitalists, the billionaires, the bourgeoisie, can no longer rule in the old way. They now have to change their method of rule, especially as it is well known now that the three richest men in the country have amassed as much wealth as the bottom half of the population. This is to say that those three men, members of the class of people we call the bourgeoisie, are worth as much as two hundred million Americans. It is not enough, and now that Trump and the members of his class, the bourgeoisie, have passed a tax cut for members of their own class, they will soon be ever more wealthy.

They are also well aware of the numerous government investigations which are underway and are now frantic to divert the revolutionary movement. So now they may decide to whip up the old patriotic fervour by going to war and calling for all Americans to put aside any petty differences they may have and stand united behind their president, and by extension, their bourgeoisie, and crush the common enemy.

It should be noted that their idea of petty differences are acts of fraud, money laundering, lying under oath, conspiracy to defraud the American government and place a puppet in the white house, one who is indebted to a foreign power and this is called collusion, in this case with the Russians.

Just how a small country half a world away, one which minds its own business, can be a threat to the American way of life is not entirely clear, but that is not about to make any great impression on the American imperialists. They just think that working people are supremely stupid and are prepared to swallow any lie which is fed to them, at least as long as the lie is big enough. To suggest that Korea is a threat to America certainly qualifies, as it is about as big a lie as the moon landing.

But to this day there are people who still believe that Americans walked on the moon, just as these same people believe that Oswald acted alone in the murder of Kennedy, and that a man living in a cave, half a world away, orchestrated the slaughter of several thousand innocent Americans on nine eleven. The people responsible for these lies and atrocities do not live half a world away and they are certainly not hiding in Korea. They are right here in North America and they are the enemy. They are the monopoly capitalist, the imperialists, the bourgeoisie, currently led by Trump, and they have got to be destroyed. This can only be accomplished through revolution and establishing a subsequent dictatorship over them, exercised by the working class, the proletariat, the Dictatorship Of the Proletariat. The monopoly capitalists, the billionaires, the bourgeoisie, must be first overthrown and then crushed by the working class, the proletariat. It is only then that the people responsible for various crimes, such as the murder of Kennedy and the slaughter of nine eleven, can be brought to justice.

Out of respect to the people who have been deceived by the lies of the imperialists, we can only point out that the American flag which was planted on the moon was waving in the breeze, which is rather strange as there is no atmosphere and therefore no breeze on the moon. Further, as is well known, the assassination of Kennedy was caught on film, completely by chance, and while the quality of the film is poor, it is clear that the bullet which killed him came from in front and below, as the bullet exited out the back of his head at a slightly upward angle. We know this because the material from his head, which is to say his brains and bones, were on video flying in that direction. I mention this not because I enjoy being crude and vulgar, and not because I am trying to offend anyone, but only because this is one of those things which has to be said.

The fact is that the bullet which killed Kennedy was fired by a shooter who was hiding in the sewer. The opening to that sewer was twenty or thirty yards from the point where Kennedy was shot, so it is entirely possible that the shooter did not even use a scope sighted rifle. He may have shot Kennedy with a rifle complete with iron sights. I say this to stress the fact that the shot which killed Kennedy could not possibly have come from on high, which is to say the top floor of the book depository building, as the bullet exited from the back of his head, so it was not fired by Oswald.

As for those people who are presumably honest, hard working, law abiding citizens who think to this day that Bin Laden was responsible for 911, I can only refer you to the fact that it was not just the twin towers that collapsed that day in New York, but also tower 7, a forty nine story sky scraper. No plane hit that building, just as no plane hit the pentagon. The fact is that there was no wreckage of any plane at the pentagon and further, such a large plane which supposedly struck the pentagon could not possibly have left such a small hole in the wall. That hole was made by a cruise missile, fired by the American military. I have gone into that in other writings so there is no need to dwell further on that particular set of lies.

It is to be hoped that the working class of America, which is now at the forefront of the international working class movement, will succeed in preventing Trump and the members of his class, the class of monopoly capitalists who are technically referred to as the bourgeoisie, from going to war with the country of Korea. That is one country which is fully prepared for war, and the American military analysts anticipate the American losses, in such a war, to be catastrophic. To the American imperialists, the monopoly capitalists, the bourgeoisie, that is a matter of no consequence. They consider it a small price to pay in order to stay in power.

As a pretext for war, we can expect the imperialists to resort to tricks which have been tried and proven in the past, such as claiming the Koreans have attacked them. It was in just this manner that President Johnson used the "Gulf of Tonkin incident" as an excuse to go to war with Viet Nam, claiming that North Vietnamese gunships had attacked American warships. It was only years later that they were forced to acknowledge that such an incident had never taken place, that no such attack had happened. They just generated an imaginary incident as an excuse to go to war.

The immediate problem is to prevent Trump and the members of his class, the bourgeoisie, from going to war with the country of Korea. The only way in which this can be done is with sufficient pressure from the working class. The best way to apply this pressure is by first making the members of the working class aware of themselves as a class, complete with their own class interests, which are diametrically opposed to the interests of the bourgeoisie.

As I have mentioned in another article, we have a splendid weapon which can be used in our struggle with the monopoly capitalists, the imperialists, the bourgeoisie, and that is the internet. It is certainly not being used, at least not to its full potential. Recently it was revealed by the bourgeois press that the top three richest billionaires in America are worth as much as half of the population of the rest of the country.

I can only suggest that this very valuable admission, by members of the bourgeois press, be placed on the internet and sent to as many working class people as possible, or at least the most advanced members of the working class, and sent by people more accustomed to use of the internet than myself. At the same time, it could be mentioned that we are all part of the same class, the working class, the proletariat, and we all have a common enemy, the monopoly capitalists, the billionaires, the imperialists, the bourgeoisie. As for those member of the working class who express an interest, we can suggest starting with reading an excellent work by Lenin, Imperialism, the Highest Stage of Capitalism. It is supremely well written, east to understand, and a fine place to start.

As I have stressed in other articles, the working class is not aware of itself as a class and that has to change. The members of that class have got to learn that fact as well as the technical terms which I have repeated, time and time again. As for those who find that most tiresome, I can only say that we learned the alphabet by repetition, and I am looking forward to the day that I do not have to repeat myself. That will be the day the working class is aware of themselves as a class, the proletariat, and also aware that the billionaires are also a member of a class, the bourgeoisie. By that time, they should also be aware that it is class war.

But now we have the world wide revolutionary movement, one which is being led by American working class women. It is their sons and brothers and husbands whom Trump and the members of his class, the bourgeoisie, plan to sacrifice on the alter of American imperialism. We can fully expect these revolutionary women to take a dim view of these proceedings, and to respond accordingly. In fact, this could well trigger a full scale revolution, one which will likely spread to other countries of the world. It is also possible that the American service men and women will revolt and refuse to go to war with a country with which they have no quarrel, and instead turn their weapons on the true enemy, starting with their own officers.

In such cases, the people who claim to be Marxist tend to reveal their true coloUrs. Those who are secretly in the service of the imperialists, the bourgeoisie, call for the country to first deal with the enemy, to unite behind "their own" imperialists, and only after the enemy is defeated, then deal with domestic issues. They neglect to mention that the enemy is a domestic issue, our very own home grown capitalists, the bourgeoisie.

For the moment, the fact is that there are progressive people who are calling for the impeachment of Trump and there are a great many people who call themselves Marxists who are joining in the chorus of calls for his removal from office. As a result of this, Trump will very likely soon find himself out of office and facing very serious criminal charges. The fact that the most reactionary elements in the country have worked themselves up into a frenzy is an indication of just how seriously they are taking this attack on their grip on power. The imperialists, the monopoly capitalists, those who are completely reactionary, the bourgeoisie, are desperately trying to hold on to power and Trump is merely their figurehead. To remove him from power is a step in the right direction but only a step, as the bourgeoisie, which is the class which is currently ruling the country, will remain in charge. To remove Trump from office is merely the first step, as without doubt a different flunky of the imperialists will be placed in the white house and press for war, either with Korea or some other country.

It is absolutely necessary to overthrow the class of parasites which are currently in power, crushing and exploiting the working class, the proletariat. This can only be accomplished by revolution, by destroying the existing state apparatus which has been set up to crush the working class, and a new state apparatus must be established with the goal of crushing the desperate and determined resistance of the monopoly capitalists, the bourgeoisie. The working class must suppress the bourgeoisie, exercise Dictatorship over them, the Dictatorship Of the Proletariat. This is explained quite clearly in another fine work by Lenin, State and Revolution.

The true Marxists will make this quite clear while the phoney Marxists will deny this, saying that it is only necessary to remove Trump from office. In this way, they perform a very valuable service to the bourgeoisie, diverting the revolutionary movement onto a path of harmless social reform. The members of the working class can then distinguish the true Marxists from the phoney Marxists, the agents of the bourgeoisie.

Now it is up to the American workers, led by women, to prevent Trump and his class of parasites, the bourgeoisie, from taking the country into a war which will be a disaster for America. As

I mentioned in other writings, it is imperative for the American working class to use the internet to get organized and work together to stop Trump and his class of monopoly capitalists, the billionaires, the imperialists, the bourgeoisie, from going to war with Korea. The alternative is a war which America cannot possibly win.

The working class must be made aware of itself as a class, the proletariat, and made aware that the billionaires are members of a class which is their enemy, the bourgeoisie. There is no need to go half way around the world to fight the enemy. They are right here in our own back yard. The members of the working class who are able to read and understand the fine works of Lenin, previously mentioned in this article, State and Revolution as well as Imperialism, the Highest Stage of Capitalism, are well on their way towards class consciousness. Such members of the working class, very likely advanced workers, will no doubt lead the revolutionary working class movement. They will then be aware of the necessity of overthrowing the bourgeoisie and establishing the Dictatorship Of the Proletariat.

To the American working class women who feel overwhelmed by the burden of leading the international revolutionary movement, starting with the removal of Trump from office and preventing war with Korea, I can only say that you have earned the right to lead. It is an honour and a privilege, and I have no doubt that you will perform this duty in a truly honourable manner. My only regret is that I am unable to meet you in person, tell you that I am proud of you, and shake your hand.

To such women I can only say, from the bottom of my heart: GOD BLESS YOU.

CHAPTER 4

DOGS, MANS BEST FRIEND

It has often been said that dogs are mans best friend, and there is some truth to this. Whereas other domesticated animals, such as cattle, horses, water buffalo, goats, sheep, geese, chickens and ducks, have been put in the service of man, either as draft animals or as a food source, sometimes both, dogs are frequently nothing more than a pet, practically a member of the family. This is so commonplace, those of us who live in North America tend to take this for granted, while people in other parts of the world tend to question our sanity.

In fact, this is one of the strangest inter species relationships of all time. It is best to remember that the animals which we refer to as dogs are not a separate species at all, but they are in fact nothing other than a species of wolf. These wolves have been selectively bred over a period of many thousands of years, but the fact remains that the animals which we refer to as dogs are nothing other than domesticated wolves.

The scientists are of the opinion that wolves were the first of all the animals to be domesticated. They suspect that as the wolves were thrown scraps from the campsites of the early stone age people, the wolves gradually became accustomed to people, eventually coming right into the camp and becoming down right tame. As anyone who knows anything at all about wolves can testify, such an explanation borders on the ridiculous.

Our ancestors, of possibly ten thousand years ago, hated wolves most passionately, and with good reason. Wolves are very intelligent predators, and preyed upon people on a regular basis. As pack hunters, they were very likely the worst enemies of our ancestors. To this day, they still prey upon us, although far less frequently.

Yet the fact remains that the transition from hated enemies to "best friend" happened, and must be explained. With that in mind, let us examine wolf society.

Every pack has a strict hierarchy, with a male leader, called the alpha male, and a female leader, called the alpha female. It is the alpha female who does most of the breeding, while the alpha male makes sure that all members of the pack know their place. Those who refuse to accept their place are promptly expelled from the pack. This same male is also responsible for ensuring the pack is supplied with a plentiful supply of meat. With that in mind, the alpha male ensures that the territory of the pack is well respected, with any intruders in the form of wolves from a different pack promptly expelled. Any sign of weakness on his part is met with a challenge from another member of the pack. Wolf society is very similar to human society. This helps to explain the reason domesticated wolves, which is to say dogs, fit so neatly into human society. It does not explain how they became domesticated.

Early humans were in a constant state of war with wolves, their worst enemies. It is safe to say that humans hated wolves, and possibly that hatred was returned, much as it is now. The suggestion that humans first threw scraps to the wolves which came too close to their campsites is absurd. The humans threw spears, rocks and arrows at the wolves, but not scraps. Yet something else attracted wolves to the camp sites of our ancestors, and for some reason, our ancestors tolerated this, at least up to a point. That something else is our excrement, our filth.

It is not well known that dogs, which are nothing other than domesticated wolves, actually prefer our filth. We may find this disgusting, but we have no right to judge another species by our standards. It may help to think of this disgust as nothing more than taste prejudice. There must be a great deal of nourishment in this filth and at the time of our stone age ancestors, it was plentiful and readily available. It was only quite recently that we have become aware of the importance of properly disposing of our filth, as otherwise it becomes a breeding ground of disease, leading to epidemics, sickness and death. Of course our stone age ancestors had no knowledge of this, but it is safe to say that they at least developed a certain prejudice against living in filth.

This brings us to the outcast from the wolf pack, the lone wolf, as it is rather accurately called. This is the wolf which did not accept his place in the pack and was cast out. To this day such an animal is supremely dangerous because it is generally half starved, alone, running from all other wolves, scampering around the edges of the territory of all wolf packs. The pack which cast this erring member out is not content to chase him out of the pack. It is necessary to chase him from the territory of the pack. If they find him in their territory, they will kill him. The trouble is that all other wolf packs feel the same way.

These lone wolves can be compared to the "outlaws" of the old west. As the name suggests, these men were outside the protection of the law and generally had a price on their heads. They were literally wanted, dead or alive. The only thing a bounty hunter had to do was bring their body in to a law enforcement agency and receive a reward. They were frequently murdered, killed in cold blood. As a result of this, they could trust no one, running and hiding, avoiding all other people, desperate, generally on the edge of starvation.

Thousands of years ago these lone wolves, who were equally desperate, approached the camps of humans. Near these camps there was lots of food in the form of our filth, and the close proximity of humans offered a measure of protection from packs of wolves. The people in these camps killed wolves at every opportunity, so wolf packs tended to keep a proper distance. On the other hand, people recognized the fact that these lone wolves were keeping the campsite clean, by consuming their filth.

This resulted in a very strange symbiotic relationship, in that two species, normally the most bitter of enemies, found that they had a use for each other. More accurately, the social outcasts of one species, that of wolves, was at least tolerated by members of another species, that of humans, as long as they kept a proper distance. The outcast wolves were allowed to consume the waste of humans and received some protection from other wolves, while the humans benefitted from the proper disposal of waste, resulting in less sickness and death.

It should be pointed out that these stone age people were nomads, which does not mean that they were constantly travelling. It is true that if they spent any too much time in one location, they would soon exhaust their food supply, because they were members of a hunting – gathering society. It is also true that there were exceptions to this rule. One such exception occurs in the Pacific north west, in that various species of salmon swim up the rivers to spawn in the spring and summer, providing a rich source of food for several months. In such cases, with people camped out in one location for that length of time, the filth piles up at a rather alarming rate. Under such conditions, a waste removing animal was very likely at least tolerated, if not welcomed.

This was the beginning of the relationship, and it is logical to assume that other wolf outcasts joined the wolf that was tolerated close to the camp of people. At first, these wolves were careful to keep their distance from people, and those that did not, or were too aggressive, were killed by humans. The wolves which survived formed the nucleus of a new pack, but with a difference. This new pack was no longer primarily a hunting pack but a scavenging pack. They scavenged the filth of humans. Further, this pack did not stake out a claim to a huge area, but only to a rather small area around the human campground.

The wolves which were most likely to survive and breed, thereby passing on their genes, were no longer the most vicious, aggressive wolves, but the most docile wolves. The most aggressive wolves were more likely to be killed by humans, and very likely consumed. Not only were these wolves consumers of human filth, but they were also a valuable food source.

As the human nomads moved to a different location, as inevitably happened, the wolves which had attached themselves to these people followed along. To stay behind was to face almost certain death from the resident pack of wolves, while sticking with the humans provided them with food and a measure of safety. After a great many generations, a relatively docile pack of wolves was created. These animals gravitated ever closer to humans. They were able to identify the dominant male within the human society, and recognized him as the leader of the pack and submitted to him. Then as the wolves bred, the more aggressive pups were killed by humans and eaten. This is one of the earliest forms of selective breeding. The barking ability of wolves was also encouraged, as it provides a valuable warning. The wolves were also used for hunting purposes, and later as pack animals.

Now, after countless generations of selective breeding, these domesticated wolves, whom we refer to as dogs, are famous for their ability to bark. Almost all breeds of dogs have this ability, while very few are able to howl. This is nothing other than a result of selective breeding.

We now refer to them as our best friends, which they are not, although they can be most useful. They are now used by the police and army for security purposes, among other things. Still, it is best to bear in mind that this "friendship" began when it was discovered that these animals can be most useful. These animals were not domesticated because people were looking for company. They were domesticated because they were found to be useful for sewage disposal.

We have now come full circle. These same animals which we originally domesticated for purposes of sewage disposal are now spreading filth. Those which serve no useful service, animals which are kept as pets, should be killed most humanely. These animals were domesticated in order to dispose of filth, and now they are spreading filth. This completely defeats the purpose of domesticating those animals in the first place.

We should quit keeping them as pets. They are not our friends, any more than cattle and sheep are our friends. They are domesticated animals and as such should be respected and not abused.

CHAPTER 5

CONCERNING ABRAHAM LINCOLN

Since the publication of my book The Second American Revolution, it has been suggested that I have not been entirely fair with that president. With that in mind, I have decided to re-examine the man and the time in which he lived.

The fact is that in 1861, the United States of America was deeply divided. The northern states had embraced the industrial revolution, which is to say that they had embraced capitalism. New mills, mines and factories were created in order to mass produce vast quantities of goods to be sold, and railroads and shipping lines were also built in order to get these goods to market. This led to the creation of new classes in America, that of capitalists or bourgeois, as that is their correct scientific name, and workers or proletarians, as that is their correct scientific name. It is the capitalists who have all the money, and as any worker can testify, money talks. In fact, it talks loud and clear.

The capitalists of the north wanted to expand, to develop capitalism in the southern states. They were well aware that the south was rich in natural resources and further, also had an abundant source of cheap labor. They were anxious to take advantage of this and invest their capital in those areas. The trouble was that the southern slave owners were determined to maintain the south as the agrarian society that it was, with plantations based on the exploitation of slave labor. They wanted no part of industrial development. This is another way of saying that capitalism and classical slavery are incompatible. The friction built up between the two classes, that of the northern capitalists and the southern slave owners for many years until in 1861, it broke out into open warfare. The eleven southern states separated from the union and announced the creation of the Confederate States of America. The forces of the north, referred to as the Federals or Yankees, promptly went to war with the Confederates or Rebels. It is referred to as the Civil War and it happened not because the country was indivisible and not because the capitalists were opposed to slavery. It happened because the capitalists were eager to expand into the southern states and invest their capital. The only obstacle was the southern slave owners and the capitalists were determined to crush them.

At that time the country was composed of 36 states, including the eleven southern breakaway states. Of the remaining twenty five states, the twenty northern most states had already abolished slavery while the five so called "border states" of Delaware, West Virginia, Maryland, Missouri and Kentucky chose to stay with the union, even though they allowed slavery. These are also referred to as "slave states". As they lived close to the northern states, they were likely well aware of the industrial capacity of those states, and assumed that there was no point in fighting a war they could not win.

As a result of this, these five slave states became united with the capitalists of the northern states in the war to expand capitalism into the southern slave states. The northern capitalists decided, quite reasonably, that the best way to destroy the southern slave owners was by depriving them of their slaves. No slaves, no slave owners. This makes perfect sense.

The decision to abolish slavery in America was not based on humanitarian grounds, but as simple expediency.

At that time the president of the United States was Abraham Lincoln and as such, was the Commander in Chief of the armed forces. He had also taken an oath to "preserve, protect and defend the Constitution of the United States". It was the Supreme Court that decided on the legality of various laws, based on their interpretation of the constitution, and their decision was final. The president was obligated to abide by their ruling, whether he liked it or not.

There were a great many people who strongly disagreed with the 1857 ruling of the supreme court, the Dred Scott decision. It is widely considered the worst decision the Supreme Court has ever made. Be that as it may, at the time of the civil war, it was the law, and the law was that American citizens had the right to own slaves. These slaves were property, not people. The trouble was that the president does not have the authority to amend the constitution. The only way this can be done is with the approval of two thirds of the states.

This is not to say that Lincoln was personally opposed to slavery. He made his views quite clear in a speech he delivered on September 18, 1858. "I will say then that I am not, nor have ever been, in favour of bringing about in any way the social and political equality of the White and Black races. That I am not nor have ever been in favour of making voters or jurors of Negroes, nor of qualifying them to hold office, nor to intermarry with White people; and I will say in addition to this that there is a physical difference between the White and Black races which I believe will forever forbid the two races living together on terms of social and political equality. And inasmuch as they cannot so live, while they do remain together there must be the position of superior and inferior, and I, inasmuch as any other man, am in favour of having the superior position assigned to the White race."

This is clearly the studied opinion of a well educated, politically powerful racist. Lincoln was a racist to the very core of his being.

As for those who think that possibly it was merely a speech, given in the interests of becoming elected, may I draw your attention to a letter written on August 22, 1862, at the time Lincoln was president. It was addressed to Greeley, of the New York Tribune. Apparently Greeley was pressuring Lincoln to emancipate the slaves, under a law referred to as the "Second Confiscation Act". As Lincoln stated: "My paramount object in this struggle is to save the Union, and is not either to save or destroy slavery. If I could save the Union without freeing any slaves I would do it, and if I could save it by freeing some and leaving others alone I would also do that."

This brings us to the Emancipation Proclamation of January 1,1863, in which the slaves of the Confederate slave owners were emancipated. The slaves of the five border states, which had remained with the Union, were not emancipated. Lincoln did precisely that which he threatened.

To this day, Lincoln is honoured as the man who abolished slavery. In fact, he did nothing of the sort.

CHAPTER 6

PREPARING FOR THE DICTATORSHIP OF THE PROLETARIAT

It has been less than a year since Trump was elected president and his administration has already lived up to the expectations of almost everyone. It is, without doubt, the most corrupt administration since that of Richard Nixon. The only difference is that Trump and his flunkies are proving themselves to be far more stupid than Nixon and his clowns were, on their worst days.

As for anyone who disputes that previous statement, I can only refer them to the tweets Trump keeps spitting out. They are not only offensive but equally embarrassing. To think that a head of state would stoop to such depths! In no other country of the world would such behaviour be tolerated. Trump is completely contemptible and the fact that his lackeys continue to follow him speaks to their moral fibre as well as their stupidity. Then there are the emails which they crank out, in which they openly plot against the American government.

At present, a special prosecutor for the FBI, Robert Mueller, is investigating the Trump administration. He and his team of seventeen lawyers are mainly looking into the allegations of possible "collusion" with the Russian government, in that it is alleged that members of the Trump team worked with the Russians in an attempt to "fix" the federal election of 2116. They are also looking into such not so little details as fraud, tax evasion and money laundering, among others. These others include possibly the most troubling charge of all, in that it is alleged an "obstruction of justice" may have taken place, in that Trump fired the director of the FBI, James Comey, because Comey was investigating Trump and his financial dealings.

As for those who are not familiar with the meaning of the word collude, it quite simply means "conspire, to come to a secret understanding for a harmful purpose". In short, at least two former members of the Trump team are currently charged with conspiring with representatives of a foreign country, in this case Russia, against the United States. In most countries of the world, this is considered an act of treason.

The members of the public are closely watching this spectacle, if only because it is so entertaining. It is also disgusting, not to mention confusing, as in addition to the investigation of the FBI, there are no less than four Congressional committees conducting a similar investigation, two for the Senate and two for the House of Representatives. The fact that five different organizations, all of whom represent the same American government, are looking into the dealings of the Trump administration, shows just how seriously the various government officials are taking this gross abuse of power. It also displays the breadth and depth of the incompetence of the American bureaucracy.

In America, it is against the law to lie to any Congressional committee or to the FBI, and the penalties for doing so are severe. Those who are being questioned tend to resort to faulty memories, or early onset Alzheimers, or CRS – Cant Recall Shit—, as the wits among the law enforcement agencies refer to it, in an attempt to not answer the questions while avoiding an outright lie.

It is the FBI investigation, led by Robert Mueller, that is of particular concern to Trump and his merry men, and with good reason. Mueller is a seasoned investigator with vast experience in securing convictions against high ranking mobsters. His method involves identifying a weak link in the chain, generally a low ranking member of the organization, and threatening that member with a stiff prison term. He then presents the alternative of working with the government in return for a reduced sentence.

This is precisely the method he is using against Trump and his associates. In particular, George Papadopoulos, a low ranking member of the Trump administration, was given the choice of a lengthy prison term or cooperating with the government. He chose to cooperate, or "flipped", to put it politely, but as the mobsters phrase it, he "became a rat". The government officials refer to this as becoming a "proactive cooperator", which sounds so much nicer. It also very likely means that he wore a wire, recording conversations with other members of the Trump team, possibly over a period of several months.

More of less as a result of this, the former Trump campaign manager, Paul Manafort, is facing twelve charges, including conspiracy against the United States government, conspiracy to launder money, and acting as an unregistered agent of a foreign power. His deputy, Rick Gates, is facing similar charges, and each is currently under house arrest and facing up to fifteen years in prison. More charges may be forthcoming.

Legal experts are of the opinion that this is just the beginning, and they expect more charges any day now, and on people even closer to Trump. These include his son in law, Jared Kushner, who is alleged to have met with a Russian banker appointed by Putin. It is also alleged that he and Donald Trump Jr. met with the Russian lawyer Natalia Veselnitskaya, in an attempt to get "dirt" on Hillary Clinton.

Of course, there are numerous others, but these are the people who are closest to Trump. It is not too surprising that most White House officials have hired personal lawyers. As more charges come down, we can expect these lawyers to advise their clients to make a deal with the prosecutors, which is bad news for Trump. No doubt some of these government officials will inform on Trump and he too will be facing similar charges.

As the head of state, he cannot be charged, at least not while in office. This does not mean that he is immune from prosecution. As Richard Nixon said, "When the president of the United States breaks the law, it is not a crime." Except that it is a crime, as Trump and his flunkies are now becoming aware.

As the members of the public are watching these proceedings very closely, the pressure is on the elected leaders, the politicians, to take action. Their first instinct, that of sweeping it under the rug, is not an option. The American Constitution is quite clear that it is up to the Congress to keep the president in line, as no one is above the law. By the Congress is meant the House of Representatives and the Senate, acting together. If the House has reason to believe the president is guilty of "treason, bribery or other high crimes and misdemeanors", then the president can be impeached. All it takes is a simple majority vote of the House, and as there are 435 members of the House, a mere 218 members have to vote to have him impeached.

Then the president goes on trial by the Senate. A special committee appointed by the House acts as prosecutors. For the defence, the president has his own battery of lawyers. The Chief Justice of the Supreme Court presides over the trial and the Senate acts as the jury. To be convicted of any crime requires a two thirds vote of the Senate, and as there are 100 senators, that means 67 must vote that he is guilty. In that case, the president can be removed from office and the vice president, Mike Pence, becomes president.

After the president is removed from office, he can possibly face criminal charges in a court of law. Then again, the president has the authority to issue a pardon at any time to any one, for any violation of federal laws. At least, that is what they think, although the lawyers who are working with Mueller are of a different opinion. If Trump issues a pardon to himself or any of his flunkies, then the government attorneys are prepared to challenge that on constitutional grounds. If successful, the pardons could possibly be over turned and Trump could be facing an extra charge of obstruction of justice.

Another option is to take a page from the book of Richard Nixon. He knew that he was about to be impeached and almost certainly removed from office. After removal, he would then have to face criminal charges and prison time. So Nixon considered his options and made a deal with his Vice President, Gerald Ford. Nixon agreed to resign as president, which would automatically establish Ford as president, if Ford agreed to grant him, Nixon, a presidential pardon. Of course Ford agreed to this and Nixon was spared a prison term.

That was then and this is now, and things have changed. Just because Nixon and Ford got away with that, does not mean that Trump and Pence can get away with it. If such a similar deal is arranged in that Trump agrees to resign as president and

Pence in turn agrees to give Trump a presidential pardon, then both could be charged with obstruction of justice. No doubt the Mueller lawyers are preparing for that possibility.

It is significant that Nixon, as president, could have first issued a pardon to the people, his flunkies, who had carried out his orders to engage in burglary, and were then caught and sent to prison. Nixon did not issue that pardon, as he did not care in the slightest for those people. It is characteristic of people such as Nixon and Trump, those who rise to positions of authority, that they care only for themselves, and when called to account, are concerned only with saving their own skins. They demand loyalty from their subordinates, while giving no such loyalty in return.

The flunkies of Trump would do well to bear this in mind. When the wolves were closing in on Nixon, he merely threw his flunkies "under the bus", as is the current popular term used to describe the manner in which executives blame their subordinates. Trump also can be expected to throw his people under the bus, in an attempt to save his own skin. Any show of loyalty on their part, to Trump, is misplaced.

The fact remains that Trump is on his way out. This will mean a victory for the working class, a step in the right direction, but only a step. It is important to remember that this just means that a different set of politicians will continue to rule from Washington. The ruling class, the monopoly capitalists, the imperialists, the billionaires, the bourgeoisie, as that is their scientifically correct name, will continue to crush and exploit us, the working class, the common people, the members of the public, the proletarians, as that is our scientifically correct name. It remains up to us, the progressive working class, to overthrow the capitalist class, the completely reactionary class of parasites which contributes nothing to society, the same class which crushes and exploits us.

They must be overthrown and it is up to us to destroy them, to remove them from power, to crush them under the iron boot of the working class. It is necessary to establish the Dictatorship Of the Proletariat. That is a fundamental tenet of Marxism.

The stage is now set for a successful socialist revolution. The ruling class can no longer rule in the old way and the members of the working class are finding it impossible to live in the old way and are demanding change. Countless members of the public, those who have formerly been apathetic, are now taking an interest in this government crisis. They are tired of seeing the billionaires, those who live in the lap of luxury, continue to amass an ever greater wealth while not paying taxes, while at the same time we, the working people, are barely scraping by, in danger of losing the little bit we have.

This is another way of saying that the working class is now politically active, taking an interest in their lives, demanding change, no longer content to be ruled in the old way. As the wits among the working class phrased it during the occupy movement, "we woke up". And so we have. The occupy movement may have fizzled out, but it is flaring up again in this, the second American revolution, part of a world wide revolution which is being led by the American working class, and in particular American women. They call it Pussy Power, a name which was inspired by Donald Trump.

All across the country, working class women are taking action, either running for office as Independents, or as Democrats, or as Independent Socialists. This is most commendable, and it is reasonable to assume that most of these women are veterans of the occupy movement. They should be encouraged and supported in this attempt to become elected to one office or another.

Also as a result of this revolutionary uprising led by women, a great many women are being inspired to speak out against sexual assault, coming forward with stories of such sexual assaults in various fields, including political and entertainment. This is referred to as the "Me Too" movement. A well known comedian has allegedly been raping women for more than fifty years, after first drugging them. A politician running for federal office has allegedly been sexually assaulting young women and girls for many years. There are a great many more women coming forward with allegations of sexual assault against the rich and powerful, including politicians and celebrities, going back a great many years. Clearly, women are taking a stand, drawing a line, letting human predators know that they have had enough. Whether or not these sex offenders know it, the worst is yet to come. The revolution is just getting underway.

As yet, this uprising can still be classified as spontaneous, or class consciousness in an embryonic form. People understand, or at least sense, the necessity for collective resistance and are in the process of abandoning their submission to their superiors. They are becoming aware of the antagonism between workers and capitalists, the billionaires, the bourgeoisie, but the workers are not, and can not, be aware of the fact that they are members of a working class, or proletarians, and that our interests are diametrically opposed to that of the capitalists. We say they cannot be aware of this because such consciousness can only be brought to them from outside the working class.

As Lenin pointed out in What Is To Be Done?, "The theory of socialism grew out of the philosophic, historical and economic theories that were elaborated by the educated representatives of the propertied classes, the intellectuals. According to their social status, the founders of modern scientific socialism, Marx and Engels, themselves belonged to the bourgeois intelligentsia."

It is only the intellectuals who can bring to the working class the awareness of itself as a class, complete with the implacable hatred of their class enemies, the bourgeoisie, and the destiny of the working class, the proletariat, to overthrow the capitalists, the bourgeoisie, and establish dictatorship over them, the Dictatorship Of the Proletariat. So for those members of the working class who are prejudiced against the bourgeois intellectuals, I can only say: GET OVER IT!

We live in a class society so there are really only two ideologies. There is no middle ground. It is either bourgeois or proletarian ideology, so, as Lenin stated it, "to belittle socialist ideology in any way, to deviate from it in the slightest degree means strengthening bourgeois ideology . . . The spontaneous development of the labor movement leads to it becoming subordinated to the bourgeois ideology . . . for the spontaneous labor movement is pure and simple trade unionism . . . and trade unionism means the ideological enslavement of the workers to the bourgeoisie. Hence our task, the task of Social-Democracy is to combat spontaneity, to divert the labor movement from its spontaneous trade unionist striving to go under the wing of the bourgeoisie, and to bring it under the wing of revolutionary Social-Democracy."—Please note that Lenin refers to Social-Democracy and I refer to it as Marxism or Communism.

As for those who may wonder why the spontaneous movement, which we are now experiencing, can be expected to lead to the domination of bourgeois ideology, it is simply because the bourgeois ideology is far older than proletarian ideology, more fully developed and possesses immeasurably more opportunities for being distributed. After all, it is the bourgeoisie which controls the press.

This means that the revolutionary movement now sweeping America, as it stands now, is doomed to failure, as the working class is not aware of itself as a class, and not aware that the capitalists have to be first overthrown and then crushed under the Dictatorship Of the Proletariat. This awareness can only come from outside the working class, from middle class intellectuals. It is necessary that the working class be made aware of itself as a class, with the duty to overthrow the billionaires, the capitalists, the bourgeoisie, and then smash the existing state apparatus, one which was sit up to crush us, the proletariat, and then set up a new state apparatus. That is the one and only way the revolution can succeed, the only way the desperate and determined resistance of the bourgeoisie can be crushed. The revolution can only succeed through the Dictatorship Of the Proletariat.

The problem is that while the working class is spontaneously gravitating towards socialism, the bourgeois ideology constantly reasserts itself, diverting that movement onto some harmless path of social reform. By this we mean that social reform is harmless to the capitalists, the billionaires, the bourgeoisie. They have the wealth and the power and fully intend to hang on to both. A few meagre reforms will not change that in the slightest.

On the other hand, they are aware of the movement towards socialism and are responding with the time honoured method of slander, in which they are dragging the names of the revolutionary leaders through the mud.

As merely one example of this, we can point out the response of the capitalists to the spontaneous revolutionary movement, which is the portrayal of Lenin, Stalin and Mao as equivalent to Hitler and Saddam Hussein. These "documentaries" are frequently shown on television. Nothing could be further from the truth, and yet it is widely distributed. The fact of the matter is that the working class spontaneously gravitates towards socialism, while the more wide spread bourgeois ideology deliberately imposes itself on the working class still more. We must oppose this bourgeois ideology with the help of the middle class intellectuals, including those who have been ruined by capitalism, forced to join the ranks of the proletariat. It matters not whether these former members of the middle class fight the billionaires, the bourgeoisie, voluntarily, as a matter of principle, or because they have been forced into poverty, and have no choice in the matter. They are aware of class distinctions and can and will help to educate the working class. Bear in mind that the members of the working class who are prejudiced against the middle class intellectuals, are also prejudiced against Marx, Engels and Lenin, and are therefore working in the interests of the bourgeoisie.

Still, the ruling class, the billionaires, the monopoly capitalists, the bourgeoisie, the completely reactionary class of people who are currently running the country, will now have to alter their method of rule. The problem, as they see it, is one of democracy. Citizens are now exercising their democratic rights, not only that of voting, but also the rights of assembly and of free speech, and will not be quiet. So now they are focused on restricting all of our democratic rights, even further.

By contrast, a great many citizens, common people, are furious that the Democratic candidate, Hillary Clinton, won the popular vote but lost the election. This means that she won the majority of votes but won fewer electoral votes than Trump, and as the election is decided by the majority of electoral votes, she lost the election. The Americans have a peculiar election system.

These same Americans are looking to Hillary Clinton to straighten out the mess created by Trump and his flunkies, but this is not about to happen. She is the former first lady, the wife of a man who was formerly president and is also alleged to be a sex offender, former Senator, former Secretary of State, and a loyal, faithful servant of the "establishment". This is to say that she is devoted to the billionaires, the monopoly capitalists, the bourgeoisie. She knows better than to "rock the boat".

It is true that of the estimated five million Americans who took part in the demonstrations of January 2017, immediately after the inauguration of Donald Trump, the vast majority were women. No doubt many of these women identify with Hillary Clinton, which is completely understandable, and they feel cheated because Hillary did not win. Be that as it may, even if she had won, nothing of consequence would have changed. Merely a different flunky of the ruling class, albeit a female, would have taken up residence in the White House.

That is the bitter truth which a great many people, those who are classified as members of a minority group, have already faced. They honestly thought that with one of their own elected as president, meaning of course Barrack Obama, then things would be different. After eight years of his administration, those same people had to face the fact that he was no different from any other president, aside from skin colour. Now the people who have placed such faith in Hillary are going to have to face that same harsh reality.

It is very likely that the political career of Hillary is over, as the investigations of Mueller and the congressional committees may well expand to her alleged involvement in the multi million dollar donations, by the Russians, to the Clinton foundation, as well as the more recent email scandal. It is suspected that the Russians were supporting the candidates of both parties, Democratic as well as Republican, which makes complete sense. That way, regardless of which party came to power, the Russians would win, as the winner would then be obligated to the Russians.

There are progressive people, most notably Michael Moore, the very accomplished film maker, who are now urging people to run for political office, possibly as Independent candidates or Independent Socialists or as members of the Democratic party, against Trump and the Republican party. This is an excellent idea, and we encourage working people to do just that. We would also encourage working people to join both parties, Democratic and Republican, as card carrying members, and run for political office, on behalf of both parties. It is a rather common mistake to regard the Democratic Party as somewhat progressive, when in fact they are every bit as reactionary as the Republican Party. After all, they serve the same class. Both are mere lackeys of the monopoly capitalists, the bourgeoisie.

But then, if even a sizeably minority of working people join the two parties, and choose candidates to run for office, then we should encourage them to do so, especially if they run as socialists. No doubt many of them will be elected and, once elected, they and their supporters will learn that it makes no difference. The billionaires are in power and have every intention of hanging onto that power.

This in no way changes the fact that the ruling class can no longer rule in the old way, so that it is now necessary to change their method of rule. As the working class has spontaneously gravitated towards socialism, the ruling class, which is to say the monopoly capitalists, the billionaires, the imperialist, the bourgeoisie, may well decide to offer the "Independent Socialists", as that is the way in which they refer to themselves, as an alternative to capitalism. From a scientific viewpoint, these people are technically called utopian socialists.

We can expect this of the capitalists, because they are as predictable as they are reactionary, and they are completely reactionary. In times of crisis, such as the one they are now facing, they can be expected to dream up that which has been tried on numerous previous occasions. This is their idea of being original. With that in mind, perhaps it is best if we examine our revolutionary history.

It is not by chance that one of the first utopian socialists made his appearance in Germany, in 1875. His name was Dr. Duhring, and he and his socialist party, as well as his philosophy, arose partly in response to Marx, who was also German, and his revolutionary theories. The theories of Duhring are anything but revolutionary, and were the subject of Engels in his excellent pamphlet, Socialism: Utopian and Scientific.

As Engels pointed out, it is the belief of the utopian socialists that "socialism is the expression of absolute truth, reason and justice and has only to be discovered to conquer all the world by virtue of its own power." It would be so nice if that were true. These utopian socialists, or Independent Socialists, as they now refer to themselves, actually believe that a display of "absolute truth" will impress the capitalists, the class of people who are currently running the country, that they will amend their ways and peace and harmony will prevail. Fat chance!

Engels goes on to say that "all past history, with the exception of its primitive stages, was the history of class struggles; that these warring classes of society are always the products of the modes of production and of exchange—in a word, of the economic conditions of their time; that the economic conditions of society always furnishes the real basis, starting from which we can alone work out the ultimate explanation of the whole superstructure of juridical and political institutions . . . socialism is no longer an accidental discovery of this or that ingenious brain, but the necessary outcome of the struggle between two historically developed classes—the proletariat and the bourgeoisie."

As opposed to the utopian socialist idea of exposing absolute truth as a means of conquering the world, there is the scientific belief, put forward by Karl Marx, who started with the materialist conception of history. As Engels phrased it "the production of the means to support human life and, next to production, the exchange of things produced, is the basis of all social structure; that in every society that has appeared in history, the manner in which wealth is distributed and society divided into classes or orders is dependent upon what is produced, how it is produced, and how the products are exchanged. From this point of view the final causes of all social changes and political revolutions are to be sought not in mens brains, not in mans better insight into eternal truth and justice, but in changes in the modes of production and exchange. They are to be sought not in the philosophy but in the economics of each particular epoch . . . While the capitalist mode of production more and more completely transforms the great majority of the population into proletarians, it creates the power which, under penalty of its own destruction, is forced to accomplish this revolution. While it forces on more and more the transformation of the vast means of production, already socialized, into state property, it shows itself the way to accomplish this revolution. The proletariat seizes political power and turns the means of production into state property."

This very nicely explains the reason the working class, the proletariat, has spontaneously gravitated towards socialism. As the economic base is now socialized, it is only natural to assume that the political super structure should also be socialized. It is also natural to assume that the people in charge of the super structure, the capitalists, the bourgeoisie, most emphatically disagree with this assessment.

Now we have got to face the current situation, which may not be pleasant, but then life never is terribly pleasant. To borrow a gambling expression, we have got to "play the cards we have been dealt".

First we have got to face the fact that the socialist Russian revolution of October, 1917, led by Lenin, was a great success. We also have to face the fact that after Stalin died, the capitalists were able to restore capitalism in Russia. Further, the Chinese socialist revolution of 1948, led by Mao, was also a great success, despite the fact that after the death of Mao, the capitalists were also able to restore capitalism in China. The fact that the current leaders may call themselves Communists or Marxists is not too surprising, as they are typical capitalists, which is to say, they are liars.

This has led to considerable confusion among members of the working class. There are a great many people who call themselves Marxists or Marxist – Leninists or Communists or Bolsheviks or Social-Democrats, while in fact they are anything but that. This calls for a little explanation. As for those who find this tiresome, I can only suggest you skim through this. Bear in mind, I am writing for all members of the working class, not just those who are young and well educated. As for those who may find that offensive, bear in mind that I am not a spring chicken.

Marx and Engels worked in the mid to late nineteenth century, and were the first to examine capitalism in its pre-monopoly stage. Their theories are commonly referred to as Marxist. The most significant revolutionary motion of that time was the revolt of the workers of Paris in 1871, and the subsequent Paris Commune, as the workers in revolt referred to themselves as Communards. This is the origin of the name Communist.

Then, at the turn of the century, which is to say at the beginning of the twentieth century, capitalism reached its highest stage, which is to say the age of monopoly, commonly referred to as imperialism, and imperialism has its own peculiar features, somewhat different from pre-monopoly capitalism. It was Lenin who examined these features of capitalism in its highest, most decadent form, that of imperialism, and his theories are commonly referred to as Leninist. Those who claim to be followers of Marx and Lenin call themselves Marxist-Leninists. It is also true that Lenin was a founding member of the Social Democratic party of Russia, which is where we get the name Social Democrat. At that time the party very quickly split into two sections, the Bolshevik section, led by Lenin, and of course this is where we get the name Bolshevik. The other section of the party was completely devoid of principle, or opportunist, and referred to as Menshevik.

For those who are not familiar with the term opportunist, it is defined as "a person who exploits circumstances to gain immediate advantage rather that being guided by consistent principles or plans." It should come as no surprise to anyone that capitalists are consummate opportunists. The closest a capitalist ever comes to principle is learning to spell the word. They would not know a principle if they tripped over it. Sadly, they have also polluted the revolutionary working class movement, so that there are now working class leaders who are also just as corrupt, just as devoid of principle, as their capitalist masters.

There are people who are somewhat discouraged because the socialist Soviet Union was overthrown by the capitalists, and the socialist country of China followed suit. To such people, I can only say that no one promised you a rose garden. Get over it! A great many revolutionaries fought and laid down their lives in the interest of a better future for their descendants as well as for workers of different countries, which includes us. The least we can do is honour their memory by carrying on, following in their footsteps, picking up the torch and fighting the capitalists. We must be inspired by their sacrifice and yes, we must also learn from their mistakes. Bear in mind that the capitalists, the billionaires, the bourgeoisie, are part of a class which is old and rotten, in decay, destined to be overthrown by the progressive working class, but still desperate to preserve their decadent way of life, determined to continue to exploit and crush us and continue to live in the lap of luxury, at our expense, of course.

This is our current situation and it has been compared to the time in which Marx and Engels worked. There are comparisons, in that at present there are no socialist countries in the world, but there are also major differences. We have the experience of the Russian as well as the Chinese revolution, and the theories of Lenin and Mao. We also have the Chinese Cultural Revolution, a ten year revolution. This too requires a little explanation.

The socialist Soviet Union was held in the highest regard, especially after their successful defeat of the German Nazis. So it came as a great shock when the revisionists restored capitalism in the Soviet Union and it became socialist in name only, which is referred to as social chauvinism.

The Chinese response was most instructive. In an attempt to prevent a similar return to power, by the capitalists, in China, they launched the Cultural Revolution. As a result of this, the capitalists who were hiding in various fields of culture were purged.

In my opinion, this was a great success, but did not go far enough. The capitalists who were hiding in various fields of science remained in power, and helped to take part in the restoration of capitalism in China, after the death of Mao.

At the time of the Cultural Revolution, the then socialist Chinese Communist Party was well aware that mass movements happen under socialism, just as they happen under capitalism. They were also well aware that even after the revolution, classes continue to exist. The revolution is merely the first step, and then it is a matter of exercising proper Dictatorship over the bourgeoisie.

As the mass movement was picking up in China, the Central Committee of the Communist Party passed a resolution, one which is unheard of under capitalism. They ordered that the police and army units were to allow the citizens to carry on as they saw fit, interfering only in cases of arson, rape or murder. Aside from those major crimes, the people taking part in that revolution were allowed to do as they pleased, and they pleased to expose, humiliate and ridicule their class enemies, the capitalists and the working class traitors who supported them. In short, the revolutionary movement was given free reign.

For ten years, the revolution raged and the working people of China were schooled in the class struggle. They learned that the capitalists, the people who have been overthrown, never resign themselves to their fate.

As a result of this, Mao was of the opinion that any capitalist return to power in China was unlikely, but if it did happen, it would be short lived, as the public had been well schooled in the class struggle. At worst, it could last only several decades. In fact, it has been several decades since the capitalists returned to power in China, so the country of China is overdue for a revolution. Then too, as the capitalists have tied together the economies of the world, they have also very likely tied together the mass movements of the world. The current revolutionary movement which is sweeping the world, being led by the American women, is very likely also sweeping China. As the Chinese ruling class has kept a tight muzzle on the press, it is very difficult to get any idea of the revolutionary motion which may be taking place. Either way, if it is not taking place now, it soon will be.

Never in the history of the world has such a situation existed. All previous revolutions were confined to one country or at best, several countries in one part of the world. Now we have a revolution, or at least revolutionary motion, sweeping the world, and it is being led by Americans, and mainly American women. Those women have every right to be proud. Very soon this revolution will break out into open rebellion, open class warfare.

Now that the capitalists, the billionaires, the bourgeoisie, are about to change their method of rule, we can expect them to offer the working class, the proletarians, a safe but harmless alternative, a utopian socialist, in the form of Senator Bernie Sanders. He refers to himself as an Independent Socialist and is very popular with the working people, with good reason. He is apparently a fine, honest, dedicated individual who considers himself a socialist and is determined to change the system from within. This is another way of saying that he is a utopian socialist, not a Marxist, and does not believe in revolution or the Dictatorship Of the Proletariat, which is the ultimate goal of all Marxists. As Sanders is a member of the Senate, he is very likely just the fellow the capitalists are looking for, and so too are we.

This requires a little explanation, as it may seem strange that we, Marxist, would agree with the imperialists on any matter. Yet here we are, and the fact is that the most advanced strata of the working class has spontaneously embraced the idea of socialism. This is excellent, without a doubt, and is a big step in the right direction, but only a step. It does not go far enough. The working class has got to learn, and can only learn from their own experience, that there is a difference between utopian socialism, which is the socialism of the so called Independent Socialists, and scientific socialism, which is the socialism of the Marxists. Further, the working class will also have to learn to distinguish between true Marxists and the phoney Marxists.

That is where Sanders and other Independent Socialists can prove to be quite useful. He and other honest but misguided people should be encouraged to run for political office, whether it is on a local, state or federal level. I use the word encourage, because such people have to be encouraged, as they are afraid of their success. And many of them will succeed, running as Independent Socialists, because the vast majority of working class people are fed up with capitalism, are demanding change, and the only alternative to capitalism is socialism. Then, as democratically elected members of the government, they can try their hand at changing the system from within. This is not about to happen. They will very quickly learn, and members of the working class will also learn, that the monopoly capitalists, the bourgeoisie, are in charge and they fully intend to stay in charge. The working class will continue to be exploited and crushed. There will be no fundamental change. The bourgeoisie have the wealth and power and fully intend to hold on to both.

These people, the completely reactionary class of degenerates who are currently running the country, are not about to part with their wealth and power, at least not without a fight. Such people have never done an honest days work in their lives and are not at all anxious to start. It is necessary to persuade them, just as it was necessary to persuade the British nobility and British capitalists to part with their wealth and power in the American colonies, in the first American revolution of 1776.

As for those who consider this a bit harsh, it is best to bear in mind that the founding fathers of the United States have given the citizens of that country the right to abolish any government which does not represent them. This right is guaranteed in the Declaration of Independence. The country was founded on revolution, and will soon abolish the current government, through revolution, and replace it with a socialist government which does represent them, in the form of the Dictatorship Of the Proletariat.

With that in mind, in the interests of educating the working class, it is up to the Marxists to support the Independent

Socialists, encourage them to run for office, at the same time making it clear that a vote for an Independent Socialist is better than a vote for Trump or one of his flunkies, a member of the GOP, Grand Old Party, or even a vote for Clinton, who is also a well established flunky of the capitalists. At the same time we can make it clear that the Dictatorship Of the Proletariat is far superior to the dictatorship of the Trumps, disguised under the name of "bourgeois democracy". The fact must be stressed that this is class war, a war between the capitalist class and the working class, between the dictatorship of the bourgeoisie and the Dictatorship Of the Proletariat. It is one dictatorship or the other, and there is no middle ground.

Our first order of business must be to make the working class aware of itself as a class, complete with its own class interests. This may sound strange, as all other classes are aware of themselves as a class, but the working class is not, and that is just the way it is. The nobility are certainly aware of their class, which they consider superior, and rub it in our faces at every opportunity. In a similar manner, the billionaires, the monopoly capitalists, the bourgeoisie, the class of people who evolved from the burghers of the middle ages, are also aware of themselves as a class. They are commonly referred to as the new American nobility, and much as they would love to be granted titles of nobility, cannot do so if only because they are prohibited by law. Besides, the nobility have closed ranks and are not about to allow themselves to be polluted with the blood of commoners, regardless of how rich those commoners are.

Lower down on the social scale, we have the middle class, otherwise known as the petty bourgeois, and they too are equally well aware of themselves as a class. These are the people who own a small business, usually employing several workers and frequently manage to live rather comfortable lives, at least until the monopoly capitalists, the bourgeoisie, put them out of business. This happens on a regular basis, but as long as they stay in business, they entertain themselves with visions of joining the ranks of the bourgeoisie. But just as the ranks of the nobility are closed, so too the ranks of the bourgeoisie are closed and possibly shrinking, as the capitalists steal from each other. They also take great delight in ruining the middle class people, the petty bourgeois, driving them into the ranks of the working class, the proletariat.

The peasantry are at the low end of the social scale but also extremely well aware of themselves as a class. That just leaves the working class, the proletariat, and in highly industrialized countries of the world, is the most numerous class. This in no way changes the fact that the working class is not aware of itself as a class.

Our current political leaders tell us that those among us who are relatively well off, even managing to make ends meet, are middle class people, which is simply not true. Those of us who work for wages are working class people, proletarians, and of course the capitalists do not want us to be aware of this.

That being said, the fact remains, and must be driven home to any and all members of the working class, that those of us who work for wages are workers, technically referred to as proletarians, and we are members of the working class, complete with our own class interests. It is not a matter of race, religion, ethnic background or any other superficial difference. It is the capitalists who exploit and crush us, and they do not care in the slightest about such differences. They care only about their profit, and the harder they work us and the less they pay us, the higher their profit. It does not take a genius to figure that our differences are diametrically opposed. This is another way of saying that we are natural class enemies.

We, the Marxists, may consider our first order of business that of making the working class aware of itself as a class. At the same time, we have got to educate the workers, get them familiar with the scientific terms, as our class enemies are supremely well aware of these terms and use our ignorance against us. This may not be as difficult as it may sound, as we all learn through repetition. That is the way we learned the alphabet.

The careful reader may have noticed that I tend to be redundant, and that is not by chance. It is deliberate. It is also best to bear in mind that time is not on our side, as the revolution could break out any day now and the working class will have to face it, ready or not.

It bears repeating that the revolution can only be successful if it is guided by a proper revolutionary theory, which is to say a Marxist theory. Perhaps it would be best to think of revolutionary theory as a road map, as a proper guide to a goal, which is precisely what it is. The point must be driven home to the working class that we live under the dictatorship of the bourgeoisie, which is to say the dictatorship of the capitalists, the billionaires, and this is completely unacceptable. We must replace this with a working class Dictatorship, the Dictatorship Of the Proletariat.

Under the dictatorship of the bourgeoisie, we have democracy for the monopoly capitalists, the imperialists, the billionaires, of whom there are only a relative handful, possibly no more than four hundred in all of North America. For the rest of us, and most of us are wage labourers, proletarians, as the peasantry and middle class have pretty well been wiped out, it is a dictatorship, the dictatorship of the bourgeoisie. It is necessary for us, the working class, the wage labourers, the proletarians, to replace this dictatorship with another dictatorship, the Dictatorship Of the Proletariat. We have got to overthrow the capitalists, the billionaires, the bourgeoisie, and crush them under the iron boot of the working class, the proletariat.

This will result in a new democracy, a democracy for the proletariat but a Dictatorship over the bourgeoisie. It will truly be a government of the people, by the people and for the people, in that the people are the working class. At the same time, we must preclude any effort on the part of the bourgeoisie to return to power, as they no doubt will make every effort to do just that. It would never occur to them to resign themselves to their fate, to perform useful, productive work. Manual labor, or any kind of labor for that matter, is beneath their dignity. But then that is where the Dictatorship comes into play.

In a perfect world, one in which we certainly do not live, we would first educate the workers, or at least the most advanced strata of the proletariat, persuade them of the necessity of the Dictatorship Of the Proletariat and only then prepare them for the coming Dictatorship. But as this is not a perfect world – no kidding, you say – we do not have that option. More or less as a consequence of this, we now have to prepare for that Dictatorship, which may happen any day now. The bourgeoisie may well force the revolution on the workers, and they will no doubt respond.

This will almost certainly result in the defeat of the capitalists and the Dictatorship Of the Proletariat will immediately be established. This means that workers with very little training, or no training at all, will be placed in positions of authority. This will be part of a new state apparatus which can and must be set up, a state apparatus for the purpose of crushing the desperate and determined resistance of the imperialists, the monopoly capitalists, the billionaires, the bourgeoisie, the insignificant minority of parasites who are currently crushing and exploiting the vast majority, the working class, the proletariat. The old state apparatus which was set up to crush the working class must be destroyed and a new state apparatus must be established, with the aim of crushing the capitalists, the billionaires, the bourgeoisie.

So now we have the dual goals of making the workers aware of themselves as a class, one which is destined to overthrow the bourgeoisie and establish the Dictatorship Of the Proletariat, and that of training the most advanced members of that class, in preparation for that Dictatorship. This is spelled out quite clearly in that excellent book by Lenin, State and Revolution. This new proletarian government will require leaders, and almost certainly workers with little training, or even no training at all, will have to rise to the occasion. The more training we do now, the better prepared we will be after the revolution.

In preparation for the coming Dictatorship Of the Proletariat, the most advanced workers should be encouraged to assume leadership roles in working class organizations, such as sports clubs and trade unions. The fact is that there are no natural born leaders, just as there are no natural born organizers, contrary to the belief of the billionaires, the bourgeoisie, and the flunkies who serve them so faithfully. Of course, when they refer to natural born leaders, they are referring to themselves.

This brings us to a tool which previous revolutionaries did not have, and that is the internet. I can only encourage people who are Marxists to use the internet to get in touch with each other, to coordinate activities such as demonstrations, as well as sharing videos and literature. This could also lead to the formation of a true Marxist Communist Party in North America, as there are no true Marxist parties of which I am aware, just parties which claim to be Marxist.

Those who are interested in scientific socialism, as opposed to utopian socialism, are encouraged to read The Communist

Manifesto, by Marx and Engels. That is a fine place to start. Then there is Socialism: Utopian and Scientific, by Engels, which is most relevant. One of the finest works of Lenin is Imperialism, the Highest Stage of Capitalism, which explains in simple, clear cut language, the features of monopoly capitalism, which is imperialism. Another work of Lenin which is today most relevant is State and Revolution, in which it is explained that one of the goals of the revolution is to destroy the current state apparatus. Then there is the not so little matter of the phoney Marxists in our midst, those who claim to be Marxists but are not. Lenin criticizes them most strongly in What Is To Be Done? It should be noted that these trends in socialist thought are not new and original but merely the same old clap trap which was dished up many years ago.

As Lenin pointed out in State and Revolution, "the class struggle is acceptable to the bourgeoisie. Those who recognize only the class struggle are not yet Marxists; they may be found to have gone no further than the boundaries of bourgeois reasoning and bourgeois politics. To limit Marxism to the theory of the class struggle means curtailing Marxism, distorting it, reducing it to something which is acceptable to the bourgeoisie. A Marxist is one who extends the acceptance of the class struggle to the acceptance of the Dictatorship Of the Proletariat . . . This is the touchstone on which the real understanding and acceptance of Marxism should be tested."

The phoney Marxists are those who openly deny the necessity of the Dictatorship Of the Proletariat, or more commonly, those who do their best to avoid the issue. It is now fashionable, in phoney Marxist circles, to not mention revolution or the Dictatorship Of the Proletariat, on the grounds that the working people are not discussing this. Well of course the working people are not discussing this, for the very fine and simple reason that they are not aware of it! It is up to us, the true Marxists, to make them aware. That will likely rouse the bourgeoisie to a fury, and that is a sight to behold.

It is best to bear in mind that the Dictatorship Of the Proletariat is the absolute worst nightmare of the capitalists, the billionaires, the bourgeoisie. These are the same people who own and control the press, and determine just what we see and hear. This is to say that the news is completely censored, and the propaganda is relentless, non stop. They rarely use the word capitalism, instead using words such as entrepreneurs or democracy, trying their best to confuse people. Their idea of democracy is a democracy of the capitalists, the billionaires, the members of their own class, the bourgeoisie. They refer to the president as the "leader of the free world", when what they really mean is leader of the capitalist world. As if capitalism is equivalent to freedom! The monopoly capitalists, the billionaires, are never referred to as the bourgeoisie, as they do not want working people to be made aware of class distinctions. In fact, they tend not to acknowledge the existence of classes. They generally refer to themselves as businessmen or entrepreneurs.

That is the current state of affairs, and the fact is that a great many working class people, or at least a sizeable minority, are not aware of the existence of classes, or at least not here in North America. This speaks to the effectiveness of American propaganda, and simply means that this stratum of workers, those who are not aware of the existence of classes, should be identified and appropriate literature sent to them. This literature should be popular but entertaining, while explaining that the capitalists make their profit from our labor power and further, the harder they work us and the less they pay us, the higher their profit. Those who are most familiar with the internet can perform a fine service in this area.

There are a great many more workers, even the most advanced, who are unaware of the Dictatorship Of the Proletariat. This strata of workers should also be targeted and literatures sent to them, although in a form which is perhaps less popular.

The younger generation, or at least those who are young from my rather advanced viewpoint, are quite familiar with computers and assure me that there are search engines which can identify demographics, which is to say statistical data relating to the population and particular sectors within it. While I am not sure what that means, it sounds most impressive and I believe I have all the technical terms correct.

This same younger generation assures me that leaflets and going door to door is "old school", by which I suspect they mean obsolete. Now a far more efficient method of educating the public, the members of the working class, is with the tools available on the internet, including face book, you tube and various other social networks. I am sure they have a point, but I still think there is a place for leaflets.

The point is that there is now a fine tool available to reach the workers and we would be fools not to take advantage of this. Most workers now have a computer and the vast majority are set up for email and also use face book. Of course we all do the same thing, which is to say we associate with our own kind, people with interests similar to our own. It stands to reason that the more advanced workers associate with other more advanced workers, sharing view points and ideas. These are the workers who will lead the revolution and the less advanced workers will listen to them. These more advanced workers are the workers of whom we are mainly concerned, although we certainly do not want to neglect the less advanced. We want to bring to these workers the awareness of themselves as members of a class, and of the necessity of revolution and the subsequent Dictatorship Of the Proletariat.

The equivalent of leaflets can be sent to these workers, in the form of emails, and they can in turn be passed on to their friends, merely with the push of a button. As long as these emails are interesting, they will in turn pass them on and discuss them. It is up to us, as Marxists, to ensure these emails are interesting. For those workers who are less advanced, we can also send emails, although perhaps in a more popular form. The less advanced are not to be ignored but raised to a higher level.

The advanced workers who take part in this sort of activity, reaching out to all members of the public, young and old, employed and unemployed as well as underemployed, can correctly be considered to be training for the Dictatorship Of the Proletariat, as after the revolution, a great deal of such work, including work with a computer, will also be required.

These same advanced workers, especially those who are rather young and politically active, are very likely well accustomed to use of the internet. We should encourage them to use this most handy tool to get in touch with people just like themselves, to spread the word, to coordinate demonstrations and protests. The equivalent of leaflets can be contained in emails and sent to countless people. These advanced workers are no doubt able to target select groups of workers and send them literature which appeals to them. For workers who are somewhat less advanced, the literature can be more popular but never vulgar.

As an example of the use which can be made of the internet, by those who are far more familiar with it than I am, I can suggest posting the video of a great many executives of American corporations, those who were gathered together at the request of members of the press. These executives were then asked what they would do with the anticipated windfall of cash which will soon be coming their way, as soon as the proposed tax cuts went into effect, at least if Trump has his way. The journalist asking this question was clearly surprised at the response, in that most executives said they would give it to their stock holders, in other words pocket the money, rather than invest it in creating more jobs.

Perhaps the journalist thought that just because Trump said that this windfall of capital would be used to create jobs, then it must be true. Of course, it is not, and the corporate executives are under no obligation to create jobs. Their loyalty lies with the class of people they serve, the capitalists, the billionaires, the bourgeoisie, and in fact they are dedicated servants. They do not care in the slightest for working class people, as those who do care for working people are not allowed to become corporate executives. It is my opinion that videos such as this should be made widely available on the internet, as a means of exposing the lies of Trump, to the effect that tax breaks for corporations and billionaires will result in more jobs for working people. It most certainly will not. It will only serve to enrich the billionaires and corporations still further.

As for those who object that everyone knows this, everyone knows that Trump is a liar, everyone knows that tax breaks for the corporations and billionaires will only serve to further enrich the capitalists, at our expense of course, I can only respond that such is not the case. While the more advanced members of the working class are supremely well aware of this, there are a great many working class people, those who are somewhat less advanced, but still a considerable minority, who are not yet aware of this. Perhaps they choose to believe that Trump has their best interests at heart, if only because they want to believe this. These workers tend to be honest, hard working people, law abiding tax paying citizens, and they tend to believe the best of everyone.

They cannot believe that the people they elected to office would lie to them. It is up to Marxists to persuade them that when it comes to the bourgeoisie, there is no point in believing the best of them, because there is no best.

One of the best ways to expose the billionaires, the bourgeoisie, is to use their own words against them. On occasion they trip themselves up, speaking the truth.

It is for that reason I frequently watch the news, not because I believe their lies and propaganda, but to see just what sort of a mess they have worked themselves into. Besides, a great many working people, or at least those who are more advanced, are also watching the news.

This brings us back to those workers who would prefer to run for office, perhaps as Independent Socialists. In that case, as Marxists, we should encourage this. If elected to positions of authority, this could provide valuable experience for these workers in the coming Dictatorship Of the Proletariat. Marxists can also run for office, as Communists, although we must be careful not to run against workers who are running as Democrats or Independents or Independent Socialists. We do not want to ruin their chance of becoming elected, in that running against them may split the vote, allowing a Trump supporter to become elected. We should be careful to run for political office only in safe districts, safe in the sense that there is no chance of an Independent Socialist becoming elected. The important thing is not that we or an Independent Socialist becomes elected, or how many become elected, but that the working class become aware of itself as a class, a class at war with the capitalist class, and the absolute necessity of overthrowing the bourgeoisie and establishing the Dictatorship Of the Proletariat. The platform of running for office will provide us with an opportunity to explain all this to the working people.

These people are the natural and desirable allies of Marxists in so far as the democratic tasks are concerned. But an essential condition for our support must be the complete liberty for the Marxists to reveal to the working class that its interests are diametrically opposed to the interests of the bourgeoisie, that our goal is revolution and the establishment of the Dictatorship Of the Proletariat.

These candidates are not the enemy, just as the Independent Socialists are not the enemy, merely people who are making an honest mistake. It is absolutely essential that we get them on our side, as we can use all the help we can get. Failing that, a position of benevolent neutrality would be an improvement.

The fact is that the enemy, which is the monopoly capitalists, the billionaires, the imperialists, the bourgeoisie, are very powerful, deeply entrenched, determined to hold on to power. They control the press and constantly swamp the working class with their bourgeois propaganda, which is to say their lies. To overthrow this class of parasites will not be easy.

This brings us to the not so little matter of the phoney Marxist, those who claim to be Marxist but are not. Of course they too are free to run for office but there is no way that we can support them. Their goal is to divert the revolutionary movement onto some harmless channel of social reform. They perform an invaluable service to the capitalists, the billionaires, the bourgeoisie, their lords and masters, by confusing the working class. They are agents of the bourgeoisie within the ranks of the working class, and are of the opinion that Marxism must be revised. They deny the necessity of the Dictatorship Of the Proletariat and some of them even admit this. Other phoney Marxists do not admit this, but are careful to avoid any mention of revolution or the Dictatorship Of the Proletariat or anything else which may offend their political masters. They are well aware that the

Dictatorship Of the Proletariat is the worst nightmare of the billionaires, the bourgeoisie. It bears mentioning that in return for this act of self degradation, they can expect precisely the same reward that the flunkies of Trump can expect, which is to say, absolutely nothing.

It was Lenin who carried on a most merciless war with these phoney Marxists, those whom at that time referred to themselves as Mensheviks. As Lenin stated in What Is To Be Done?, it is the position of such people that Social-Democracy, as that is the term they used at that time, "must change from a party of the social revolution into a democratic party of social reform . . . the possibility of putting socialism on a scientific basis and of proving that it is necessary and inevitable from the point of view of the materialist conception of history was denied . . . the very conception, ultimate aim, was declared to be unsound, and the idea of the Dictatorship Of the Proletariat was absolutely rejected. It was denied that there is any difference in principle between liberalism and socialism. The theory of the class struggle was rejected on the grounds that it could not be applied to a strictly democratic society . . ." Such was the position of the Mensheviks, opportunists one and all, completely devoid of principle, at the time of Lenin, and such is the position of so many people who claim to be Marxists to this day. In that respect, not a great deal has changed.

The whole purpose of that book was to expose the bankruptcy of that nonsense, put forward in the name of Marx, even though it is absolutely revisionist and completely acceptable to the monopoly capitalists, the billionaires, the bourgeoisie. Yet to this day there are people, in almost every country of the world, who preach this Menshevik, reactionary claptrap, and in the name of Marx and Lenin, no less!

In order for the revolution to be successful, it needs a revolutionary theory. This point must be stressed and we must face the fact that at present, there is no revolutionary party of the working class, at least not here in North America. I deliberately use the word revolutionary, by which I mean Marxist, because those parties which do exist, while claiming to be Marxist, are in fact mere parties of social reform. On the one hand they may admit that they are revisionists, which is to say that the theories of Marx, Engels and Lenin must be revised, or they deny being revisionists but are non revolutionary in actions. This is to say that they are absolutely opposed to revolution and the subsequent Dictatorship Of the Proletariat. They are the most loyal, devoted servants of the capitalists, the imperialists, the billionaires, the bourgeoisie, and the most stupid. They are most determined to keep the working class unaware of itself as a class, unaware of revolution and the subsequent Dictatorship Of the Proletariat. The billionaires merely accept this bit of self degradation as their due.

Then too, perhaps the phoney Marxists, those who are technically referred to as social chauvinists, which is to say socialist in words but chauvinist in deeds, think the working people are not capable of understanding the necessity of revolution, of seizing political power and crushing the desperate and determined resistance of the bourgeoisie, through the Dictatorship Of the Proletariat. As proof, they may point to the fact that the workers are not talking about this. These same phoney Marxists refuse to acknowledge that the workers are not aware of this. It is up to us, the Marxists, to bring them this awareness of themselves as a class and the necessity and inevitability of the revolution, along with the subsequent Dictatorship Of the Proletariat. The working class must emancipate itself, and that cannot be done by a bunch of well meaning reformist middle class intellectuals.

This is not to denigrate intellectuals, whether of the middle class or any other class—and I am an intellectual—as such people can and do perform a very valuable service to the revolution. A great many middle class people have been ruined by capitalism, and their ranks are growing on a daily basis, as the bourgeoisie continue to tighten their grip on society, eliminating any and all competition, no matter how insignificant. In other words, they run middle class people out of business, ruining them, forcing them into bankruptcy, forcing them into the ranks of the working class.

A recent example of this is provided by the taxi companies. A few of those taxi companies are rather large, at least by the standards of working people, while many are owner-operators. Almost all have been ruined, forced into bankruptcy, due to competition from Uber.

As details are so important, it should be pointed out to working people that formerly, a taxi medallion in New York City was selling for well over a million dollars. Now those same medallions are selling for a quarter million. Many people who invested in a taxi medallion, with the idea of becoming small business people, middle class, working hard and possibly expanding, have since been ruined.

As soon as Uber came into existence, the income of all taxi owners fell dramatically. Yet the payments on their medallions remained the same, even as the value of the medallions took a nose dive. Very soon, they owed far more on their taxis than they were worth. Almost all were forced into bankruptcy, so that the billionaires became ever more wealthy.

This can be used to drive home the point that the middle class is being wiped out. The billionaires allow no competition, regardless of how slight. The lesson for the working class is that there is no point in trying to go into business, to become middle class. Any and all such attempts are destined to fail. The monopoly capitalists will make sure of that.

As these—former-middle class people are forced to join the ranks of the proletariat, they are supremely well aware of class distinctions and are quite capable of bringing this class awareness to the working class. To such people, former members of the middle class, we have only one thing to say: Welcome!

These new members of the working class can perform an invaluable service to the proletariat, as they bring with them the awareness of classes and are well aware of the lies and schemes of the capitalists, the billionaires, the bourgeoisie. After all, they can speak from experience. They can help to inform the working class of the mentality of these parasites, and can also explain that after the revolution their resistance, that of the billionaires, will increase ten fold, as they make every effort to regain their "paradise lost". After the completion of the revolution, the only way to prevent a return to power is to crush them under the iron heel of the working class, the proletariat, which is correctly referred to as the Dictatorship Of the Proletariat. The capitalists must be overthrown and absolutely crushed. Under no circumstances should they be allowed to return to power, as happened in the Soviet Union, after the death of Stalin, and in China, after the death of Mao. It is up to us to learn from the mistakes of the Russians and Chinese and not to repeat their mistakes.

We respect the honesty of the Independent Socialists and have no problem with them. We have a real problem with the phoney Marxists who run for political office while claiming to be Marxists. Our attitude towards these people, these agents of the billionaires within the ranks of the working class, must be one of unwavering struggle. We must constantly draw a clear line between the fake Marxists and the true Marxist, as that is the only way to educate the members of the working class.

It is to be expected that many of the working people who are currently running for office are veterans of the occupy movement and have no illusions. They have been tempered in the class struggle and know what to expect. They are no longer content to be ruled in the old way and are demanding change. They are not satisfied with the manner in which the elected officials have betrayed them. Rather than sit back and complain, they are taking action. This is most commendable. I can only suggest that the younger generation assist them in running for office. They can be of great service in this regard, with their knowledge of computers and the internet. This will also provide the younger generation with valuable experience which will be be of great benefit after the revolution, after we establish the Dictatorship Of the Proletariat.

As members of the working class run for office, either as Independent Socialists, as Democrats or as Marxists, we can expect that under the current political climate, where so many working class people are demanding change, embracing socialism, many of these candidates will be elected to office. They will then learn from bitter experience, that it is not possible to enact any meaningful change. The Marxists are already well aware of this, and can use the elections as a means of educating the members of the public, which is to say the working class, as we all have to learn from our own experience.

The capitalists, the billionaires, the bourgeoisie, are in charge, and no change of faces in any elected office is going to change that. That is the painful lesson that the Independent Socialists will have to learn, as well as their supporters, the honest members of the working class. Then from their own bitter experience they will learn that the Marxists are right, and come around to being our strongest supporters. It is also very likely that Marxists who run for office will also be elected, not that it matters a great deal. The important thing is that the working people be made aware that any elected official, under capitalism, changes nothing. It remains the dictatorship of the bourgeoisie.

As for those who think that it is not right for Marxists to be elected to office, I can only draw attention to the fact that in the fall of 1917, at the time of the successful socialist Russian revolution, there were Marxists who had been elected to the Russian Constituent Assembly, and they played an invaluable role in the revolution. They then used that office to educate the working people, to let them know that officials democratically elected to office was better than no officials elected to office, but the government still remained under the control of the capitalists, the bourgeoisie.

After the revolution, these same people took part in dissolving that Constituent Assembly and setting up the Dictatorship Of the Proletariat. That is the proper Marxist approach.

Bear in mind that immediately after Trump was sworn into office in January, approximately five million American women marched in protest, and in most countries of the world, a great many other women marched in support of their American sisters. This gives us an indication of the strength of the international working class movement, one which is being led by American women.

We can only offer them our most sincere gratitude and support. They have every reason to be proud.

CHAPTER 7

CURRENT AMERICAN REVOLUTION

Jun 9, 2020

The death of another unarmed Black man, at the hands of the police, has apparently triggered another American revolution. His murder was caught on video, by a bystander who recorded this on her cell phone. The video has gone "viral", and has been shown around the world. Countless people are outraged, not just in America but in numerous other countries. Protests have taken place all across America, in cities and small towns. Statues which have stood for years, in honour of such people as the Confederate General Robert E. Lee, are now being torn down. General Lee was a slave owner and staunch supporter of slavery. It was his firm belief that Black people were an inferior race, and he fought at the head of an army, in an effort to preserve the institution of slavery. Statues in honour of such people are an insult to all Black people, as well as to all minorities. For that matter, they are an insult to all those who fought for the Union in the Civil War. The sacrifice of those valiant soldiers should not be marred by honouring the memory the slave owners, the very people whom they destroyed.

The mass movement against violent police repression and racism has even spread overseas. In England, the statue of a man who lived several centuries ago was torn down and thrown into the river. The reason is that the statue honoured a man who was a slave trader. There too, the people are taking action, doing the "right thing", even if that right thing is not strictly within the absolute letter of the law. Some things just have to be done.

In America, the movement is very broad and deep. Even the journalists are now using the word revolution, if only in whispers, so to speak. It is clear that the word is cause for embarrassment. They are having a difficult time facing the fact that the current uprising, the protests, the marches, the calls for an end to police brutality and racism, is nothing less than a full scale revolution.

Never in the history of the country have so many distinguished figures, including former high ranking members of presidential administrations, as well as former high ranking military men, spoken out so clearly and passionately, against a sitting president.

One former four star general referred to the current protests as "the beginning of the end of the American experiment". This statement is perhaps not so much clear, as it is passionate.

It is characteristic of such people that they cannot bring themselves to use the word capitalism, much less socialism. The general used the expression "American experiment", as a reference to capitalism. Also, his expression "the beginning of the end" is a reference to the end of capitalism. Of course, it will soon be replaced by socialism, and that will only happen through revolution, but that is a thought which the general finds too terrible for words.

A former Secretary of Defence referred to Trump as a "threat to the Constitution", someone who "tries to divide us". In this, he is absolutely correct.

The current Secretary of Defence has just openly disagreed with Trump on the question of using the American military against the protesters. The Defence Secretary considers it to be an "abuse of executive authority". Trump, by contrast, has no concept of abuse of executive authority. As far as he is concerned, he has absolute authority, and fully intends to use it, as he sees fit.

Even a high ranking member of the American Senate, a former candidate for the presidency and a member of the same political party as Trump, has marched with Black Lives Matter. He is perhaps the one and only such politician to go to that great length.

For the benefit of working people who are just now becoming politically active—welcome, my brothers and sisters, my comrades!—I will mention that there is a law referred to as the Posse Comitatus Act, which forbids the use of American military against American citizens. Trump responded to this by saying that the Insurrection Act of 1807 allows him to use the military within the country, in case of an "insurrection", as he sees fit. According to the same law, federal troops can be sent in to each state only at the request of the governor of that particular state. Trump has his own interpretation of the law. As far as he is concerned, if the governors are not doing their job, then he will do it for them!

Trump refers to himself as the "law and order president", yet his latest stunt made a mockery of law and order. In the interests of a "photo op", which is shorthand for photo opportunity, he had his Attorney General, the "top cop" in the country, clear an area,

Lafayette Park, next to the White House, so that he could march to a nearby church and have his picture taken.

The park was occupied by peaceful protesters at that time, those who were exercising their democratic right to express their disapproval, as is guaranteed in the Constitution. The Attorney General of the country then gave the illegal order and the police responded by attacking those law abiding citizens with pepper spray, tear gas, shields and clubs. So much for law and order!

Trump then very proudly marched to the church and waved around a bible. He also posed with his closest aides. The journalists were quick to point out that all were White, although one of them was a female.

Trump is able to justify this by accusing all protesters of being "terrorists", members of an organization he refers to as Antifa. That is short for Anti Fascist, and very likely such an organization does not even exist. If it does exist, then it stands to reason that our parents and grandparents, those who fought the Nazis in World War 2, were terrorists! Such nonsense! It is also an insult to the millions of brave men and women who fought the fascist Nazis.

As mentioned in a previous article, cracks are beginning to appear in the American Empire. Several republics are starting to take shape. On the east coast and the west coast, the two population centres, states have come together. Also, in the midwest, the industrial heartland of the country, seven states have also formed an alliance. One of those states is Minnesota, home to Minneapolis, the city in which George Floyd was murdered. In other words, the epicentre of the revolution.

That is most significant, because the City Council of Minneapolis has just decided to take revolutionary action. In particular, they have decided to disband the Minneapolis City Police! They plan to replace it with a "new model of public safety". Now people across the country are calling for the "defunding" of various police agencies.

As for those who are confused concerning this "new model of public safety", there is a good reason for this. It has yet to take shape! It is a new creation of the revolution! The precise form it will assume remains to be seen.

The mayor of Minneapolis is dead set against this as he is in the service of the capitalists, but the City Council is reported to have a "veto proof majority".

It is to the credit of the journalists that they interviewed a young lady—clearly a leader—who stated that people were at first confused, suspecting that the police were not working the way they were supposed to work. But then they had second thoughts and came to the conclusion that the police are doing precisely that which they are supposed to be doing!

This is a huge step forward in the revolutionary working class movement. The members of the public are now aware, if only on an instinctive level, that the role of the police is not to protect and serve but to crush the working class! The police are nothing other than members of a state apparatus that is set up by the capitalists, the billionaires, the bourgeoisie, to crush the working class. It has nothing to do with "serve and protect"!

Now it is absolutely necessary to read the Essential Works of Lenin. May I suggest starting with State and Revolution, a book which was written immediately before the November 7 revolution of 1917. That was the revolution which brought the proletariat, the workers, to power in Russia. That book is as relevant now as it was then. Working people must be made aware that the capitalists, the billionaires, the bourgeoisie, are in charge. The capitalists make sure that the working people are kept under control. In fact, they have a fine apparatus set up to keep the working people suppressed. As Lenin put it, "A standing army and police are the chief instruments of state power". (my italics)

The point being that the more advanced members of the working class, the proletariat, are correct in thinking that the police are behaving precisely the way they are supposed to behave! They are the "chief instruments of state power"! It is the police and standing army, and in particular the National Guard, that is responsible for crushing the working class, the proletariat! It is the police and standing army that must be disbanded! Those are the "chief instruments of state power" which the capitalists use to crush the workers!

In Russia, 1917, it was only after the successful November revolution that the police and standing army were disbanded. Then the separate independent socialist republics took shape. At that time, it was first necessary to crush the capitalists under the newly created state apparatus, the Dictatorship Of the Proletariat, and only then was it possible to disband the police and standing army.

By contrast, here in America, 2020, several independent republics are already taking shape. As well, the working people are more aware that the police are crushing them. Even before the revolution, they are taking the proper steps to disband the police departments. As the City Police are one of the "chief instruments of state power" of the capitalists, there can be no doubt that the capitalists will take a "dim view" of the attempt of the City Council to disband one of their most useful tools. The resistance the City Council is about to encounter in trying to disband the City Police will prove to be most valuable training.

This will serve them well after the revolution, as they assume positions of authority, under the Dictatorship Of the Proletariat.

Further preparations must be made for the Dictatorship Of the Proletariat. Workers, or at least the most advanced workers, must be encouraged to become members of any and all organizations, those which allow working class membership. This includes sports clubs, trade unions and political parties, especially the two mainstream parties, Democrats and Republicans. As card carrying members, party bosses, they can then run for any and all political offices. The purpose is to gain valuable experience in the class struggle, not to secure socialism through democratic elections. Regardless of what the social chauvinists say, socialism cannot be secured in that manner. On the other hand, such elections are a useful tool, to be used in the interests of raising the level of awareness of the working people.

There is also a desperate need for a true Marxist political party to lead the workers, the proletariat. Such a party can distinguish itself from the chauvinist parties by openly calling for the Dictatorship Of the Proletariat.

As for those individuals who are referred to as "conscious people", which is to say people who are well aware of the revolutionary theories of Marx and Lenin, may I suggest that you perform your duty. To paraphrase the old expression, "to whom much has been given, from whom much is expected". You have the education and training. Use it. Feel free to form a true Marxist political party:

American Communist Party, Dictatorship Of the Proletariat.

CHAPTER 8

WOMEN'S EQUALITY UNDER CAPITALISM

July 30, 2020
Gerald McIsaac

For many years, in America and Western Europe, women in all emancipation movements have put forward the demand that obsolete laws be annulled, so that men and women are made equal under the law. This has been going on for decades, if not centuries. As a result of this, progress has been made, at least in certain countries. In some cases, laws have been passed, but it is safe to say that none of these laws have been fully put into effect.

The reason for this is quite simple. In September of 1919, in a speech to working women, Lenin laid out the tasks of the working women's movement. At that time, only two years after the successful socialist revolution, the country was in grave peril. The four years of the First World War was followed by civil war, which was still raging. The country was in ruins and victory was certainly not assured. The socialist government needed all the help it could get. With that in mind, Lenin explained the tasks of the working women's movement in the Soviet Republic.

As he put it, "wherever there is capitalism, wherever there is private property in land and factories, wherever the power of capital is preserved, the men retain their privileges". He went on to say that this private property of land and factories "even where there is complete political liberty, even in the most democratic republics, keeps the working people in a state of what is actually poverty and wage slavery, and women in a state of double slavery". (my italics)

It was Marx who made it clear that the only way to effect the complete emancipation of women and make her the the equal of the man, is through the socialization of the economy! . In that way, women can and will participate in common productive labour. Of course, this is only possible through socialism, under the Dictatorship Of the Proletariat. At that time, women will occupy the same position as men.

This is not to say that women will be expected to perform the same work as men, and produce the same results. Lenin made this quite clear when he stated: "Here we are not, of course, speaking of making women the equal of men as far as productivity of labour, the quantity of labour, the length of the working day, labour conditions, etc., are concerned; we mean that the woman should not, unlike the man, be oppressed because of her position in the family."

This brings us to the demand of so many women for an amendment to the constitution, in order to secure complete equality. The trouble is that then women would be expected, and even required, to be the "equal of men as far as productivity of labour, the quantity of labour, the length of the working day, labour conditions, etc." As they are also so often required to perform the house work, this amendment could only backfire, placing an additional burden on women.

Lenin went on to point out that the drudgery of house work, which is generally the lot of the housewife, is not only arduous, but "does not include anything that would in any way promote the development of the woman . . . the building of socialism will begin only when we have achieved the complete equality of women and when we undertake the new work together with women who have been emancipated from that petty, stultifying, unproductive work". With that goal in mind, the new socialist republic was busy setting up "model institutions, dining rooms and nurseries, that will emancipate women from housework". It was the duty of the women to help establish these model institutions.

Of necessity, the building of these "model institutions", was not proceeding at a rapid pace. The country was in a state of ruin, and it was not at all clear that the revolution would be successful. Still, Lenin took the time to offer encouragement to the working women. He considered their input to be that important.

Lenin went on to say: "We say the emancipation of the workers must be effected by the workers themselves, and in exactly the same way the emancipation of working women is a matter for the working women themselves . . . In order to be active in politics under the old, capitalist regime special training was required, so that women played an insignificant part in politics, even in the most advanced and free capitalist countries. Our task is to make politics available to every working woman".

Perhaps it would be best to bear in mind that Lenin spoke to those women one hundred years ago. The situation has changed dramatically since that time, so that women in many parts of the world have made great strides. That includes America, and in that country the women are leading the revolution! They are indeed active in politics! They are not only effecting the emancipation of working women, but also the emancipation of the working class! They have proven themselves to be excellent organizers!

To the women who have done such an excellent job in organizing and taking part in marches and protests, I can say that was well done. I can also say that now is not the time to "rest on your laurels". The monopoly capitalists, the bourgeoisie, are still in charge. They have not "changed their stripes". They are still crushing and exploiting the working class, the proletariat. They still regard women as members of their personal harem. Nothing of substance will change until the whole class, the bourgeoisie, is overthrown and crushed under the Dictatorship Of the Proletariat. The sad fact of the matter is that the upper stratum of the American proletariat, or at least a great many of them, have been bribed, bought off by the capitalists. Now it is up to you, the American working women, to "take up the torch" and carry the battle to the enemy, the capitalists, the bourgeoisie.

Granted this is not the "way it should be", it is not "fair", it is not "just". It is the way it is, and life is not fair. Working women, and in fact all women, will continue to be crushed, exploited and even abused by the capitalists, as long as they remain in power. Further, as it is clear that the working men are prepared to tolerate this, that leaves the "ball in your court".

I hope you will excuse the mix of metaphors, but feel free to take consolation in the fact that as an old time male chauvinist, it pains me deeply to state that the men are not leading.

The fact remains that women are now, and will remain, in a "state of double slavery", as long as we live under capitalism.

Women will be freed of the drudgery of housework and able to take part in productive labour only under socialism. Then and only then will she be truly the equal of any man.

At the time Lenin spoke to the working women, the tasks of the working women's movement was far different from that which it is today. Now that the revolutionary movement is in "high gear", the task of the working women is to lead the whole working class. It is necessary to raise the level of awareness of all workers so that they are class conscious, aware that they are members of a class of people, the proletariat, in opposition to the capitalist class, the bourgeoisie. The most advanced workers must be raised to the level of Marxists. We must prepare for the Dictatorship Of the Proletariat. All working people, and especially women, must assume positions of leadership. Join the two mainstream political parties as card carrying members. Run for any and all political office, as candidates of both parties. Fight to abolish the electoral college. Organize marches and demonstrations. Ridicule and humiliate the members of the administration. Give the capitalists no peace. Any and all skills working people learn now will be put to good use after the revolution.

At that time, the bourgeoisie will have to be crushed under the Dictatorship Of the Proletariat. Workers will be placed in positions of authority. Any training they receive now will prove to be most valuable. It is very likely that most of those workers will be women, if for no other reason than that most men are simply not qualified for the task. It is my most fervent hope that in the near future, many men will rise to the challenge, and prove me to be mistaken.

Ladies, I realize that is a heavy burden I am placing on your shoulders. I regret that the only alternative is to resign yourselves to a life of drudgery, wage slavery and abuse of every kind. I am sure you will agree that such a life is not worth living. Allow the posters and banners to proclaim:

Onward to the Dictatorship Of the Proletariat!

Scientific Socialism!

Workers of the World, Unite!

CHAPTER 9

NOVEMBER ELECTIONS AND REVOLUTION

Aug 7, 2020

As I write this, the press is preoccupied with the countdown to the November presidential election. They would have the American public believe that the end to the "nightmare" which is currently gripping the country is right around the corner. Of course the name of the "nightmare" is Trump, the "serpent" who has weaselled his way into the White House. But now, lo and behold, they see a Knight in Shining Armour on the horizon! This hero, in the form of the Democratic presidential candidate, is destined to slay the dragon and restore peace and tranquility to the country. The Age of Aquarius is right around the corner!

Granted, the members of the press, the journalists, do not present the news in quite that manner. Yet all seem convinced that the salvation of the country lies in the upcoming elections. They foresee the Democrats winning a resounding victory in both House and Senate, as well as a landslide defeat for Trump. Then in January, with head down and tail between his legs, Trump will be placed in chains and marched off to prison.

Countless people may take some consolation in the thought of a new president being sworn in, followed immediately by the police slapping the handcuffs on Trump. As the president, head of state, it is doubtful that Trump can be charged, at least for now. But as a former head of state, it becomes "open season" on Trump. Without doubt, various law enforcement agencies have gathered a great deal of evidence, and are prepared to charge him with various crimes, both federal and state. At the same time, the members of his family and close friends will also be charged.

These happy thoughts should be put aside, as such a fairy tale has no place in the real world. Trump has no intention of relinquishing power, surrendering to the authorities and facing numerous, very serious criminal charges. Such a course of action would almost certainly result in him spending the rest of his life in prison. The man knows this, as he is not entirely stupid.

It should be noted that the president has the legal right to pardon anyone for breaking any federal law—possibly even himself!—but no right to pardon anyone for violating any state law. Trump is well aware that he is looking at federal charges of abuse of power and tax evasion, among other things. As well, the state of New York is now examining his "financial records", with a view to possible fraud and money laundering. As the man is a habitual liar, it is not beyond the realm of imagination. To imagine Trump as a man of honesty and integrity, is well beyond such a realm.

Trump is already laying the ground work for his continued occupation of the White House, regardless of the results of the November elections. He has no intention of vacating the premises. He has already suggested an "election delay", due to the Corona Virus. Then there is the "bogus" of mail in voting, in which "Russian interference" will lead to "false results". When asked by his friends at a news channel, he refused to admit that he would honour the election results, saying instead that he "would see" after the election. The Attorney General, a loyal Trump boot licker, testified to Congress that he would honour the election results, but only "if the results are clear". No doubt, the only "clear" results are those which place Trump back in power for another four years.

This is not to say that Trump is the problem, because he is not. He is merely the most visible presence. He represents the capitalists, the class of people whose scientific term is the bourgeoisie. In fact, he is a member of that class. All members of that class are reactionary, completely devoid of principle, and Trump is clearly no exception. He is merely more arrogant than most, boasting that he can sexually assault any women he pleases. There are numerous women who allege that he has done just that. What is more, he has gotten away with it, at least for now.

This brings us to the class opposite the capitalist class, the working class, the proletariat. The capitalists have done a fine job of decimating all other classes, so that mere remnants of the peasants, or farmers, remain in existence. The nobility was eradicated many years ago, and now the middle class, technically referred to as the petty bourgeois, is in the process of being wiped out. This class of people, small business owners, cannot compete with the monopolies. The optimists who try to establish a small business are quickly crushed by the monopoly capitalists. The capitalists are not about to tolerate any competition, no matter how slight.

The current pandemic of the Corona Virus is not sparing America. On the contrary, it is devastating the country. One quarter of all the infections and deaths around the world are happening in America. People are complaining that Trump is not being a leader. Such people are mistaken. Trump is very much a leader, and countless people are following him.

Those who are familiar with American history are well aware of numerous leaders. In the "old west", the James – Younger gang was led by Jesse James and Cole Younger. Billy the Kid had quite a following. Wes Hardin was well known as a gun fighter, as was Wyatt Earp. The only difference between the two was that Earp carried a badge and used it to commit murder. In more modern times, during the Great Depression, we have been blessed with Public Enemy Number One, John Dillinger, Ma Barker and her sons, Machine Gun Kelly, Baby Face Nelson, Mad Dog Vachon and Scarface Al Capone. More recently, John Gotti, the Teflon Don has become a household name, as has Sammy the Bull Gravano. Charles Manson had quite a following, including several lovely young ladies.

The point being that these people were leaders and countless people followed them. In fact, they followed them to the gallows, to the grave and to prison. The girls who followed Manson were able to "cheat the hangman", but only at the expense of spending the last fifty years in prison.

So for those who say that people need leaders, I can only respond that you are mistaken. People need proper leaders, and there is a big difference between the two. Trump is a leader of the capitalists, the bourgeoisie. Common people, working people, proletarians, need leaders for the working class, and the one and only people who can provide that leadership is the scientific socialists, the Marxists. That is always the case, now more so than ever.

The reason I say this is because the situation is truly revolutionary. The Corona Virus is raging unchecked across the country. Countless people are unemployed, partly as a result of the virus and partly as a result of the fact that the country is now entering another Great Depression. Any day now the stock market will crash. The bourgeois economists expect this crash to be even more intense than the famous crash of 1929. The latest "stimulus package", which offered a measure of relief to a great many people, has just expired. Those same economists expect that a third of all Americans will soon be unable to meet their payments for housing, either in the form of rent or mortgage expenses. Tens of millions of Americans will soon be not only unemployed, but also homeless.

On the other hand, the situation now is far different from a century ago. By that I mean working people are far more aware, if still not class conscious. They are somewhat instinctively moving towards socialism. An example of this is the Capital Hill Autonomous Zone, in which people lived together communally, sharing the little they had. Another example is the fact that in three parts of the country, the east coast, the west coast and the industrial heart land of the country, various states have come together to form the nucleus of separate socialist republics. It is doubtful that the people who are taking part in the creation of these – soon to be – socialist republics are aware of that which they are doing. This is referred to as being spontaneous, and is quite common.

Spontaneous actions are perfectly acceptable for common people, members of the public, working class people, proletarians, as well as middle class people, petty bourgeois. The working class is not aware of itself as a class. This awareness has to be brought to the working class from an outside source. Of course that outside source is middle class intellectuals. As for those who are prejudiced against such people, bear in mind that Marx, Engels and Lenin were middle class intellectuals. In short, get over that prejudice!

I also mention middle class people, petty bourgeois, as a great many such people are either ruined or in the process of being ruined. Before the virus hit, they were under great pressure by the monopoly capitalists. Now, as most small businesses have been shut down for several months and will very likely be shut down again, possibly for a much longer time, the owners are ruined. They cannot possibly stay in business. They are being forced into the ranks of the working class, the proletariat. At the same time, they are bringing with them their awareness of the existence of classes, as all middle class people are class conscious.

This is not to say that they are all Marxists, as most of them are not. Some are not even aware of the theory of the Dictatorship Of the Proletariat, although many are aware of such Marxist theories. All are quite capable of helping to raise the level of awareness of the working class. Those who are aware of the revolutionary theories of Marx and Lenin should bring that awareness to the working class, the proletariat. Such people have nothing to fear. As proletarians, they are free to take part in the revolution and the subsequent Dictatorship Of the Proletariat. In fact, I strongly recommend this.

Trump is becoming ever more brazen, first forcing peaceful protesters out of Lafayette Square and now sending government agents, in plain clothes, into the city of Portland to arrest protesters and carry them away in unmarked vans. These are reported to be "police" from DHS, Department of Homeland Security. Perhaps it would be more accurate to refer to them as Secret Police.

The fact is that the country is deeply divided, as almost everyone is prepared to admit. It is set to explode, or to put it in scientific terms, the contradictions are sharp and clear. Civil war could break out at any day. This is to say that time is not on our side. The level of awareness of the working class must be raised. Workers must be prepared for the Dictatorship Of the Proletariat.

Now is the time for workers to join the two parties, Democrats and Republicans, as card carrying members. Assume positions of responsibility. Run for any and all political office.

Perhaps of even more importance, it is necessary to organize. The women and students have proven their ability in the past, and now an even greater effort is required. There are reports that the leaders of the women's movement of several years ago may have sold out to the capitalists, becoming members of a corporation. If so, no doubt others can take their place.

Feel free to take inspiration from other female revolutionary leaders, such as Rosa Luxembourg and Clara Zetkin. They set a fine example.

Of critical importance is the creation of a truly Communist Party, one which calls for the Dictatorship Of the Proletariat. Only in that way can it be distinguished from the social chauvinists and the centrists. Those people would sooner crawl on their bellies over broken glass, rather than endorse the Dictatorship Of the Proletariat.

All workers, or at least all advanced workers, should read the Communist Manifesto by Marx and Engels, as well as the Essential Works of Lenin. In this manner, such workers will receive a fine grounding in Marxism. As the middle class intellectuals are as yet silent, it is up to workers to take the initiative. They can take part in the formation of a truly Communist Party, Dictatorship Of the Proletariat.

Bear in mind that Lenin referred to America as the "freest and most civilized country . . . a democratic republic. But what do we find? The brazen rule of a handful, not even of millionaires, but multimillionaires, while the people are in slavery and servitude".

As this was written a century ago, it is now correct to say that we have the "brazen rule" of billionaires and multi billionaires, while still "the people are in slavery and servitude".

Just as Lenin was the leader of the Marxist party of Russia, which came to be known as the Communist Party of the Soviet Union, so too we are in desperate need of an American Communist Party, Dictatorship Of the Proletariat. Only such a party can provide the proper leadership!

Bear in mind that as Lenin stated, it is easy to start a revolution in a "petty bourgeois" country, as was Russia in 1917, but far more difficult to carry it through. By contrast, it is far more difficult to start a revolution in a "cultured" country, as is America, but far easier to carry it through.

Perhaps it would be best if I ended this article with a slogan coined by Lenin:

Victory or Death!

CHAPTER 10

CATTLE KILLED AND MUTILATED IN STATE OF OREGON

Aug 11, 2020

Of late, the press has been reporting that a great many cattle, both bulls and cows, are being killed and mutilated, in the state of Oregon. If nothing else, this is a somewhat welcome change from the reports of the political gong show in Washington. Aside from that, the speculation as to the cause of the death of these animals is nothing less than an embarrassment.

In the eastern part of the state, there are very few ranches, but those which do exist are huge, covering many thousands of acres. The cattle are allowed to range freely. It is on these huge estates that the cattle are being discovered, dead and mutilated. There is no shortage of theories to explain these strange events.

Each time this happens, the local police are called in to investigate. In one case, the police report stated, there was "no indication it had been shot, attacked by predators or eaten poisonous plants. The animals sex organs and tongue had been removed. All the blood was gone".

Here we have an example of an incomplete police investigation. In fact, just because there was no blood around the wound sites does not mean that the "blood was gone". The blood was precisely where it was supposed to be, inside the carcass. If the police had conducted a proper investigation, that would have been confirmed.

In the case of four bulls being discovered dead, the local press reported that: "There were no tracks around the carcasses. Ranch management and law enforcement suspect that someone killed the bulls. Ranch hands have been advised to travel in pairs and to go armed". As there were no tracks or signs of human activity around the carcasses, the conclusion is illogical. The bulls were clearly not killed by people.

In almost all cases, the genitals of the bulls have been removed, with "surgical precision", so that it is speculated that the bulls were "killed to get the organs of the free ranging bulls". It is further speculated that the bulls were "darted with tranquilizers that knocked them out. While some people acted as lookouts, others bled the animals by inserting a large gauge needle into the tongue and into an artery, then removing the organs after the heart quit beating."

Once again we have an incomplete investigation, in that it is assumed that the blood is missing. Also, there was no sign of human activity, a fact which was conveniently ignored. As the country is supremely dusty, any tracks are immediately apparent. That rules out human involvement. As well, they are correct when they say that "It is not bears, wolves, cougars or poisonous plants. Nor were the animals shot . . . not one drop of blood". Yet they are determined that people were responsible for this!

Strangely enough, these same people are the first to admit that it is simply impossible to move around that "dusty country" without leaving tracks. On the one hand, their investigation rules out human activity, yet on the other hand, they still blame people.

In the case of the death of one cow, according to a deputy conducting the investigation: "No dart puncture, no bullets, no strangulation marks, no rope burns, no tire tracks, no signs of poison". From that rather thorough investigation, the same deputy reached a rather strange conclusion: "definitely foul play involved in this animals death". Once again, we have incorrect conclusions derived from incontrovertible facts.

Then there is the idea of "people attacking the animals to cause financial harm to the ranchers". We could point out that there are easier ways of causing "financial harm", but even that brainstorm is better than the more popular belief, that "the animals are being levitated into a space ship, mutilated, and then dropped back to the ground".

It is to the credit of one of the ranchers that he joked about this. He said he was "flattered that aliens from distant galaxies would travel all the way to planet earth, just to kill and mutilate my cattle." He is one of the few ranchers to still maintain a sense of humour.

As local law enforcement is stumped, the FBI has been called in. They in turn report that a similar situation took place in the 1970's. As they put it, at that time, "in the West and Midwest, thousands of cattle were killed and mutilated, from Minnesota to New Mexico. There have been sporadic cases since then". The investigation of that august agency concluded that "there is no indication that anything other than common predators were responsible." As the investigations have proven conclusively that the animals are not being killed by bears, wolves or cougars, it is clear that the FBI considers some other "common predator" to be responsible. They neglect to say just what predator that may be.

Here we have a very clear cut example of well meaning, honest, professional, highly respected people, including members of various law enforcement agencies, stating the problem clearly, investigating carefully, and then coming to conclusions. The trouble is that the conclusions they reach are in complete contradiction to the facts. This can only be described as shoddy work.

All are correct when they note that there is no blood around the injury sites. They are also correct when they note no sign of human interference, such as "bullet wounds, puncture wounds, strangulation marks, rope burns or foot prints". Also no sign of predation from "common predators". From this they conclude that the "blood was drained from the animal", or "foul play was involved", or as the FBI stated, "common predators were responsible". All are mistaken, although the FBI is closest to the truth.

Perhaps someone should tell these Dick Tracy sorts, these ace detectives, that which all school children know. Once an animal dies, the heart quits beating. There is no blood around the wound sites because the animal was dead when it was mutilated! Dead animals do not bleed! They correctly point out that there is no indication of the animal being killed by a human, of "foul play", because there was no foul play. The police have done a fine job of ruling out the impossible, but failed to take the crucial step of facing the one and only alternative! The animals are being killed by poison gas!

There is only one animal which can release poison gas, strong enough to kill cattle. This poison gas, commonly referred to as a "cloud of smoke", is not smoke at all, but supremely toxic. The fact that it uses this poison to kill cattle is proof of that. Then it consumes the parts of the animal it can easily gather, including the tongue and genitals. It also frequently rips out the large intestine, a very nourishing part of the anatomy. It is strange that the press does not report this, perhaps because they are concerned with the sentiments of the readers. Or perhaps the animal has changed its behaviour.

Of course the animal to which I am referring is the pterosaur, commonly called the pterodactyl. As it is nocturnal, it is rarely seen. It also flies, so that it is very light, with huge paws, to that the tracks it leaves are very difficult to spot. It has also clearly developed a taste for beef, at least in Oregon. As long as livestock is left outside after sunset, those animals will continue to be preyed upon by this prehistoric monster. I regret I do not have better news.

To the law enforcement officials, I can only say that there is no law against wild animals killing livestock. In other words, no "foul play" involved. To the FBI, I can say that the pterosaur is hardly a "common predator", but it is certainly a predator.

That brings us to the not so little matter of proving the existence of this "not so common predator". May I suggest taking a sample of the blood from the carcass and sending it to a laboratory. As long as the blood is extracted from the animal within 24 hours of the death of the animal, then it is very likely the lab can determine the poison used to kill the animal. At the same time, swab around the wound sites and send the swab to a lab, for a DNA analysis. No doubt the test result will confirm that the wound was made by a reptile. Equally without doubt, those test results will be challenged, so it may be best to send the samples to three independent labs. This is my idea of a thorough investigation.

These test results will confirm that the livestock is being killed by a blast of poison gas and consumed by a reptile. Law enforcement personnel can take comfort in knowing that the ball will then be taken from their court and placed where it belongs, in the court of the scientists. The death and mutilation of this livestock is not a crime. It is a problem to be faced by the scientists. It is high time they did their job.

CHAPTER 11

CRISIS SEEN AS OPPORTUNITY

Aug 20, 2020

The Corona Virus pandemic is raging around the world. In America, it is almost completely out of control. It is estimated that over five million Americans have been infected, with the death rate at over 170,000. The number of dead is expected to double within the next several months. As well, the stock market is expected to crash any day now, as the country enters a second Great Depression. The "economic stimulus package", in the form of six hundred dollar weekly payments to families, has just expired. Within a month, landlords will be issuing legal eviction notices. It is estimated that an additional forty million people will soon become homeless. The presidential elections are on the horizon, and Trump and his henchmen see the havoc caused by the virus as an opportunity!

The Democratic candidate for president has chosen a woman as his "running mate", as the candidate for Vice President. She is a member of a minority, a "woman of colour", in that she is considered to be "black and brown". This is considered to be a politically correct way to say that her father was from Jamaica and her mother was from India. Or as the press politely phrases it, she is "Black and East Indian".

For the benefit of those who are just now becoming politically active, I will mention that the American Indigenous people were formerly referred to as "Indians", a term which is objected to by both Indigenous people and people from India. That is the reason the press refers to people from India as East Indian. Apparently it is now politically correct to refer to "Afro Americans" as Black. Bear in mind that these expressions are not mine.

Be that as it may, Trump and his advisors have wasted no time in slandering this woman. They claim that she is not "qualified" to run for the office, as she "was not born in America". They offer no shred of evidence to support this charge.

This is not too surprising, as Trump is just as much a racist as he is a liar. And of course Trump lies constantly. Even when his lips are not moving, he lies, in the form of tweets. The only thing he hates more than minorities are female minorities, especially those who do not "know their place". As far as Trump is concerned, every woman has her place, and that place is prone. That is the reason he surrounds himself with attractive young women, those who do not object to being "groped", which is a polite term for sexual assault.

Perhaps it is ironic to think that Trump had no ambition to become president. He ran for president on an impulse, that which entertainers refer to as a "publicity stunt". Bear in mind that Trump is, first and foremost, an entertainer. Also bear in mind that most people did not expect him to win. Yet win he did, and perhaps no one was more surprised than Donald Trump. As a result of this, he has since found that he enjoys the power, and has no intention of relinquishing that power. As his popularity is currently "nose diving" in the polls, that creates a little problem. But as Trump is a resourceful man, he has developed a plan to "win" the upcoming election.

The medical experts are all agreed that we should exercise "social distancing", to stay at least six feet apart, and avoid gatherings. The trouble is that in order to vote, it is frequently necessary to wait in line. That simply cannot be done, while exercising social distancing. The only alternative is to vote by mail.

The crisis caused by the virus, the illness and death of countless Americans, is seen by Trump as nothing less than an opportunity! As most people will be forced to vote by mail, he is making arrangements to ensure that a proper vote will never take place! The votes which are cast by mail will never be counted by the deadline! Trump can then declare that the election was fraudulent! Trump plans to remain in power, and not just for another four years, but indefinitely!

As part of his plan to sabotage the election, he has recently placed one of his loyal henchmen in charge of the post office. The new manager of the post office just discontinued numerous sorting machines. Various public blue post office boxes have been placed in storage. Employees are required to close the post offices on a regular basis, cutting the hours of service. Now the budget of the postal service is cut to the point that "snail mail" is no longer a joke. People are already complaining about the time it takes to receive their mail. At the time of the election, when there is anticipated to be an avalanche of additional mail, in the form of ballots, the newly appointed head of the postal service will make sure that few of them reach their destination, at least not before the deadline. That will give Trump a chance to proclaim that the election was a fraud, null and void, and he will continue to "serve" as president. Mission accomplished.

Perhaps someone should tell Trump that the American people are not about to put up with this. Then again, it would not do any good. Besides, he is about to learn this the hard way. The American people are heroic, with a proud history of revolution. Very soon, they are about to stage another revolution, the Second American Revolution. The upcoming presidential election, which Trump plans to declare fraudulent, could well prove to be the spark which triggers the revolution.

Once again, I will mention, for the sake of those working people who are only now becoming politically active—and I hope there are a great many of you!—that there was a time, commonly referred to as the "stone age", in which classes did not exist. It was not the "golden age" of humanity, as people did not live in a "Garden of Eden". On the contrary, life tended to be short and brutal. So there is no need to become nostalgic over that which existed long before we were born. The "good old days" it was not.

Those days ended with the beginning of civilization. The first classes appeared, in the form of slaves and slave owners. As can be well imagined, there was conflict between the classes. That which was in the best interest of one class, say the slave owners, was in the worst interest of the slaves, and of course the opposite is true. In short, as soon as classes came into existence, class conflict appeared. In fact, we cannot have classes without class conflict. In due time, slavery by and large gave way to the feudal system, which was not a vast improvement.

Then a strange thing happened. Around or about the years 1720 to 1740, in Great Britain, there appeared an industrial revolution. It quickly spread to other countries, and in fact it is still spreading. This industrial revolution created two new classes. The burghers of the "middle ages" became transformed into the class of capitalists, or "bourgeois", derived from the word burgher. These newly minted capitalists in turn needed workers to run their machines, and these workers became hourly employees, "proletarians". In short, the industrial revolution gave birth to two new classes, bourgeois and proletarian. As usual, the two classes immediately came into conflict. That class conflict has in no way abated. On the contrary, it is now raging at a fever pitch.

At first, no one could understand this new creation, that of capitalism. It took the genius of Karl Marx to explain it, in his book Capital. Then in 1848, he and his friend and collaborator, Friedrich Engels, wrote the Communist Manifesto. Remarkably enough, it is as true today as when it was first written.

The introduction of the Communist Manifesto expresses the terror of all bourgeois:

"A spectre is haunting Europe – the spectre of Communism."

The only difference now is that this "spectre" has spread around the world, including America. To this day the bourgeois live in mortal dread of Communism. As Communism is the worst enemy of capitalism, there is a reason for this. It goes on to say that:

"The history of all hitherto existing society is the history of class struggles. The modern bourgeois society that has sprouted from the ruins of feudal society has not done away with class antagonisms. It has but established new classes, new conditions of oppression, new forms of struggle in place of the old ones."

That is quite clear. Now that the revolution is on the horizon, it is important to bear in mind that Trump is not the problem. The problem is that the bourgeoisie, the monopoly capitalists, the imperialists, are in charge. Trump is merely a member of that class, and as Lenin stated it, "imperialists are completely reactionary". We can expect nothing progressive from them. It is therefore up to the working class, the proletariat, to overthrow the bourgeoisie and crush them, under the Dictatorship Of the Proletariat.

The Communist Manifesto lets us know what to expect during a revolution. It goes on to say:

"Our epoch, the epoch of the bourgeoisie, possesses however, this distinct feature: it has simplified class antagonisms. Society as a whole is more and more splitting up into two great hostile camps, into two great classes directly facing each other – Bourgeoisie and Proletariat."

That is certainly true now, more so than ever before. The peasants, in the form of the family farmer, have been all but wiped out, at least in North America. That leaves the middle class, the petty bourgeois, and they are being squeezed ever tighter by the monopoly capitalists, the bourgeoisie, or the imperialists, as that is the correct technical term. The remainder of the middle class is "living on borrowed time". As the stock market crashes and the country enters another Great Depression, as ever more millions find themselves homeless as well as unemployed, so too ever more small businesses will face bankruptcy. The owners of those businesses will find themselves joining the ranks of the working class, as proletarians.

This was forecast by Marx and Engels in the Communist Manifesto:

"The lower strata of the middle class—the small tradespeople, shopkeepers and retired tradesmen generally, the handicraftsmen and peasants, —all these sink gradually into the proletariat, partly because their diminutive capital does not suffice for the scale on which Modern Industry is carried on, and is swamped in the competition with the large capitalists, partly because their specialized skill is rendered worthless by new methods of production. Thus the proletariat is recruited from all classes of the population . . . These also supply the proletariat with fresh elements of enlightenment and progress. Finally, in times when the class struggle nears the decisive hour, the progress of dissolution going on within the ruling class, in fact within the whole range of old society, assumes such a violent, glaring character, that a small section of the ruling class cuts itself adrift, and joins the revolutionary class, the class that holds the future in its hands. Just as, therefore, at an earlier period, a section of the nobility went over to the bourgeoisie, so now a portion of the bourgeoisie goes over to the proletariat, and in particular a portion of the bourgeois ideologists, who have raised themselves to the level of comprehending theoretically the historical movement as a whole."

This is of exceptional importance because the working class, the proletariat, is not aware of itself as a class. This class awareness can only come from an outside source, and that outside source is of course the bourgeois intellectuals, or "ideologists", as Marx refers to them. Only such people, former members of either the middle class, the petty bourgeois, or the upper class, the bourgeoisie, can raise the consciousness of the working class, the proletariat, to the level of that of Marxists. The members of the working class who are true Marxists are few and far between.

No doubt the "decisive hour" is fast approaching, as the class struggle is assuming a "violent, glaring character". The current "ruling class", in this case the bourgeoisie, is already starting to splinter. It is safe to say that cracks are beginning to appear in their "united front". It is the bourgeoisie that owns the press, and the journalists are allowed to report only that which their employers want them to report. At the "news conferences" with Trump, they are allowed to ask only general questions. Certain questions are strictly forbidden. Yet at a recent news conference, a journalist asked Trump the question which was previously forbidden: "Do you regret all the lying you have done to the American people?" Trump was so shocked that the journalist had to repeat the question. Then of course Trump refused to provide an answer.

That question is an indication that the bourgeoisie is beginning to quarrel among themselves. The people who own the news outlet, for whom that journalist worked, allowed him to ask that question. Those people are members of the bourgeoisie, and they have taken a stand, against the other members of their class.

It is clear that "a small section of the ruling class", in this case the bourgeoisie, has separated itself, or "cut itself adrift" from the rest of the class, and has now "joined the revolutionary class", in this case the proletariat, the "class that holds the future in its hands". Without doubt, the "class struggle nears the decisive hour", and as that is the case, we should know what to expect. No doubt, not all members of the working class, the proletariat, will become revolutionary. In fact, we can expect some of them to oppose the revolution.

The Communist Manifesto goes on to let us know what to expect:

"the dangerous class, the 'lumpen proletariat', the social scum, that passively rotting mass thrown off by the lowest layers of the old society, may, here and there, be swept into the movement by a proletarian revolution; its conditions of life, however, prepare it far more for the part of a bribed tool of reactionary intrigue."

As we have no shortage of "lumpen proletariat", those who have been "thrown off" by the old society, if only through no fault of their own, we know what to expect. No doubt the bourgeoisie will attempt to use them to their advantage, as a "bribed tool of reaction", to try to crush the revolution. We can only hope the proletarian revolution is strong enough to sweep them up into the movement.

This brings us to Section II, Proletarians and Communists:

"In what relation do the Communists stand to the proletarians as a whole?

"The Communists do not form a separate party opposed to the other working class parties.

"They have no interests separate and apart from those of the proletariat as a whole.

"They do not set up any sectarian principles of their own, by which to shape and mold the proletariat movement.

"The Communists are distinguished from the other working class parties by this only 1: In the national struggles of the proletarians of the different countries, they point out and bring to the front the common interest of the entire proletariat, independently of all nationality. 2. In the various stages of development which the struggle of the working class against the bourgeoisie has to pass through, they always and everywhere represent the interest of the movement as a whole.

"The Communists, therefore, are on the one hand, practically, the most advanced and resolute section of the working class parties of each country, that section which pushes forward all others; on the other hand, theoretically, they have over the great mass of the proletariat the advantage of clearly understanding the line of march, the conditions, and the ultimate general results of the proletarian movement.

"The immediate aim of the Communists is the same as that of all other proletarian parties: formation of the proletariat into a class, overthrow of the bourgeois supremacy, conquest of political power by the proletariat."

From this it is clear that the Communists are intellectuals, aware of the existence of classes and the role the working class must play in overthrowing the capitalists, the bourgeoisie, and setting up the Dictatorship Of the Proletariat. They refer to themselves as "conscious people", as they are well aware of the class struggle, of the fact that the working class spontaneously rises up against the bourgeoisie. This is to say that the working class, the proletariat, gets into motion, by the millions, without knowing what it is doing! The social scientists refer to this as a "spontaneous uprising", while I refer to it as an Act of God.

The Communists are equally well aware that the members of the working class, the proletariat, are not aware of themselves as a class. The conditions of life of a proletarian do not lead to this awareness. It is therefore the duty of Marxists, most of whom are current or former members of the "propertied classes", to bring this awareness to the workers, to raise the working class, or at least to raise the most advanced workers, to the level of awareness of Marxists.

It is also clear that the one and only way to "overthrow the bourgeois supremacy", to achieve the "conquest of political power by the proletariat", is through revolution. As for those who doubt that, feel free to consider all the wars the American government has been involved in, including the present wars. At the same time, consider the virus which is devastating the country, the homeless and unemployed, soon to be augmented by millions of more Americans. Feel free to compare that to the homes and lifestyles of the billionaires, the bourgeoisie. Bear in mind that Trump is merely one member of the bourgeoisie, and he represents their interests. The rest of his class are about as anxious to part with their wealth and power, as he is.

The Communist Manifesto goes on to say "the theory of the Communists may be summed up in the single sentence: Abolition of private property . . . In one word, you reproach us with intending to do away with your property. Precisely so; that is just what we intend."

No wonder the capitalists so passionately hate the Communists! This hatred of the Communists is matched in intensity only by their love of their property!

That brings us to one of the strongest accusations against us:

"The Communists are further reproached with desiring to abolish countries and nationality.

"The working men have no country. We cannot take from them what they have not got. Since the proletariat must first of all acquire political supremacy, must rise to the leading class of the nation, must constitute itself the class, it is so far, itself national, though not in the bourgeois sense of the word.

"National differences and antagonisms between peoples are daily more and more vanishing, owing to the development of the bourgeoisie, to freedom of commerce, to the world market, to uniformity in the mode of production and to the conditions of life corresponding thereto.

"The supremacy of the proletariat will cause them to vanish still faster. United action, of the leading civilized countries at least, is one of the first conditions for the emancipation of the proletariat.

"In proportion as the exploitation of one individual by another will also be put an end to, the exploitation of one nation by another will also be put an end to. In proportion as the antagonism between the classes within the nation vanishes, the hostility of one nation to another will come to an end."

The fact of the matter is that the bourgeoisie love war. If nothing else, war is most profitable, or as they put it, "good for business". As a result of war, the factories run at full capacity and the war material thus produced tends to be quickly destroyed, resulting in an ever greater demand. This greater demand gives rise to an increase in price, according to the well known capitalist "law of supply and demand".

Of course, it remains for the working class to fight the wars of the bourgeoisie, to kill workers of other countries. They would have us believe that this is an act of patriotism, true "defence of the motherland". It is only the Communists, the true leaders of the working class, who call for the war to be turned into a civil war, to turn the rifles against the bourgeoisie. The war must be turned into a revolutionary war.

There are other accusations against the Communists, which the Communist Manifesto documents:

"The charges against Communism made from a religious, a philosophical, and generally, from an ideological stand point, are not deserving of serious examination.

"Does it require deep intuition to comprehend that mans ideas, views and conceptions, in one word, mans consciousness, changes with every change in the conditions of his material existence, in his social relations and his social life?

"What else does the history of ideas prove, than that intellectual production changes its character in proportion as material production is changed? The ruling ideas of each age have ever been the ideas of its ruling class.

"When people speak of the ideas that revolutionize society, they do but express that fact that within the old society the elements of a new one have been created, and that the dissolution of the old ideas keep even pace with the dissolution of the old conditions of existence."

The industrial revolution has given rise to socialized production, so that it is only natural that we should think in terms of socialism. The "old ideas", that of the "blessings of capitalism", must be dissolved, along with the "old conditions of existence", which is wage slavery, for the proletariat. This is another way of saying that the bourgeoisie must be overthrown and crushed under the Dictatorship Of the Proletariat.

The Communist Manifesto makes this quite clear in the following passages:

"The proletariat will use its political supremacy to wrest, by degree, all capital from the bourgeoisie, to centralize all instruments of production in the hands of the State, i.e., of the proletariat organized as the ruling class; and to increase the total productive forces as rapidly as possible.

"Of course, in the beginning, this cannot be effected except by means of despotic inroads on the rights of property, and on the conditions of bourgeois production; by means of measures, therefore, which appear economically insufficient and untenable, but which, in the course of the movement, outstrip themselves, necessitate further inroads upon the old social order, and are unavoidable as a means of entirely revolutionizing the mode of production.

"These measures will, of course, be different in different countries.

"Nevertheless, in most advanced countries, the following will be pretty generally applicable.

1. Abolition of property in land and application of all rents of land to public purposes.

2. A heavy progressive or graduated income tax.

3. Abolition of all rights of inheritance.

4. Confiscation of the property of all emigrants and rebels.

5. Centralization of credit in the hands of the state, by means of a national bank with State capital and an exclusive monopoly.

6. Centralization of the means of communication and transport in the hands of the State.

7. Extension of factories and instruments of production owned by the state; the bringing into cultivation of waste lands, and the improvement of the soil generally in accordance with a common plan.

8. Equal liability of all to work. Establishment of industrial armies, especially for agriculture.

9. Combination of agriculture with manufacturing industries; global abolition of all the distinctions between town and

country by a more equable distribution of the populace over the country.

10. Free education for all children in public schools. Abolition of children's factory labour in its present form. Combination of education with industrial production, etc.

"When, in the course of development, class distinctions have disappeared, and all production has been concentrated in the hands of a vast association of the whole nation, the public power will lose its political character. Political power, properly so called, is merely the organized power of one class for oppressing another. If the proletariat during its contest with the bourgeoisie is compelled, by the force of circumstances, to organize itself as a class, if, by means of a revolution, it makes itself the ruling class, and, as such, sweeps away by force the old conditions of production, then it will, along with these conditions, have swept away the conditions for the existence of class antagonisms, and of classes generally, and will thereby have abolished its own supremacy as a class.

"In place of the old bourgeois society, with its classes and class antagonisms, we shall have an association, in which the free development of each is the condition for the free development of all."

It is clear that the approaching revolution will give rise to the Dictatorship Of the Proletariat, in which the current ruling class, the bourgeoisie, will be crushed. The measures which Marx outlined will lead to the abolition of class antagonisms, and of "classes generally", so that all classes will eventually disappear.

All of this was written in 1848, and at that time he referred to the "proletariat organized as the ruling class". It was only in 1871, after the experience of the Paris Commune, that he began to refer to the Dictatorship Of the Proletariat.

In 1871, the workers of Paris revolted and took over the city. They shared the little they had and set up the first workers state. They referred to this as the Paris Commune. The bourgeoisie wasted no time in crushing the rebellion. This experience, brief as it was, provided Marx with valuable information. In fact, it was so valuable that he added it as an amendment to the Communist Manifesto. The workers, once they seized control of the city, failed to crush the capitalists, the bourgeoisie, or at least not with sufficient enthusiasm. At that point, Marx stressed the point that the working class, or "the proletariat organized as the ruling class", was not being stated strongly enough. It is necessary, after the proletariat seizes political power, to crush the capitalists, the bourgeoisie, with a certain enthusiasm. In this, the workers of the Paris Commune were negligent, and was one of the reasons that the Commune was crushed. As Marx put it, the working class must absolutely crush the bourgeoisie, through a dictatorship, the Dictatorship Of the Proletariat.

I use capital letters as a means of stressing the importance of that method of rule, and as a means of drawing a clear distinction between the true Marxists, and those who merely claim to be Communists. The "phoney Marxists", technically referred to as social chauvinists, are in fact loyal servants of the bourgeoisie, and are careful to make no mention of the Dictatorship Of the Proletariat.

With that in mind, there is an urgent need for a true party to lead the working class, which can only be a Communist Party, and I can suggest that the name of the party be Communist Party, Dictatorship Of the Proletariat, or CP,DOP.

Such a party can only be formed by "conscious people", Communists, those who are aware of the revolutionary theories of Marx and Lenin. It is very likely that most of them will be former members of the "upper classes", of necessity. The bourgeoisie make a point of keeping the working class "in the dark".

To further learn from the experience of previous revolutions, we can examine the Russian revolution. In early 1917, after the Russian people had risen up and overthrown the Czar, the Russian bourgeoisie came to undisputed power. A "bourgeois democratic republic" was established, referred to as the Kerensky regime. This regime was generous with promises, such as land to the peasants, an end to the war, a Constituent Assembly, improved working conditions for workers, etc. Of course it was all a pack of lies, and Lenin was determined to carry the revolution through to its logical socialist conclusion. With that in mind, he wrote State and Revolution. This was based heavily on The Communist Manifesto, especially the stress Marx placed on the mistakes made by the workers of the Paris Commune. In particular:

"But the working class cannot simply lay hold of the ready made state machinery, and wield it for its own purposes."

The existing state machine, set up by the small minority, the capitalists, the bourgeoisie, for the purpose of crushing the vast majority, the working class, the proletariat, must be smashed. In its place, a new state apparatus must be established, for the purpose of crushing the desperate and determined resistance of the bourgeoisie. This new state apparatus is referred to as the Dictatorship Of the Proletariat.

Under the leadership of Lenin, on November 7, 1917, the Russian socialist revolution took place. The working class of Russia took the advice of Marx. The bourgeoisie were overthrown and crushed under the Dictatorship Of the Proletariat.

As it is clear that the next American revolution is fast approaching, it is vital that workers prepare for the Dictatorship Of the Proletariat. With that in mind, I can only encourage a careful reading of the Communist Manifesto and State and Revolution. The various agents of the bourgeoisie, within the working class, will do their best to divert the revolutionary movement onto a harmless path of social reform. If they succeed, nothing will change.

With that in mind, in the immortal words of Marx and Lenin:

Workers of the World, Unite!

Prepare For the Dictatorship Of the Proletariat!

Victory Or Death!

CHAPTER 12

TRUMP AS A THREAT TO DEMOCRACY

Aug 24, 2020

The Democratic National Convention has now officially endorsed Joe Biden for president and Pamela Harris for Vice President. Due in part to the Corona Virus, this Convention is far different from all previous Conventions. As large gatherings of people are ruled out, so as not to spread the virus, the celebrities have been forced to give their speeches on video.

Then too, never before has any member of the Republican party actually endorsed a Democratic candidate for president. Now numerous high ranking Republican party members have "crossed the floor" to endorse Biden and Harris. These include Governors and Senators, those who are currently in office, as well as those who formerly held those offices. A great many people, who served as loyal, high ranking bureaucrats within several Republican administrations, have now joined the ranks of the Biden supporters. Countless others are as yet remaining silent, or "straddling the fence", to use the expression of the press. As yet they have not decided "which way to jump".

Perhaps the harshest words came from a most unlikely source, the former president, Barrack Obama. He chose to speak out, in a manner which left no room for any misunderstanding. He stated that as far as Trump is concerned, "this is one big reality show. He has not grown into the job because he can't. He has no interest in putting in the work . . . only cares about himself and his friends . . . his administration is determined to tear our democracy down, if thats what it takes for them to win".

It is most unusual for a former president to speak ill of a sitting president, if not unprecedented. This is one more indication of the fact that the class of people in charge of the country, the capitalists, the bourgeoisie, are deeply divided.

Obama is correct when he says that Trump "is determined to tear our democracy down". At least, he is making a supreme effort. On the other hand, it is not true that Trump cannot grow into the job. He simply has no interest in making the effort. Further, it is not true that Trump cares about his friends, if only because he has no friends. Trump cares only about himself and his immediate family. No one else.

A great many people who helped place him in power are currently in jail, or facing serious criminal charges. The latest "associate" of Trump, who has just been charged, is his former "top lieutenant during the crime spree called the Trump 2016 campaign". He is considered to know "where all the bodies are buried", and is thought to have the moral fortitude of Trump. In other words, he is a regular "snake in the grass". As that is the case, the advisors to Trump are advising him to issue a presidential pardon, to this snake, before he "sings like a little canary".

I have chosen to use these popular expressions as they are the same expressions the politicians use, as well as the mobsters. That is not a coincidence. The American political arena is very similar to a mob outfit.

It is doubtful that Trump is worried about being "ratted out". He may issue pardons to his loyal henchmen, or he may not. It is more likely that he will "throw them under the bus", as their freedom, or incarceration, is a matter of complete indifference to him.

As president, the head of state, he is quite well immune from prosecution. He is president now and fully intends to remain president, regardless of the results of the upcoming election. In fact, he plans to remain as president, for life, and then pass the reins of power to his daughter. It is the least he can do for the American people.

The point being that Obama is right to be worried that Trump is determined to "tear our democracy down", because he is doing just that. Obama is a member of the middle class, the petty bourgeois, yet is a loyal servant of the bourgeoisie. He has reason to be concerned. Further, he and the other members of his class expect all Americans to be concerned with the loss of "their democracy".

This begs the question: What is this democracy, of which he is so concerned, and why should we also be concerned?

Lenin provides us with an answer to that question in his work, The State and Revolution. As he phrases it, "In capitalist society, under the conditions most favourable to its development, we have more or less complete democracy in the democratic republic. But this democracy is always restricted by the narrow framework of capitalist exploitation, and consequently remains, in reality, a democracy for the minority, only for the possessing classes, only for the rich. Freedom in capitalist society always remains about the same as it was in the ancient Greek republics: freedom for the slave owners . . . Democracy for an insignificant minority, democracy for the rich—that is the democracy of capitalist society . . . on all sides we see restriction after restriction upon democracy . . . in their sum total these restrictions exclude and squeeze out the poor from politics, from taking an active part in democracy."

From this it is clear that democracy, at least under capitalism, is not "majority rule". Far from it, although the ruling class, the capitalists, the bourgeoisie, would have us believe otherwise. Instead, it is "democracy for the rich", for the "insignificant minority", for the monopoly capitalists, the bourgeoisie. It is the "ideal political shell for capitalism". The trouble being, as far as the capitalists are concerned, is that Trump is a threat to the democracy of the bourgeoisie!

There is a reason the bourgeoisie are concerned with the fact that Trump plans to set himself up as "royalty", perhaps "King Donald of America". As Lenin explains, "A democratic republic is the best possible political shell for capitalism, and therefore, once capital has control of this very best shell . . . it established its power so securely, so firmly, that no change, either of persons, of institutions, or of parties in the bourgeois democratic republic, can shake it." (italics by Lenin)

Trump is not planning to change "persons or institutions or parties" within the "democratic republic". Trump is planning to destroy the democratic republic, the "best possible political shell for capitalism"! That is the reason the bourgeoisie is determined to stop him.

That answers the first part of our question, and brings us to the second part, which is the reason we should care about the destruction of the bourgeois democratic republic.

It was Engels, no less, who referred to universal suffrage as an "instrument of bourgeois rule". He referred to it as "an index of the maturity of the working class. It cannot and never will be anything more in the modern state".

As that is the case, we certainly want all members of the working class, the proletariat, to be as politically active as possible, to "take an active part in democracy". At the very least, that means voting for the candidate of their choice. But if Trump has his way, all Americans will be relieved of the burden of voting.

This has given rise to an extremely rare case of converging interests, of two opposing classes, that of the proletariat and the bourgeoisie. The bourgeoisie want to remove Trump from office, as they see that he is a threat to their method of rule, while the proletariat wants to remove him from office, as he is a threat to democracy, if not to all of humanity.

As a result of this, for the moment—strictly for the moment—the two classes have a common goal! Now it is up to the proletariat to support the bourgeoisie in their effort to stop this madman!

This is not quite as remarkable as it may first appear. There are times throughout history, when classes who are the bitterest of enemies, come together, and work together towards a common goal. Of course, as soon as that goal is reached, they go back to attempting to destroy each other.

An example of this happened in America, in 1861. At that time, the country was in the process of splitting apart. The capitalists of the north were determined to invest their capital in the south.

The slave owners of the south were determined to block this industrial development. As the capitalists are anything but stupid, they decided that the best way to destroy the southern slave owners, was by emancipating their slaves. No slaves, no slave owners. Of course, the slave owners took a dim view of this approach.

As is well known, the tension rose to the point that the "south", or at least eleven states which practiced slavery, separated from the union. That left five other states, referred to as "border states", which also practiced slavery, and were also considering separation.

As a means of "damage control", agents of the north approached the slave owners of the border states and promised them that they could keep their slaves, as long as they assisted the north in crushing the southern rebellion. The slave owners of the border states agreed to this, and the "rest is history", as is the common expression.

The war ended in 1865, the Confederacy was defeated, and shortly afterwards, slavery was abolished in America. A section of the slave owners assisted the capitalists in destroying the slave owners!

A similar situation took place in Russia, immediately after the October revolution of 1917, in which the first socialist republic was established. At that time, Russia was still at war with the Central powers, including Germany. In fact, the German forces were advancing into Russia, and Lenin knew he needed help. With that in mind, he asked the country of France to send in demolition experts, to assist the Russians, to at least slow down the German advance.

As France was also at war with Germany, they agreed to assist in this objective. Even though the French capitalists hated Lenin, and everything he stood for, they agreed to help. So the officer in charge of the French detachment of demolition experts met with Lenin. Of course they shook hands and pretended to like each other, even though each could quite cheerfully have strangled the other. Shortly afterwards, in March of 1918, Russia was able to secure peace with Germany, and of course that was the end of the alliance between Russia and France.

Now we have a similar situation, in that the capitalists, the bourgeoisie, are asking the working people, the proletariat, to assist them in stopping Trump. The working people should do just that. In the process of stopping Trump from "tearing our democracy down", they will go beyond voting, they will be "taking an active part in democracy".

Just as the American capitalists used the slave owners to destroy the slave owners, so too the American workers can assist the capitalists, the bourgeoisie, in stopping Trump and in the process, destroy the capitalists, the bourgeoisie.

In the process of stopping Trump from destroying democracy, the working people will be taking an active part in democracy! At the same time, the Marxists, the Communists, can make it clear to people that the real problem is the class of people whom he serves, of whom he is a member, that of the monopoly capitalists, the bourgeoisie.

With that in mind, I can suggest that all Americans join the two political parties, Democrats and Republicans, as card carrying members. As such, you can decide the candidates to run for any and all political offices. I can also suggest that everyone vote in the upcoming election.

As well, it is up to conscious people, those who are aware of the theories of Marx and Lenin, to form a proper Communist Party, in order to lead the working class. Those who have been most politically active in the recent past, which is to say the women and students, will have to resume their activity, but on a wider scale. The members of the public have to be made aware that the problem is the capitalist, the bourgeoisie, and not just Trump. The solution is in revolution and the subsequent Dictatorship Of the Proletariat.

Let people know that the current democratic republic is set up by the capitalists, for the capitalists. They, the bourgeoisie, are in charge, and fully intend to remain in charge. It is democracy for the bourgeoisie, a dictatorship over the proletariat. The one and only way for the working class, the proletariat, to emancipate itself, is through revolution. The capitalists must first be overthrown and then crushed, under the Dictatorship Of the Proletariat. Such a dictatorship means democracy for the working class, the proletariat, but a Dictatorship for the bourgeoisie.

It is to be hoped that when this takes place, the men will be motivated to also take part in the revolutionary motion. No doubt as the revolution grows and spreads, ever more people will be swept up into the movement.

Now is the time to take action. Be creative. Harass the capitalists wherever and whenever possible. Allow them no peace. March on their offices, homes, banks and restaurants, their resorts, where they plot and scheme to stab each other in the back, and remain in power. Make their lives supremely miserable, and preferably do so in an entertaining manner, one which also raises the level of awareness of the working class. The best way to educate people is to entertain them at the same time.

Allow the posters and banners to proclaim:

Workers of the World, Unite!

Scientific Socialism!

Dictatorship Of the Proletariat!

Victory Or Death!

CHAPTER 13

AMERICA DIVIDED

Sep 1, 2020

Once again, a black man has been shot by the police, and once again the shooting has been captured on video. This time the shooting took place in Kenosha, Wisconsin. From the video, it is clear that the man was shot in the back, at point blank range, no less than seven times. As a result of this, he is reported to be paralyzed from the waist down. It is to the credit of the medical professionals that he is not dead. It is a testament to the stupidity of the local police that they went to the hospital and chained him to the bed. Perhaps they thought he would run away!

This continuation of violence, on the part of the police, has led to an escalation in protest. The most visible indication of this is in the field of professional sports. For the last several months, a great many players have been "taking a knee" as a sign of protest, at the time of the playing of the national anthem.

Various professional athletes, in the fields of basketball, baseball and soccer have chosen to "boycott" games, at least for the days of the previous Wednesday, Thursday and Friday. As a result of this stand by the athletes, the NHL issued a statement which is supremely vague: "Black and Brown communities continue to face real, painful experiences. The NHL and NHLPA recognize that much work remains to be done before we can play an appropriate role in a discussion centred on diversity, inclusion and social justice". This is another way of saying "life goes on".

By contrast, the members of the WNBA, Women's National Basketball Association, not only boycotted the game, but demonstrated at Centre Court and issued a statement in support of the movement against violent police repression: "We are lifting the name of Black and Brown women, whose names have been forgotten . . . We will continue to use our platform to speak of these injustices that are still happening and demand action for change. Black lives matter. Say her name. Say his name. We are not just basketball players. We are so much more than that. All lives matter, including the Black lives we are talking about."

The contrast between the two statements is sharp and clear. The men issued a statement which is bland and meaningless, while the women issued a statement which is opposed to police brutality. The women are not about to "shut up and play". They are not "just basketball players". They are indeed "much more than that", and they have every reason to be proud. This is one more example of the American women leading the revolutionary working class movement.

As yet, there is no mention of class content, but the people taking part in the revolutionary uprising are moving in that direction.

Numerous government officials have pointed out that Trump is now "fanning the flames of violence". He plans to visit the city of

Kenosha, against the wishes of city officials, who fear that such a visit will give rise to more violence. The governor of the state is opposed to this visit, and is practically pleading with Trump to stay away. Of course that is all the more reason for Trump to visit. Given a chance to "stir the pot", Trump is not about to pass it up!

Trump is "appalled" at the "violence" in the city of Portland, which has been "going on" now for over ninety consecutive days. He had a few "harsh words" for the mayor of that city, to put it mildly. To put it accurately, he was downright ignorant with the man. Trump referred to the man as a "Radical Left Do Nothing Democrat", in one of his tweets. That was one of the more pleasant things he said about the man.

Such behaviour, on the part of a head of state, is nothing short of contemptible. Trump is also threatening to send in the National Guard, to "restore law and order", even though such an order could be in violation of the very law he is so anxious to "restore".

In response, the mayor of Portland has accused Trump of "creating hate and division". He is appealing to the protesters to "not tear each other apart". Although the sentiment is a noble one, it is a bit late for that. The country is already torn apart.

In addition, Trump has ordered the Director of the National Intelligence to cancel all election security briefings for the Congress. The Speaker of the House has responded by calling this a "shocking abdication of its responsibility to keep Congress informed". Of course she is right that it is an "abdication of its responsibility", but the reason she finds this so "shocking" is not clear. It is just another step that Trump is taking, in the process of setting himself up as "king".

The fact is that Trump is becoming ever more brazen. He has no intention of stepping down in January, regardless of the results of the election. If the vote goes against him, he will merely declare that the election was bogus, fraudulent, and therefore it is his patriotic duty to continue to serve as president. It is the least he can do for the American people!

It is significant that a spokesman for the military made a statement to the effect that they would not get involved in any "election dispute". As the president is the "Commander in Chief" of all the armed forces, it is quite possible that the country may soon have two people who claim to be president, both issuing orders to the military. Under such a situation, it is difficult to imagine how the military cannot "get involved"!

As a result of this insanity, on the part of Trump, even his most fervent supporters can now see the "writing on the wall". They are now "jumping ship", as there is no point is fighting for a "lost cause". The latest individual to "come to her senses" was one of his closest, most devoted advisors, who resigned from her job, in order to "spend more time with her family".

No doubt her job, that of working for Trump, put a strain on her marriage, as Trump hires only attractive young females, those who have no objection to being groped. It is very likely that her husband took a "dim view" of such "shenanigans". Then again, it is entirely possible that she had a twinge of conscience.

It is far more likely that she decided to "cut her losses". Trumps "days are numbered", and even his closest advisors are now aware of this. As they have about as much loyalty to him as he has to them—which is to say none whatsoever—they are merely walking away.

There is a reason that Trump is reluctant to part company with the reins of power. He does not want to spend the rest of his life in jail!

At best, as soon as he is no longer president, Trump can expect to be charged with numerous counts of fraud, tax evasion, money laundering and possibly abuse of power. The government can be expected to separate him from his wealth, so that his small army of lawyers will melt away as snow in June. At worst, his love and admiration for Putin may have crossed the line, if he in fact collaborated with Putin in betraying the American government. That is the very definition of treason, and that is the one thing the American people will not tolerate. If convicted of treason, all Americans, regardless of political persuasion, will be calling for his blood.

It is quite remarkable that a large part of the city of Portland is still occupied by protesters. Of course that infuriates Trump, with good reason. He sees it as a threat to his class, that of the monopoly capitalists, the bourgeoisie. They are afraid that such an occupation could spread to other cities, much as a virus spreads. In this, they are correct, and they are determined to contain it. That is the reason he has responded with his usual lies and slander.

It is perhaps not a coincidence that the people who are occupying a part of the city of Portland have established a council. Under similar circumstances, in Russia, 1917, on the eve of the Russian revolution, the workers established something similar. These similar councils were referred to as "Soviets", and of course they spread across the country.

At the same time, in Russia, under the rule of Czar Nicholas, a number of government officials came together and plotted against the Czar. This was a natural result of the revolutionary motion.

Now, in America, in a similar situation, we have a number of self described "government officials" who are also plotting against Trump. As they are being very secretive, it stands to reason that they are trying to draw no attention to themselves. This is not too surprising, as thieves love darkness.

The situation in Russia at that time was most exceptional. Among other things, the Russian people, workers and peasants, had the experience—most bitter experience—of the previous revolution of 1905. Although that particular revolution had been crushed, with the utmost brutality, it served as a "school", as a means of "educating" the Russian people. The veterans of that revolution had no illusions. They knew exactly what to expect.

By the same token, the American people, in 2020, have the experience of the Occupy Movement, as well as the Anti War movement of the "sixties". The veterans of those two previous uprisings are now veterans, and they too know what to expect. We can expect them to lead the current American revolution.

Here now in America, the ruling class, the capitalists, the bourgeoisie, are concerned that Trump is a threat to their method of rule. In fact, the "democratic republic is the best possible political shell for capitalism", according to Lenin. To have Trump set himself up as a monarch would result in the loss of the democratic republic, which is not in the best interests of the bourgeoisie. That is the reason they are determined to stop him. They are not opposed to Trump as a matter of principle, if only because they have no principles.

Now the bourgeoisie is expecting the working class, the proletariat, to assist them in stopping that madman. Even though the two classes are the bitterest of enemies, it is up to the proletariat to assist the bourgeoisie, to form a temporary alliance, as they have a common enemy.

This is perhaps not as strange as it may sound. In Russia, in early 1917, the Russian workers, peasants and petty bourgeois came together to form an alliance with the Russian capitalists, the bourgeoisie, in order to overthrow the Czar. At that time, the madman occupying the throne was Nicholas the Second, also known as Nicholas the Bloody, and he had to go. In February – March of that year, the Russian people were successful, the Czar was deposed, and the alliance was over. A bourgeois democratic republic was formed, and in the process of overthrowing the Czar, the Russian working people received a valuable lesson. It served them well in the October revolution of the same year, in which the capitalists were overthrown, and a socialist republic was established.

A similar situation is now unfolding in America. Trump has to be stopped, the democratic republic has to be defended, and that calls for the broadest possible alliance of protesters. The experience the working people are about to gain will serve them well. After Trump is deposed, those same revolutionary protesters will proceed to overthrow the capitalists and to establish a socialist republic, under the Dictatorship Of the Proletariat.

We can expect everyone on the "Left" to take part in the motion to depose Trump, including the social chauvinists, those who are socialists in words, chauvinists in deeds. This will no doubt lead to some confusion on the part of the members of the public, as they will wonder about the difference between various groups who claim to be Marxists or Communists.

The best way to distinguish ourselves from the other "Leftist" groups, while marching with them in defence of the democratic republic, is to carry signs and banners which call for the Dictatorship Of the Proletariat. As the social chauvinist are most passionate defenders of the capitalists, the bourgeoisie, they want no part of the Dictatorship Of the Proletariat.

After Trump is removed from office, no doubt the social chauvinists will call for all protests to end, as the democratic republic in "now secure". As loyal subjects of the bourgeoisie—although it would never occur to them to admit this—they want no part of revolution and the subsequent Dictatorship Of the Proletariat.

I should add that I have chosen to use these capital letter in order to stress the importance of the theory. It is the worst nightmare of every capitalist.

With that in mind, let the banner proclaim:

Workers of the World, Unite!

Scientific Socialism!

Dictatorship Of the Proletariat!

CHAPTER 14

PREPARE FOR CIVIL WAR

Sep 8, 2020

The current political situation in America can perhaps best be described as insane. If it was in the form of a work of fiction, critics would dismiss it as too ridiculous. It appears to be a mixture of comedy and horror, two forms of entertainment which do not go well together. Yet the actions of Trump and his administration would be laughable, if they were not so tragic.

It is estimated that an additional forty million people will soon be homeless, yet this is a matter of supreme indifference to Trump and his supporters. Their only concern is that he remain in power. The country is also facing another possible government shut down at the end of the month, but that too does not concern Trump.

As well, the current death toll, as a result of the Corona Virus, is approaching 200,000. By the end of the year, that number is expected to more than double, to over 400,000. That is certainly not a joking matter, but Trump sees it as an opportunity, as a means of staying in power. The virus has given rise to the necessity of "social distancing", as a means of containing the spread of the virus, so that most Americans plan to vote by mail. With that in mind, Trump has taken steps to ensure that the mail does not get delivered on time, so that he can declare the election a fraud. As well, he is encouraging citizens to vote twice, once by mail and once in person, an action which is completely against the law. That too could lead to the election being declared invalid, which is precisely what he wants.

Such actions are completely devoid of principle, an abuse of power at best, supremely contemptible, but not entirely irrational. By contrast, his suggestion of "Men in Black", an "entire plane load of looters, anarchists and rioters", of "thugs wearing black uniforms", leads people to question his sanity. Trump is also suggesting that his opponent for the presidency, the former Vice President, is "controlled by people you never heard of, people that are in the dark shadows."

As if that is not bad enough, he is also a believer in "QAnon", Apparently, "Q" is a high level, anonymous, government insider, an individual who is "running an international Satanic pedophile child trafficking ring and controlling the world".

To think that the man who is spitting out this nonsense is the American president!

More or less as a result of this insanity, numerous former members of his administration are either facing charges or are already in prison. Many other current members of the same administration will soon be joining them. One of the convicted felons has just written a book, which is already a best seller, even though it is not yet in print. Yet members of the press have received advance copies, so we know what it says.

The author, a self described "fixer" for Trump, was his former lawyer and advisor. He was apparently a close confidant of Trump, long before Trump became president. Critics say that he was the closest thing Trump had to a friend. This is reasonable, as Trump is not the sort of person who is capable of forming friendships. He is too self absorbed for that.

The fact remains that in this book, soon to be published, he refers to Trump as a "racist, a bully, a predator, a con man, a swindler, completely corrupt". He further states that "Trump can't be trusted" and "You shouldn't believe a word he utters". He also claims that Trump is determined to "leverage power to the maximum level possible". With that in mind, he accuses Trump of flattering the Russian president, Putin, with a view to building a Trump Tower in Moscow.

Of course the White House is not taking this lying down. They have pointed out that the author of that book is nothing less than a disbarred lawyer, a federal inmate, convicted of no less than nine charges, including lying to Congress. This comes as no great surprise to anyone, as only liars and crooks are qualified to work for Trump.

The author of the book does not deny being a liar, but maintains that he lied only at the direction of, and for the benefit of, Donald Trump. But then he was caught in those lies, tried and convicted. Of course, at that point Trump "threw him under the bus", as Trump cares only about himself and his immediate family.

The journalists are also reporting that at the time Trump was in France and scheduled to visit a cemetery containing the remains of American servicemen killed in the line of duty, he refused to go as he was afraid the rain would expose his bald spot. When asked about this, he mentioned that he could not go because he had to call his wife, in America. The journalists found this hard to believe as his wife was, at that time, with him in France.

In addition, a highly respectable magazine is reporting that Trump has also referred to military veterans as "suckers and losers", as they "don't know how to exploit the system and get out of serving". Clearly he has only contempt for those who serve their country, including those who have made the ultimate sacrifice. He managed to avoid the nuisance of spending time in the military by being granted deferral due to "bone spurs" on his feet. Money may not buy happiness, but it certainly buys almost everything else.

Trump has responded to these serious accusations against him, by attacking the lady who owns "controlling interest" in the magazine which made these allegations, a "billionaire philanthropist", as someone who "does not know her place". Trump is determined to make her rue the day she spoke ill of him!

As if that is not bad enough, a second book is soon to be published, written by a former FBI agent, who is suggesting that Trump was being investigated on suspicion of being a "Manchurian Candidate". That is a rather oblique way of referring to someone who is suspected of being a Russian agent. It is entirely possible that the agent was fired for pursuing that line of investigation.

Yet there are two sides to every coin, so to speak. Or as the social scientists refer to it, there are two sides to every contradiction. The press is accurately reporting the news, but from the bourgeois point of view, of course. That is one side of the coin. The flip side of the coin, the proletarian side, is the fact that people are rising up, demanding change. The Black Lives Matter movement is growing and gaining strength. People of all colours and ethnic backgrounds are now marching, against violent police repression. Professional sport games are being cancelled. The protesters in Portland are standing their ground, even under extreme pressure. The Kentucky Derby is being harassed by protesters. The protests are spreading to other cities and around the country. They are even spreading to other countries.

Perhaps of more significance, no less than three separate republics have already taken shape. As yet, they have not declared independence and formed socialist republics, but soon that will happen. On the east coast, which is one of the population centres of the country, seven states have come together. On the west coast, three states have come together, also population centres. Then in the midwest, the industrial heartland of the country, seven more states have formed a coalition. Without doubt, very soon other states will come together and form other coalitions, the nucleus of independent socialist republics.

Now the federal election is less that two months away, and the journalists are counting down the days. I have deliberately chosen to quote precisely the words they are using, in order to make a point. The journalists are clearly concerned, as they are patriotic Americans who love their country. They are also convinced that Trump is the problem, and that voting him out of office is the solution. Except that Trump is not the problem, the problem is capitalism, and as long as the capitalists, the bourgeoisie are in charge, nothing of substance will change.

There is only one solution to the problems created by capitalism, and that is to convert it into socialism. That is only possible through a revolution and the subsequent Dictatorship Of the Proletariat. The bourgeoisie has to be overthrown and crushed, as otherwise they will return to power, as they have in Russia and China. There are certain conditions that are necessary for a revolution to take place.

As Lenin put it, "It is only when the 'lower classes do not want to live in the old way and the 'upper classes' cannot carry on in the old way that the revolution can triumph." He refers to this as the "fundamental law of revolution". (italics by Lenin)

As that is the case, it is clear that the American "upper class", in this case the bourgeoisie, can no longer rule in the "old way", which is to say the two party system. Trump has no intention of stepping down, regardless of the results of the federal election. After all, the man is not entirely stupid. He knows that as soon as he is no longer president, he will be charged and convicted of numerous crimes, both state and federal, and spend the rest of his life in jail. Unless of course, he is convicted of treason, in which case he could face the firing squad.

As for the "lower classes", in this case the working class, the proletariat, they have "had enough", they are "fed up". They are no longer content to "live in the old way". They are tired of being unemployed and homeless, living in poverty, watching their fellow Americans sicken and die from the virus, while the "one percent" live in the "lap of luxury". They are demanding change. This is the very definition of a revolutionary situation!

So now, on the one hand, we have the ruling class, the bourgeoisie, squabbling among themselves, not sure of how to proceed. They just know that they cannot rule in the old way, under the two party system.

On the other hand, we have the working class, the proletariat, those who are facing massive unemployment and homelessness, resulting in extreme poverty. This in addition to the virus which is decimating the country. They just know they cannot live in the old way.

It is for these reasons that I am convinced the revolution is about to take place, and that it has every chance of success, that it can "triumph". Which is not to say that it will magically be "triumphant" by itself. It is going to require a little effort on our part.

With that in mind, I can only suggest that time is "not on our side", if you will excuse the expression. Trump has made it clear that he fully intends to remain in office, regardless of the results of the November election. In fact, he has stated that he plans to remain in office until he decides to step down. That is one of the few honest statements he has ever made! On this one point, and on this one point alone, we can believe him.

Trump no doubt plans to set himself up as a monarch, perhaps King Donald the First, of the House of Trump. Instead, he is about to receive a rude awakening.

The American people will not stand for this. We can count upon them to stand up and defend their democratic rights. It is very likely that a full blown revolution will be set in motion. Remarkably enough, we can expect the American people, the working class, to rise up in protest, along side the American capitalists, the bourgeoisie.

Such an alliance—although rare—is not unprecedented. In early 1917, in Russia, a similar alliance took place, in that the common people of Russia, workers and peasants, came together with the Russian bourgeoisie, in opposition to Czar Nicholas. It resulted in the overthrow of the monarchy, in February – March of that year. Immediately after the abdication of the Czar, the alliance was ended. Several months later, on November 7—new style calendar—the bourgeoisie were overthrown by the workers and peasants, led by Lenin and the Russian Social Democratic

Labour Party. It should be noted that at that time, such was the name of the Communist Party.

Now here in America, we can expect the working class to first assist the bourgeoisie in defeating Trump. That will give them fresh confidence in their ability to enact change. As soon as Trump is deposed, the bourgeoisie will attempt to disarm the working class, as they are well aware of the danger of armed workers. Then we can expect the working class to defend their democratic right to bear arms, as is guaranteed in the Constitution. The freshly energized proletariat will resist this new assault on their rights, and we can expect the workers to carry the revolution forward, as happened in November of 1917 in Russia, and overthrow the bourgeoisie.

That being said, it is not reasonable to expect the workers to overthrow the capitalists and establish the Dictatorship Of the Proletariat, without a little help from their leaders. That is where conscious people come in, Marxists, true Communists. That is the very thing that is lacking. Without the leadership provided by a true Communist Party, the success of the revolution is in doubt.

This brings us to the role of leaders, or at least proper leaders, which is to say scientific socialists. In other words, Marxists, as they are the only true leaders of the working class, the proletariat. Those who claim to be socialists but not Marxists, are really utopian socialists, and whether they know it or not, are in the service of the capitalists, the bourgeoisie.

As for those who are skeptical, may I suggest you give consideration to the opinion of Engels, who recognized three forms of the great struggles of the working class, that of the economic, the political and the theoretical! In fact, it was Lenin who pointed out that the "role of vanguard can be fulfilled only by a party that is guided by an advanced theory." (italics by Lenin)

This is to stress the necessity of the creation of a Communist Party. It must be created. It is the duty of conscious people, which is to say Marxists, to create a true Communist Party, as otherwise the revolution will likely not succeed.

The reason for this is quite simple. The working class is not aware of itself as a class. This class awareness must be brought to it from an outside source, from middle class intellectuals. Anyone who scoffs at the importance of the class awareness, at the revolutionary theories which can only be brought to the working class, by a true Communist party, "means, whether one likes it or not, the growth of influence of bourgeois ideology among the workers". (italics by Lenin)

Lenin goes on to say that "The working class spontaneously gravitates towards socialism, but the more widespread (and continuously revived in the most diverse forms) bourgeois ideology spontaneously imposes itself upon the working class still more". For that reason, it is up to Communists to combat bourgeois ideology with proletarian ideology.

In addition, we can expect the American empire to break up, to split into independent socialist republics, as happened in Russia. Three American republics have already taken shape, and no doubt more will soon follow. This may happen only after the socialist revolution which overthrows the bourgeoisie, or perhaps before that. As yet, we have no way of knowing. We do know that the capitalists are completely reactionary, dead set opposed to revolution and socialism, and supremely reluctant to part with their wealth and power. That is the reason they have to be crushed under the Dictatorship Of the Proletariat.

As for those who object that there already are several Communist parties in the country, I can only respond that you are mistaken. There are several parties which claim to be Communist or socialist, but none of them are Marxist. This serves to confuse the working people, as is no doubt intended. So in the interest of distinguishing ourselves from the social chauvinists, I am suggesting that the name of the party be Communist Party, Dictatorship Of the Proletariat. As all social chauvinists avoid any mention of the term Dictatorship Of the Proletariat, as if it were an infectious disease, that should help to clarify the situation.

In addition to the usual Marxist slogans, may I suggest an additional one:

American Communist Party,
Dictatorship Of the Proletariat

CHAPTER 15

AMERICA CLOSE TO CIVIL WAR

Sep 11, 2020

As we enter the final few weeks of the latest political gong show, known as the 2020 presidential elections, a series of "tell all" books have just been published. No doubt the authors deliberately waited until the election was in "full swing", so as to get as much press coverage for their books as possible. Assuming that to be the case, they are sure not to be disappointed.

The journalists are quite cheerfully reporting, even gleefully, that no less than five books are exposing the inner workings of the White House. Each book is even more damning that the previous one, to the delight of the reporters. As Trump has consistently slandered the reporters, professionals one and all, as "purveyors of fake news", who can blame them?

They are especially excited by the book authored by the famous journalist, investigative reporter and writer, one whom interviewed Trump possibly eighteen times. Each interview was recorded, at the permission of Trump, so that any denial lacks credibility. Not that any such little detail ever stopped Trump from lying before, so we can expect him to stay in form and continue to lie.

In anticipation of those lies, the press is playing the recordings, in which Trump stated, in early February, that he knew the virus was "even more deadly than strenuous flu", that it was "dangerous, highly contagious, air borne and deadly". He went on to say that he "did not want to start a panic", so he deliberately "downplayed the risks". Now that over six million Americans are infected, with nearly two hundred thousand dead, everyone knows that he was right. It is indeed "deadly". Perhaps the relatives of the deceased can take some comfort in knowing that no panic was created!

This is not to imply that Trump accepts any responsibility for the virus which is devastating the country, because he does not. As he stated in an interview in July, "The virus has nothing to do with me. It's not my fault. China let the damn virus out".

As one journalist pointed out, "Trump does not seem to grasp that a President has a responsibility to protect the public." In fact, such a "grasp" is beyond the intellectual capacity of the man. That same journalist blamed it on "hubris", which is defined as excessive pride or self confidence. Trump certainly has no shortage of that!

In addition, his niece has written a book, which is also less than flattering. Even though related by blood, she is clearly not a big fan of his. Or perhaps, given a chance to make some money with a tell all book, she just could not pass up the opportunity. Such attitudes may well run in the family. No member of the family has ever been known to stand on principle.

The journalists are also reporting that the Attorney General, the "top cop" in the country, has sunk to a greater depth. Each time they think he has hit bottom, he finds a way to go lower.

In this particular case, a certain lady, a writer, claims that Trump raped her in the nineteen nineties. Of course, the statute of limitations has long since expired, so he cannot be charged. But then, in response to her accusations, Trump called her a liar. She in turn responded by suing him for "defamation of character".

That is quite straight forward, a simple civil law suit, not a criminal matter, certainly no concern of the Department of Justice. Yet the Attorney General has seen fit to volunteer the services of that government agency, to act as personal attorneys for Trump, at tax payer expense of course.

In other news, the governor of New York state is accusing Trump of trying to "kill New York City". As Trump tweeted "Drop Dead NYC", it is clear that the governor has a point. It would appear that Trump is doing his best to provoke the North East to separate, and form a separate independent socialist republic.

As well, the Director of the National Intelligence has just told Congress that there will be no more personal briefings, at least concerning election security. When the Congress responded that this was a violation of section 6507 of the National Defence Authorization Act, the Director made no response. Apparently he takes his orders from Trump, not the Congress.

It is clear that the ruling class, in this case the capitalists, the bourgeoisie, can no longer rule in the old way. The two party system, which has served them so well for so many years, has "let them down". Trump, one of their own, no less, is now a "loose cannon" and has to be stopped. That is the reason they have allowed the publication of the books which are so critical of

Trump. Then too, the journalists have been "turned loose", and in fact are in a "feeding frenzy". They have been given the "green light" to expose Trump as the liar, crook and sex offender that he is. This they are doing with great enthusiasm.

According to Lenin, one of the requirements for a successful revolution is the inability of the ruling class to rule in the old way. That requirement is clearly being met. He further stated that the other requirement, comes at a time when the oppressed class is no longer prepared to live in the old way. That time is now.

As the journalists are focused on Trump and the upcoming presidential election, the protests which are happening around the country are being largely ignored. At best, they are mentioned largely in passing, almost as a footnote. Still, it is clear that the protests in Portland, which have now been going on for over one hundred days, are showing no sign of slowing down. On the contrary, they are escalating, with a Molotov cocktail being thrown. That is the popular term for a glass bottle, filled with gasoline and fitted with a cloth fuse. Then the cloth is lit and the bottle thrown. As the glass breaks, the gasoline catches fire and the results can be most unpleasant. That is certainly a dramatic escalation of the protests.

Trump and his administration are so concerned with the protests that they are sending in federal troops, dressed in plain clothes, driving in unmarked vehicles, with the goal of quelling the "uprisings". The fact that this is against the law, or unconstitutional, to put it in legal terms, does not concern Trump. Breaking the law is his idea of restoring law and order.

By law, the federal government can send in federal troops, usually in the form of the National Guard, only at the request of the governor of the state. As numerous governors are reluctant to call in such troops, Trump has decided to go around the governors. With that in mind, he has created something called PACT, or Protecting American Communities Task Force. Officially, they have been created to "protect American monuments, memorials and statues and combatting recent criminal violence". As a result of this, any protesters who are arrested can be charged with a more serious crime, as the violation of the "order to disperse" is now a federal offence.

This too is an escalation in the class struggle, in response to the "protests", which is nothing more than revolutionary action. This escalation has the effect of alienating certain members of the bourgeois class, so that we can expect some of them to join the revolutionary movement. This is an indication of the strength of the revolution, just as predicted by Marx.

A further indication of the unwillingness of the working class to live in the old way is being played out on the far side of the country. In the city of Rochester, New York state, a mentally ill black man was killed by police. That resulted in many nights of protest, seven police officers being suspended, and the police chief was forced to resign.

In Essex, New Jersey, hundreds of families lined up for a food bank. Within a couple hours, they ran out of food. A great many people are now going hungry. Most of those people never thought they would see the day that they would have to rely on hand outs. They are out of work, soon to be homeless, and now they have been degraded. Make no mistake, they are no longer content to live in the old way.

That is the other side of the coin, the other aspect to the contradiction, to state it in scientific terms. So now we have a ruling class which can no longer rule in the old way, and a working class which is no longer prepared to live in the old way.

In short, the situation is truly revolutionary. The stage is set for a successful socialist revolution.

Now that Trump is under pressure, he is lashing out. The mayor of Rochester is absolutely correct when she says, referring to Trump, "his only desire is to bait people, to act with hate and to incite violence that he believes will benefit him politically". That lady is a fine judge of character!

This is not to say that Trump is the problem. The class of people whom he represents is the problem, and that is the monopoly capitalists, the bourgeoisie. They have to be overthrown, a socialist republic has to be established, and the former ruling class, the capitalists, those who are concerned only with their profit, the bourgeoisie, have to be crushed under the Dictatorship Of the Proletariat.

That is a fact, a fundamental tenet of Marxism, just as it is a fact that it is not reasonable to expect the working people to be aware of this. Scientific socialism and the working class motion evolve separately, and it is now necessary to merge the two. The working class movement and the movement for scientific socialism must become one movement. The only way that can happen is by having proper leaders, which is to say that we are in desperate need of a truly Communist Party, one which calls for revolution and the subsequent Dictatorship Of the Proletariat.

With that in mind, may I suggest that in 1895, in Czarist Russia, Lenin got together with a group of intellectuals, met in secrecy and led them in creating a Russian Communist Party. At that time, it was called the League of Struggle For the Emancipation of the Working Class.

Even though they met in the utmost secrecy, they were still "ratted out". Most of them, including Lenin, were immediately arrested and thrown in prison. Even under those conditions, the League of Struggle took shape, as Lenin was able to write and smuggle the illegal material out of prison.

One of these illegal works was titled Draft and Explanation of a Program For the Social Democratic Party. That is of particular interest to us, as it gives us an idea of the program of the current American Communist Party, which must soon to be created.

As Lenin put it, "The Party's activity must consist in promoting the workers' class struggle . . . to join up with the workers movement, to bring some light into it . . . to uphold the interests of the workers and to represent those of the entire working class movement".

From this it is clear that it is the duty of Marxists, Communists, to "join up" with the working class movement, and not to attempt to divert it onto some harmless path of social reform. As for the idea of "bring some light into it", this is to say that the working class is not aware of itself as a class, certainly not aware of the revolutionary theories of Marx, and the working class must be exposed to these Marxist theories.

Lenin refers to this as "developing the workers class consciousness . . . means the workers understanding that the only way to improve their conditions and to achieve their emancipation is to conduct a struggle against the capitalist and factory owner class created by the factories . . . that the interests of all workers of any particular country are identical, that they all constitute one class, separate from all other classes in society . . . that to achieve their aims they have to work to influence the affairs of state, just as the landlords and capitalists did, and are continuing to do so now".

Those who are about to create a new American Communist Party would do well to bear that in mind. Most, if not all, Leftist parties and organizations, seek to divert the revolutionary movement onto some harmless path of social reform. Whether they know it or not, and many of them are not aware of this, they are working in the service of the bourgeoisie.

Without doubt, the situation is truly revolutionary, as the ruling class can no longer rule in the old way and the working class is no longer prepared to live in the old way. As that is the case, certain bourgeois intellectuals are breaking away from their class. It is up to these intellectuals, those who are aware of the revolutionary theories of Marx and Lenin, to form a proper American Communist Party. Only such a Party is able to lead the working class, to raise their level of awareness, to make them aware of themselves as a class, of the necessity of revolution and further of the necessity of crushing their class enemies under the Dictatorship Of the Proletariat.

Only with the proper leadership, that of a true Communist Party, will the revolution succeed. The alternative is to continue to live under the rule of the capitalists, the dictatorship of the bourgeoisie. That is a fate worse than death.

CHAPTER 16

AMERICA: A HOUSE DIVIDED

Sep 20, 2020

In 1858, an American politician made a speech, in which he stated that "a house divided cannot stand". That politician was Abraham Lincoln. He was absolutely correct. He was also president at the time of the Civil War of 1861-1865. Now the "house" is once again "divided", and the second American Civil War is looming.

The current death toll, as a result of the Corona Virus, stands at 200,000 and is expected to double by the end of the year. The medical professionals are concerned that it could more than double, if as they expect, it combines with the flu virus, to create a perfect storm, a "twindemic", which could result in the death of a great many more people.

The unemployment rate is massive, but grossly underestimated, as most of the people who are out of work are not classified as unemployed. As well, a great many people are homeless, with an additional forty million people expected to be evicted from their homes soon. The "economic stimulus package", which provides some relief to people, has been reduced, and will soon be eliminated. The government is expected to shut down at the end of the month, as at that time it will run out of money, so that all government payments are expected to cease.

The people are rising up, demanding change. The movement against violent police repression, against minorities, "black and brown", has now merged with the working class movement, led by Black Lives Matter. The protests are becoming ever stronger, ever finer.

The Attorney General has responded by threatening to charge protesters with sedition. As sedition is defined as "conduct or speech inciting people to rebel against the authority of a state", that is a very serious charge. It is very close to treason, which is to betray ones country. It is clear that the Attorney General is confusing the right to peaceful protest, as is guaranteed in the Constitution, with rebellion. But then Americans have the right to "abolish any government which does not represent them". Their founding fathers gave them that right, in the Declaration of Independence. Such details are conveniently over looked by people such as the Attorney General. They are about to receive a rude awakening.

In the midst of this, Americans are faced with a federal election. All members of Congress are up for election, one third of the Senate and of course, the presidency is on the line. The press is focused on Trump, and would have us believe that removing him from office will solve the problems facing the nation.

Trump is not worried about the election, as he has no intention of stepping down, regardless of whether he wins or loses. He has that base covered. As a result of the virus, most people are being forced to vote by mail. With that in mind, he appointed a new Postmaster General, so as to ensure that the ballots are not delivered and counted on time. As well, he is encouraging people to vote twice, once by mail and once in person. Of course this is strictly against the law, so that if voters take his advice and vote twice, he can then declare the election fraudulent, assuming the vote goes against him.

Remarkably enough, Trump could still win the upcoming presidential election, even without election fraud. He is a fine demagogue, which is defined as "an orator or political leader who gains power and popularity by arousing the emotions, passions and prejudices of the people". It should be noted that Lenin referred to demagogues as "the worst enemies of the proletariat".

Trump knows how to appeal to those who are desperate, drowning in debt, unemployed, homeless, or about to become unemployed and homeless. He merely blames their plight on minorities and immigrants!

Now these desperate people, voters, are being asked to make a choice. They are being asked to choose between a man who is well known as a liar, thief and sex offender, but a leader, and a man, a former Vice President, who can best be charitably described as a follower.

The contrast between Trump and his competition is striking. Trump usually speaks his mind, rarely bothering with tele prompters. The former Vice President, the Democratic candidate for president, on the other hand, relies heavily on tele prompters. When he goes "off script". he becomes completely confused, stumbles, contradicts himself. He is the very definition of a follower.

The press is focused on the presidential election, and there is considerable speculation as to the election results. All are agreed that as soon as Trump is no longer president, he will be arrested, charged and spend the rest of his life in prison. No doubt Trump is also of that opinion, as he is not entirely stupid. For that reason, he has no intention of stepping down.

With that in mind, one journalist, a truly starry eyed optimist, suggested that Trump has no choice but to step down, if the vote goes against him, as the election result is guaranteed in the Constitution. Clearly this misguided soul failed to notice that at the time Trump took the oath of office, that of "preserving, protecting and defending the Constitution", his lips were moving, and that is a fine indication that he was lying!

Other theories have been offered, by other journalists. One has suggested that Trump may give himself a presidential pardon, which is quite possible. Another has suggested that he may "pull a Nixon", which is to say resign early, perhaps the day before his term expires, so that the current Vice President can automatically become president for a day, and grant Trump a pardon. This is highly unlikely, as there is nothing in it for the Vice President.

Even if he is granted a presidential pardon, such a pardon applies only to federal crimes, not to state crimes. Trump is anticipating numerous state charges, in addition to federal charges. Such a pardon will not keep him out of prison.

As a result of this, numerous people, those who are in positions of authority, are deeply concerned. A noted election law professor stated that "the undermining of election integrity is a most dangerous thing". He has reason to be concerned, as Trump stated on Twitter that "the election results may never be known". Further, the Attorney General, a loyal flunky of Trump, stated that he would respect the election results, but only if "the results are clear".

Numerous government officials are very nervous. Few are prepared to "go down with the ship". All are aware that Trump is prepared to throw them "under the bus", if he thinks it will serve his purpose. Many have already "jumped ship". Others are currently defying him, at the risk of being fired. The FBI director stated publicly that most protesters are peaceful, not terrorists, in defiance of Trump. A former Virus Task Force official is now accusing Trump of caring only about reelection. She accuses him of stating that the virus means that he "does not have to shake hands with disgusting people". Even the former spy chief is now advising Congress to create an election oversight commission. This sentiment is being echoed by Senator Sanders, who is concerned that "Trump may not accept the election results". Count on it!

Even the top military officials are feeling the heat. The National Guard troops are occasionally patrolling the cities, but without any weapons, against the wishes of Trump. The Defence Secretary has ordered the regular army units to return to base, not to patrol American cities. Pentagon officials have stated that they will not get involved in any election disputes.

The situation is certainly revolutionary, in that the capitalists, the bourgeoisie, can no longer rule in the old way, while the working class, the proletariat, is no longer content to be ruled in the old way. We can expect a full scale civil war, a revolution, to break out any day now. In other words, the current situation is very similar to the situation of Russia, in 1917. The important difference is that the Russian working people had truly Marxist leaders, in the form of Lenin and the Communist Party. Without that leadership, it is doubtful that the revolution could have succeeded.

In the case of the Russian revolution, it was not at all immediately clear that the revolution would succeed. The country was in ruins, after four years of war, plus the harsh terms of peace imposed by the Treaty of Brest Litovsk. That was followed by four years of civil war, in which the forces of reaction, the counter revolutionaries, referred to as the Whites, sought to overthrow the new socialist republic. Their goal was not only to restore capitalism, but also the monarchy, and to give the land back to the landlords.

Yet in the midst of this civil war, in June of 1920, Lenin wrote the Theses On the Fundamental Tasks Of the Second Congress Of the Communist International. As the situation at that time has certain similarities to the current revolutionary situation, it deserves careful study.

It may be objected that at that time, in 1920, the situation was far different. As Lenin phrased it, "the finest representatives of the revolutionary proletariat in all capitalist countries have fully grasped the fundamental principles of the Communist International, the Dictatorship Of the Proletariat and Soviet power". (I use capital letters to stress the importance of that fundamental principle, placing it on the same level as Soviet power-GM) Such is no longer the case. The most advanced strata of the proletariat no longer embrace the Dictatorship Of the Proletariat or Soviet power.

Then again, it is now the case that the vast majority of people have spontaneously gravitated towards socialism, or to the "Left", as is the common expression. This places them in a better position to take part in the revolution, as compared to the Russian proletariat, in 1917. As well, no less than three American republics have already taken shape. No doubt they will soon separate and establish independent socialist republics. By comparison, it was several years after the Russian revolution before separate republics took shape, and the Union of Soviet Socialist Republics came into existence.

In his theses, Lenin stressed the importance of the proper leadership. As he stated it, in reference to the Communist Party, "it is only under the leadership of such a party that the proletariat is capable of displaying the full might of its revolutionary onslaught, and of overcoming the inevitable apathy and occasional resistance of that small minority, the labour aristocracy, who have been corrupted by capitalism . . . it is the Communist parties' principle task at the present moment to unite the scattered Communist forces, to form a single Communist Party in every country (or to reinforce or renovate the already existing Party) in order to increase ten fold the work of preparing the proletariat for the conquest of political power—political power, moreover, in the form of the Dictatorship Of the Proletariat."

It is my opinion that at present, the most important thing, or the "key link", as Lenin phrased it, is to make preparations for the Dictatorship Of the Proletariat. The first step in those preparations is to form a proper Communist Party. Without the proper leadership provided by a truly Marxist Communist Party—and there is no other form of proper leadership—then it is doubtful that the revolution will succeed. Further, there can be no question of uniting the "already existing Party", as all parties which claim to be Marxist are in fact social chauvinists.

Now the capitalists, the bourgeoisie, are facing several crises, in the form of the virus, unemployed and homeless, an anticipated second great depression, not to mention a "loose cannon" in the form of Trump. As a result of this, they are deeply divided, not sure of how to proceed. A few members of their class, as well as a considerable number of their formerly loyal middle class, petty bourgeois supporters, have now "jumped ship" and are joining the revolutionary forces. Almost all of these people are well educated intellectuals. They are aware of class distinctions, familiar with the revolutionary theories of Marx and Lenin. Now is the time to make use of their education, training and skills. It is up to them, it is their duty, to take part in forming a truly Marxist Communist Party.

True, there are certain advanced workers who are familiar with the revolutionary theories of Marx and Lenin. Especially now that we have the internet, it is possible to become self educated. To expect these numerically small number of workers, no matter how advanced, to form a Communist Party, is expecting too much. Which is not to say that they cannot take part in creating such a Party, and in fact it is recommended.

No doubt the American Communist Party will be formed, and in the near future. The success of the revolution largely depends upon this. Bear in mind that, as Lenin stated, "the Communist Parties' current task consists not in accelerating the revolution, but in intensifying the preparation of the proletariat . . . to see that 'recognition' of the Dictatorship Of the Proletariat shall not remain a mere matter of words".

As I write this, the press is reporting that another member of the Supreme Court has just died. This may well give rise to another crisis, as Trump is determined to nominate another Supreme Court justice, a woman, and have her confirmed by the Senate, before the November elections. There is strong opposition to this, by a great many people, who prefer to wait until after the federal elections. But then Trump is determined to do whatever he wants, regardless of the will of the American people. As the revolutionary situation is so volatile, it could trigger an explosion.

No doubt, the situation of the proletariat is desperate. Most are deeply in debt, unemployed or under employed, homeless or facing eviction, with little or no medical coverage, unable to make ends meet. The petty bourgeois are also feeling the pinch. They expect the stock market to soon collapse, wiping out any savings they have set aside. As well, those who own small businesses anticipate losing them, as the depression tightens its grip, and they are forced into the ranks of the proletariat.

It is the petty bourgeois intellectuals to whom I am appealing. It is not fair that you should have to be burdened with the additional task of forming an American Communist Party. It is what it is. Fair has nothing to do with it. Call it fate, or historical development, or an act of Almighty God, if you believe in God, as I do. However you choose to refer to it, the fact remains that the working people need leaders, proper leaders, and you are the chosen ones.

I am sure you will rise to the occasion. I have complete confidence in you

CHAPTER 17

AMERICANS RECEIVE A LESSON IN DEMOCRACY

Sep 28, 2020

Lenin once wrote, in Imperialism, the Highest Stage of Capitalism, that "Crises of every kind—economic crises more frequently, but not only these—in their turn increase very considerably the tendency towards concentration and monopoly". The current situation in America is certainly proof of that statement. The country is currently facing several crises, not just an economic crisis, and political power is becoming ever more concentrated. The middle class, the petty bourgeois, is being decimated, with ever more members being forced into the ranks of the working class, the proletariat.

As far as the capitalists are concerned, they are facing a "perfect storm", a convergence of crises. The Corona Virus, which has killed over 200,000 Americans, is flaring up again, now that restrictions have been lifted, and it is anticipated to return with a vengeance, as soon as the flu joins forces with the virus to form a "twindemic". As well, the economic stimulus package, in the form of checks to alleviate the effects of the virus and unemployment, have run out and Congress cannot come to an agreement to continue such payments. This is expected to dramatically increase the unemployment rate. As well, the number of homeless is expected to skyrocket, as the laws protecting tenants from eviction is due to expire.

As a result of this, the stock market is fluctuating wildly, in anticipation of a second Great Depression. It is just a matter of time before it crashes completely, as it did in 1929. The bourgeois economists, in the simplicity of their souls, have responded with characteristic enthusiasm, as they anticipate a full "economic recovery". In fact, they perform a fine Guy Smiley imitation in the face of economic catastrophe. But then it is in their interest to pretend to be so naive.

As well, the Senate is fighting over the nomination of the next Supreme Court Justice. The protests against violent police repression, especially as regards minorities, is becoming ever stronger. To top it all off, the politicians, journalists and political scientists are finally figuring out that Trump has no intention of stepping down in January, regardless of the results of the November election. What is more, he may have found a way to stay in power, quite legally!

A noted journalist, writing for one of the most conservative, highly respected magazines in the country, was able to determine precisely the course of action Trump is pursuing. The journalist found it completely appalling, or as he stated it, "scared myself writing this story". Effectively, he merely faced the fact which he already knew, but chose to deny. For that matter, countless other journalists and politicians have also been denying the same facts, which they know to be true. The fact is that the American voters do not elect the president! The president is elected by the members of the electoral college, and the American voters do not elect the electors! The electors are appointed by the state legislature! The only requirement to legally remain in office, is to have the majority of the electors vote for Trump! The presidential vote is merely a formality! It is not legally binding!

With that in mind, Trump is approaching various state legislatures, encouraging them to appoint electors who will vote for him. They are being encouraged to ignore the popular vote. The journalist who determined this, is of the opinion that it is "quite disturbing, dangerous, not normal, not customary", that the "system is not designed to work that way", but there is "no umpire". He neglected to add that such actions are also quite legal.

Even top ranking members of his own party are accusing Trump of "taking aim at one of the election pillars of democracy." One such party member, a distinguished lawyer, is suggesting that the upcoming election "could break America." Others are saying that Trump is threatening to "push American democracy to the brink".

As Trump now openly admits his refusal to commit to a peaceful transfer of power, if the vote goes against him, their fears are well grounded.

It is very likely that the fact which irritates the bourgeois most is the fact that this threat to "break America", this threat to "American democracy", is coming, not from the Left, not from Communists, but from Donald Trump, one of their own!

One high ranking Republican Senator became quite indignant over the idea of a less than peaceful transition of power. He mentioned that such a peaceful transition of power is guaranteed in the Constitution. As if political power can be guaranteed by a mere stroke of a pen! Clearly this fellow has led a very sheltered life. He has missed his calling. As a starry eyed optimist, he really should have joined the Peace Corp!

A second such Senator is of the opinion that "the American people will not allow a dictator". In this, he is absolutely correct. There is sure to be a transition of power, but it will be anything but peaceful. No doubt Trump will merely declare himself to be president, possibly for life, and the American people will rise up in protest. After Trump is stopped and possibly arrested, the good Senator will then expect the revolutionaries to put down their weapons and disperse, like good proletarians. Not likely!

Other journalists have described this as an "authoritarian crisis", that Trump is "taking a wrecking ball to the presidency", that he is "dismantling the presidential election". Trump is being compared to the former president, Richard Nixon, who declared that the president is above the law. As Nixon put it, "when the president breaks the law, it is not a crime". That is precisely the attitude of Trump, and it took the journalists this long to figure it out!

Other comparisons have been made, in regards to the presidential election of 1972. At that time, most voters were of the opinion that they were being forced to choose between a "crook and a jerk", in that the Democratic Party nominee was not highly respected. As a result, the overwhelming majority of Americans voted for the crook and Nixon won the election in a landslide. It is entirely possible that history could repeat itself. Despite all the lies, deception and election rigging, Trump could honestly win the election, as people may once again choose to vote for the crook, rather than "Sleepy Joe"!

As long ago as May, Trump appointed a new Postmaster General, with a view to slowing down the delivery of mail, so as to ensure that the election ballots which are sent in, do not get counted on time. He is also challenging the validity of mail in ballots, and anticipates that it will end up in the Supreme Court. With that in mind, he is determined to appoint a new member to that Supreme Court, and before the November election. In short, he is covering all the bases. One way or another, he is determined to stay in power.

Lest we give too much credit to Trump, bear in mind that he has a small army of lawyers working for him. They are pointing out the loopholes in the system, clearly earning their pay.

From a Marxist perspective, the important thing is that voter interest is now reported to be "off the charts". This is no doubt true, as it is only during a time of reaction that citizens become apathetic. The current situation is anything but a time of reaction! It is revolutionary, as people are determined to enact change. For that reason, we can expect a record number of people to engage in voting. That is excellent, for as Engels stated, universal suffrage is "an index of the maturity of the working class. It cannot and never will be anything more in the modern state."

As this anticipated voter turn out is expected to set a record, it indicates a high level of maturity of the working class. We can further anticipate the votes to be universally ignored, which will no doubt infuriate most people. They will complain that this is not democratic, while in fact it is most democratic. It is bourgeois democracy. This must be explained to them.

This is where conscious people, Marxists, Communists, come into play. It must be explained to people that democracy is not majority rule, as is taught in all bourgeois schools. It is a system of government in which one class crushes another class. This is to say that it is a state apparatus, and under capitalism, it is one of the methods by which the capitalists, the bourgeoisie, crushes and exploits the working class, the proletariat. Bourgeois democracy is a dictatorship, a dictatorship of the bourgeoisie.

Now it is up to class conscious people to explain this to working people, and in words they can understand, without being condescending. Also explain that a republic does not recognize a monarch, so that America is a republic, while Canada is not, as Canada recognizes the Queen of England. Further explain that the capitalists prefer to rule under the democratic republic, as according to Lenin, "it is the best possible political shell for capitalism".

Bear in mind that certain workers are more advanced than others. It is the more advanced workers who are the leaders. The less advanced workers pay strict attention to the more advanced. This is not to say that the less advanced should be ignored, just that they should be spoken to in a manner they can understand. At the same time, at no point should there be any reference to vulgarity.

We indeed live under democracy, but democracy for the capitalists, and only for the capitalists. For the working class, the proletariat, it is a dictatorship, a dictatorship of the capitalists, the bourgeoisie, over the proletariat. The capitalists are in charge and fully intend to remain in charge. The fact that they are currently squabbling among themselves, arguing over the particular method of rule, does not change that.

It is up to the working class, the proletariat, to change things, and to change things dramatically. The capitalists, the tiny minority, those who are currently crushing and exploiting the vast majority, the working class, must be overthrown and crushed under the proletariat, the Dictatorship Of the Proletariat. Lenin also mentioned that "A Marxist is one who extends the acceptance of the class struggle to the acceptance of the Dictatorship Of the Proletariat." (italics by Lenin, capitals by author)

There is a reason the capitalists must be forcibly crushed after the revolution. The reason is that they are not about to resign themselves to their fate. In fact, such a thought would never cross their minds. They will resort to every subterfuge, every lie, deception, deceit, in order to return to power. Their resistance will be increased ten fold, as they desperately attempt to restore their "paradise lost". As Lenin states, socialist development, after the revolution, "proceeds through the Dictatorship Of the Proletariat." It is only under socialism that the working class, the proletariat, will achieve full democracy, and that is possible only when the bourgeoisie is being fully crushed. The one and only form of scientific socialism is the Dictatorship Of the Proletariat. All else is petty bourgeois, utopian socialism, and has been proven to be a failure.

Now the press is counting down the days to the election, much as children count down the days to Christmas. One makes about as much sense as the other. Perhaps the journalists think that Trump will imitate the Grinch who stole Christmas, and have a change of heart!

The working people have no such illusions. They are taking action.

In the city of Louisville, state of Kentucky, a young Black woman, an EMT, was shot dead in her own home, by police officers. No officer has been charge in connection with her death. Protests have erupted across the country, and a curfew has gone into effect in the city. As an indication of the strength of the revolutionary movement, two police officers in Louisville have been shot. As well, a state of emergency has been declared, and the Kentucky National Guard has been mobilized.

The uprising has spread to other cities, with rocks, bottles and fireworks being thrown at police. One officer had his helmet cracked by a baseball bat. Protesters have gathered at the home of the Majority Leader of the Senate, as well as at the memorial of the late Justice of the Supreme Court. At the memorial, Trump tried to speak, while protesters were chanting "Vote Him Out!".

This harassment of the capitalists, at their homes and places of business, is most encouraging. They are learning to hit the capitalists where it hurts. Now the working people have got to learn to carry signs and posters containing class content. That is where the proper leaders come into the picture, class conscious people, Marxists, Communists. As ever more of the middle class, the petty bourgeois, are ruined, many of them will no doubt cast aside any illusions they may have of once again becoming successful, and carry the Marxist awareness to the proletariat.

As most class conscious people, Marxists, are current or former members of the petty bourgeois, it is up to them to get active. Create a proper American Communist Party. At the same time, join other organizations, those which are active in the revolutionary movement. Give proper direction to the movement. Suggest that the posters and signs reveal class content. Expect the social chauvinists to oppose this, as they are the devoted servants of the bourgeoisie, working within the working class.

It is important to distinguish between the centrists, those who may be utopian socialists, who may think that socialism is a good idea, and the social chauvinists, those who are determined to strive only for paltry reforms. The centrists are not the enemy, but allies. We want as many of those people on our side as we can persuade. On the other hand, the chauvinists are agents of the bourgeoisie, and they are the enemy.

Remember that it is far more difficult to start a revolution in a highly industrialized country, a cultured country, than it is in a petty bourgeois country, an under developed country. On the other hand, it is far easier to carry the revolution through, in an industrialized country, than in an underdeveloped country. Hopefully, this will offer encouragement to those who are discouraged by the—temporary—turn of events in the Soviet Union and in China, in which capitalism has been restored.

Bear in mind that the less advanced workers are not the enemy. Such people tend to be followers, not leaders, and for the most part, have merely been mislead. With such people, patience is required. Given time, we can expect them to listen to the more advanced workers. Focus on the more advanced.

We can expect the social chauvinists to say that the working class is not prepared to seize political power. There is some truth to this, as under capitalism, the working class will never be fully prepared to seize political power. The capitalists will make sure of this. Then again, the Russian proletariat was even less prepared to seize political power in 1917. Yet it was forced upon them, and they rose to the occasion.

Very soon, the revolution will also be forced upon the American proletariat. Trump will see to that. There is no time to waste. Any training workers receive now will prove to be of great value after the revolution. At that time, such workers, and even workers with no training, will be placed in positions of authority. With that in mind, I will close with my usual advice:

Prepare For the Dictatorship Of the Proletariat!

CHAPTER 18

AMERICANS RECEIVE ANOTHER LESSON IN DEMOCRACY

Oct 4, 2020

The first presidential debate of the 2020 election is history, and most of the world is having themselves a great laugh. Two elderly men, one a sitting president and the other a former vice president, both vying for the top political office in the country, have succeeded in making great fools of themselves. The journalists are comparing this to two kindergarten children, fighting in the school yard. Those journalists are the kind ones.

The journalists who are less kind, but perhaps more accurate, are referring to the debate as a disgrace, chaotic and combative, complete with interruptions and personal insults, a train wreck complete with cross talk, a monstrosity, a disaster, an insult to the American people. They also said that it was difficult to refer to this debate without resorting to expletives. That did not stop one lady from describing it as a gong show, although the word she used was not "gong". All agreed that it was an insult to the American people.

This is all very true, just as it is also true that a great many Americans were watching this spectacle. As that is the case, it is up to class conscious people, Marxists, Communists, to explain to people that this is a very clear cut example of bourgeois democracy. Such childish behaviour, including name calling and personal insults, usually takes place behind closed doors. Then the bourgeois politicians come to an agreement and present a united face to the public. The fact that this behaviour is now being openly displayed is an indication of the strength of the revolutionary movement, and the fact that the bourgeois is now deeply divided. They can no longer rule in the old way!

The moderator tried to pin down Trump, to the statement that he would commit to a peaceful transfer of power, in the event of losing the election. Of course, Trump refused. But then, Trump is not legally obligated to honour the election results of the presidential vote! Such a vote is merely a formality. The real power rests with the few hundred Electors, the members of the Electoral College. Their vote is the only vote which matters.

The Twelfth Amendment to the Constitution makes it quite clear that the President, as well as the Vice President, are elected by the members of the Electoral College. It should be stressed to the working people that the tens of millions of voters do not elect the president, but that the few hundred Electors do elect the president. Further, the Electors are not accountable to the state which they represent. They are under no legal obligation to vote for the candidate who won the most popular votes.

No doubt many voters, or at least the more advanced voters, will object that this is hardly the case. Many states, if not all, have laws passed which require the Electors to vote for the candidate who receives the majority of popular votes. Equally without doubt, the lawyers who represent Trump are prepared to argue, in the Supreme Court, that these laws are unconstitutional!

The fact is that Trump has a small army of lawyers working for him. Some of them are experts in Constitutional law, which is the reason he hired them. They have been assigned the task of making sure Trump is re-elected, and they are determined to do just that. They are prepared to argue that no state has the right to interfere in any federal election. As that is the case, any and all state laws which require the Elector to vote in a manner which the state demands, is unconstitutional. It is very likely that the Supreme Court will agree with them, and rule in their favour. It is also very likely that the ruling will be unanimous.

The opposing lawyers will likely argue that this is traditional, that it is customary for the Electors to vote for the candidate who receives the most popular votes in the state. Yet the Supreme Court justices will reply that they are concerned with the Constitution, the law of the land, and not with custom and tradition. The only reason these state laws have not been struck down before now is because no one has challenged them!

It is perhaps ironic that Trump, one of the finest, most successful liars, cheats and swindlers of modern times, may be able to weasel his way into a second term as president, using legal means! He merely has to persuade various state legislatures to appoint two hundred seventy Electors to vote for him. The popular vote be damned!

The press is now counting down the days to the election. They would have us believe that it is the sacred Day of Salvation, the day upon which society will be relieved of the burden of the Spectre of Trump. Such is hardly the case, but as the working people watch the news, and are interested in the election, it presents us with an opportunity to raise their level of awareness.

The federal election, "or election day", to which it is being referred, is on November 3. On that day, or more accurately that evening, it is customary for one of the candidates for the presidency to declare victory, while it is also customary for the other candidate to rather graciously concede defeat. This year, that is not about to happen.

Both candidates, as well as the press, are focused upon the Electoral College. Each state has a certain number of "Electoral Votes", based upon the population of the state. This means that the more people in the state, the more Electors the state can nominate to vote for the next president. It is the Electors who vote to determine the next president, not the citizens.

It is customary for the candidate who wins the majority of popular votes in any particular state to receive all of the Electoral votes for that state. This means that the Electors from that state are required to vote for that particular candidate, either Republican or Democrat. It is referred to as the two party system, and it has served the bourgeois well, for a great many years. In certain states, there is even a law to that effect. In this way, on election day, each candidate is able to determine the number of Electoral votes they are about to receive. The popular vote is important only in that it determines the candidate for whom the Electors from that state are obligated to elect. As the successful candidate is required to receive two hundred seventy Electoral votes, that is the "magic number".

At least, that is the way it is supposed to work, and has worked for many elections, since the days of the Civil War. The only flaw in the system is that it is strictly against the law. That is the argument the lawyers for Trump are prepared to make to the Supreme Court.

It is very likely that Biden, as the Democratic candidate for president, will declare victory on election night. He will announce that he has the majority of Electoral votes. We can expect Trump to deny this, as the popular vote does not determine the Electoral vote!

In addition, due to the fact that most citizens plan to vote by mail this year, it is anticipated that the vote count will be delayed. As Trump has gone to great lengths to delay mail delivery, this is not too surprising. Still, by law, all votes must be counted by December 8. This is referred to as the "safe harbour" day. Any ballots not counted by that day, will never be counted.

The next step in the complicated process to elect a president takes place on December 14. On that day, the Electors, in the various states, cast their ballots for president. Yet even that does not end the process. On December 23, the votes arrive in Washington. Then after New Years, on January 6, the Electoral votes are counted in Congress. It is only at that point, two months after the election, that a new president is determined.

The system was set up in the days of horse and buggy, so to say that it is obsolete is an understatement.

Trump and his team of legal eagles have detected a few flaws in the system, which they fully plan to exploit. The only votes he requires for re-election is that of the Electors, and a mere two hundred seventy of them. Any state interference can and will be challenged in the Supreme Court, as no state has the right to meddle in a federal election. Or at least the lawyers will make those arguments.

This also helps to explain the reason Trump is so determined to appoint another Justice to the Supreme Court. He no doubt thinks that the Justice he appoints, will rule in his favour. That remains to be seen.

The final step in the presidential gong show will not take place until January 20. On that day, by Constitutional law, a new president will take the oath of office. If it cannot be determined which candidate should be president, the Speaker of the House, Nancy Pelosi, will become the next president, as a "place holder". The expression is not mine.

It is entirely possible that there will never be another president of the United States. Some of the most highly respected members of the bourgeois press are of the opinion that American democracy is "teetering", that the country has lost its "moral compass". They are afraid that the American empire is on the verge of collapse, and in this they are absolutely correct. This is not to say that the American imperialists have lost their "moral compass", because they have not. They never had a moral compass, so they could not possibly have lost it.

It must be explained to working people that we live in a class society, and that those who own and control the factories, mills, mines, railroads, airlines, press and internet, are the capitalists, referred to as the bourgeois, and that those of us who work for them are workers, referred to as the proletarians. We are members of different classes, and our interests are diametrically opposed. This is to say that they are completely opposite. It is in the interest of the capitalists to work us as hard as possible, while paying us as little as possible, while it is in the interests of the workers to earn as much as possible. The capitalists are concerned with their profit, their "bottom line", while workers are concerned with putting food on the table.

The conditions of life of the working class do not lead to the awareness of itself as a class, so that this awareness must be brought to the proletariat. As the vast majority of working people are now concerned with the presidential election, now is the time to use this controversy as a means of raising their level of awareness.

We may also point out that the capitalists, the bourgeois, are careful to not use the word "capitalism". They refer to themselves as "entrepreneurs", as people engaging in "free enterprise", and the political system as that of "democracy".

There is a particle of truth to this, in that we indeed live in a democratic republic. It is indeed democracy, but democracy for the capitalists, the tiny minority of the population, the billionaires, the "one percent". For the working people, the proletariat, it is a dictatorship, the dictatorship of the bourgeoisie.

It may be objected that there are many capitalists who are not billionaires. That is true, and such small time capitalists, or middle class people, are referred to as petty bourgeois. They form a separate class, and are under increasing pressure, as the monopolies become ever stronger, ever more complete. Most of these "small business owners" are now bankrupt, or in the process of going bankrupt. The current crises in capitalism are destroying this class, forcing the members of the middle class into the ranks of the proletariat.

The "good news" is that the petty bourgeois is well aware of themselves as a class. In the process of being financially ruined, they are forced to abandon their hopes and dreams of becoming billionaires, members of the bourgeoisie. It is with bitterness and despair that they join the ranks of the proletariat, kicking and screaming, as it were, but joining the ranks nonetheless. They bring their awareness of the existence of classes with them.

Most of these people are well educated, aware of the revolutionary theories of Marx and Lenin. As such, it is the duty of these freshly minted proletarians to bring this class awareness to the working class.

As a means of encouragement, perhaps it would be best to bear in mind the words of Lenin, that which he refers to as the "fundamental law of revolution". He explains that a revolutionary situation is one in which "the exploiters should not be able to live and rule in the old way". In addition, "It is only when the 'lower classes' do not want to live in the old way and the 'upper classes' cannot carry on in the old way that the revolution can triumph". (italics by Lenin) That is precisely the situation in which we now find ourselves!

At the risk of being accused of pointing out the obvious, even the most highly respected members of the ruling class, the bourgeoisie, have basically admitted that they can no longer rule in the old way. The two party system is being destroyed by Trump, one of their own, no less. They are now being forced to change their method of rule! They just have no idea what changes to enact.

The current crises in capitalism have served to not only devastate the middle class, but also to further impoverish the working class. Of course I am referring to the Corona virus, which has currently killed over 200,000 Americans, and that number is expected to double by the end of the year. As well, the stock market is expected to crash at any time, which will give rise to a second Great Depression. Countless people are out of work, with almost no prospects of a job. The "economic stimulus checks" are about to expire. As soon as it becomes legal for landlords to issue eviction notices, the number of homeless is expected to skyrocket.

A similar situation existed in the "dirty thirties", at the time of the Great Depression. For no less than a decade, ten years, our grandparents suffered through unemployment, homelessness and starvation. The suffering of the working people was terrible, yet they failed to rise up in revolution. Part of the reason for this is because, as Engels pointed out, "without a revolutionary theory, there can be no revolutionary motion". The working people had no Marxist leaders!

It was Lenin who stressed the importance of the theoretical struggle, in his work, What Is To Be Done?, where he stated that the "role of vanguard can be fulfilled only by a party that is guided by an advanced theory." (italics by Lenin) This is to stress the importance of a truly Marxist, Communist Party, one guided by the revolutionary theories of Marx and Lenin. Without such a Communist Party to guide the working class, it is doubtful that the revolution can be successful.

The social chauvinists have a particular hatred for that article. It deserves careful study, as Lenin condemns those whom he refers to as "Economists". Such people claim to be socialists or Marxists, while arguing that working people should fight only for improved wages, living and working conditions. They disapprove of even any mention of the existence of classes!

As for those who are of the opinion that there is no harm is fighting for such paltry reforms, I can only respond that such a struggle will not lead to class consciousness. Of course they are important, mainly as a means of raising the level of awareness of the working class. I would even go so far as to say that the struggle to abolish the Electoral College, which I would classify as a political reform, is acceptable to the Economists, as such a political reform is not a threat to the rule of the capitalists.

Without doubt, the current situation is revolutionary, as the ruling class, the capitalists, cannot rule in the old way, and the working class is no longer content to be ruled in the old way. This does not necessarily guarantee the success of the revolution, as the working class is grossly contaminated with bourgeois ideology. As Lenin phrased it, "to belittle socialist ideology in any way, to deviate from it in the slightest degree means strengthening bourgeois ideology."(italics by Lenin)

The one and only way the revolution can succeed, to lead to a socialist republic, is to raise the level of awareness of the working class. The working class has to be made aware of itself as a class, a proletarian class, with its own class interests, as opposed to that of the capitalists, the bourgeois. They must be given the Marxist awareness, or as Lenin phrased it, "A Marxist is one who extends the acceptance of the class struggle to the acceptance of the Dictatorship Of the Proletariat". (italics by Lenin)

It is now up to conscious people, Marxists, Communists, to raise the level of awareness of the working class, the proletariat. Such expressions as Scientific Socialism and Dictatorship Of the Proletariat must become common place, at least among the more advanced workers. In other words, preparations must be made for the Dictatorship Of the Proletariat.

It is very likely that a great many middle class people will consider this to be a none too subtle hint to get active, to take part in forming an American Communist Party. To such people I can only respond—guilty as charged. It may help to think of yourselves as the "chosen ones". You are aware of the revolutionary theories of Marx and Lenin. You are also well aware that your dream of joining the ranks of the bourgeoisie have just evaporated. Even your former, rather comfortable middle class life style, is a thing of the past, never to return. In your "previous life", you were admired, well respected, a true professional. You never thought this could happen to you, yet here you are. You have been cast down, into the ranks of the proletariat, through no fault of your own. As bad as it is, you suspect that things are about to get worse, much worse. And you are right.

With your training and experience as a former middle class professional, you know well the mindset of the bourgeois. People are mere tools, to be used, until no longer needed, and then cast away. There is no room for sentiment in the world of business, of capitalism. There are only "users" and the "used". You are now one of the used. Your world has just come crashing down. Your standard of living has just been reduced to nought. You are consumed with bitterness and frustration. Now is the time to choose between suicide, as many of your friends have, or you can choose the way of action.

You have an opportunity to make a huge difference, to take part in creating a better world. That better world is one of socialism, a world in which people do not stab each other in the back. A world of democracy for the working class, the proletariat, a world in which the capitalists, the bourgeoisie, are crushed under the Dictatorship Of the Proletariat. It is a world which you can help to create, and one in which you will once again be admired and respected. The choice is yours.

With your talent, skills and training, you can take part in the creation of a truly American Communist Party, Dictatorship Of the Proletariat. As a member of the Communist Party, you can help to guide the revolution to a successful socialist republic. In the process, you will regain your self respect. It will restore purpose to your life. Bear in mind that three separate republics have already taken shape, and others will soon follow. They just need to be guided onto the proper socialist path.

The revolution is bound to break out any day now. Trump and his followers will see to that. There is no limit to their greed or their arrogance. The only thing they understand is brute force. Revolution is not the time or the place for the faint of heart, the squeamish. We can count on violence and bloodshed. This is not the time for pacifists. Only the determined, the resolute, need take part in the formation of the Communist Party. Only those who are prepared to lay down their lives for socialism, for a better future, for the Dictatorship Of the Proletariat.

The choice is yours.

CHAPTER 19

NOW IS THE TIME FOR INSURRECTION

Oct 10, 2020

A great many Americans woke up recently to some rather refreshing news. The president of the United States, Donald Trump himself, has now contracted the virus! Countless people were giddy with delight, shedding tears of sheer joy. Even the journalists were deeply touched (or especially the journalists), although most performed a reasonable imitation of sympathy and concern for their Commander in Chief. Some even went to the length of wishing him a speedy recovery!

Trump in turn has risen to the occasion. Even though sick, he has allowed the medical people to administer to him a drug cocktail, including steroids. Properly pumped up on these drugs, he proudly announced that he now "understands" the virus. He then left the hospital and made a great display of removing his mask, at the entrance to the White House. In his ensuing speech, he offered encouragement to his faithful followers, as he "feels better than twenty years ago". He then advised people, "don't be afraid of covid".

As the press was quick to point out, this is an insult to the families of the hundreds of thousands of people who have lost a member to the virus. In addition, countless others are about to be infected. It is anticipated that as soon as the flu season strikes, the combination of flu and the virus will likely increase the daily death toll dramatically.

This has given rise to open speculation that the Twenty Fifth Amendment to the Constitution may soon be put into effect. That comes into play when it is determined that the president is incapacitated, due to physical or mental inability to perform his job. The more charitable people suspect that Trump no longer has the mental acuity to perform his job. The less charitable are of the opinion that he was never capable of doing his job!

The Chairman of the Federal Reserve has even weighed in on the matter. In the face of all the suffering and death caused by the virus, he is warning of an "economic tragedy" if America cannot control the virus. This is "economist speak" for another Great Depression, which is right around the corner. It is also the true voice of capitalism, in that there is no place for sentiment. The only thing that concerns the capitalists is their capital. The suffering of millions of people concerns them only in so far as it affects their profits.

This has not stopped Trump from "returning to work". He is now back in the Oval Office at the West Wing of the White House, according to journalists. One lady, who makes a career of reporting on the disfunction within the presidential palace, stated that the situation is completely chaotic, more so than usual, "and that is really saying something". Sadly, she was not even trying to be funny. She was merely stating a fact.

The Secret Service agents, those highly trained professional people who are prepared to take a bullet for the president, are not at all happy. It is one thing to take a bullet for the president, and something else entirely to take a bullet from the president, so to speak. Of course, the "bullet" to which they are referring is the virus Trump is carrying. The Secret Service people were forced to drive Trump around the White House grounds in an enclosed vehicle, while he was infected. Even with personal protective equipment, those agents were in danger of contracting the virus.

The American military is also feeling the pinch, with the Joint Chiefs of Staff in isolation. Some, or possibly all of them, may have been infected by the virus, perhaps due to contact with Trump.

Even the bourgeois intellectuals are concerned. They choose their words carefully, in order to make no mention of classes and certainly not of class conflict. Instead they stretch their imaginations to the limit, performing an impressive act of verbal gymnastics, and in the process, inventing such terms as "moral compass", "soul of the nation", and a country that is "spiralling out of control." As if it is possible to have a country without classes!

By contrast, the press is reporting that as a result of the crises facing the nation, the wealth of the "super rich", the "billionaires", has increased dramatically. The more deeply the common people sink into poverty, the more enriched become the capitalists. Of course, as loyal servants of the bourgeoisie, the press is careful to make no mention of such a word, as that would suggest the existence of classes.

These intellectuals dare not state that which is really bothering them: Revolution. They suspect that the lawyers for Trump are prepared to "go nuclear", to bypass the electoral college somehow, if necessary, and force the presidential election into the House of Representatives. In that case, it does not require a majority of votes to determine the next president, but a majority of states! As there are fifty states in the union, and each state has one vote, it requires a mere twenty six votes in the House to determine the next president.

Those same bourgeois intellectuals are afraid that the American working class people will not stand for this. Their fear is that Trump is determined to trigger a revolution, whether he knows it or not. Not that Trump cares. His concern is solely with his own personal ambition, and that means staying in power. The oath of office he took, upon becoming president, was a mere bit of idle verbiage.

In response, the bourgeois have turned one of their "big guns" upon Trump. They have enlisted one of the former "first ladies", in an attempt to discredit him, hopefully with the result of voting him out of office. It is her opinion that "our country is in chaos", that Trump is "not up to the job", that he is a "racist, spreading fear and division, fails to take the virus seriously", that the country is "spirally out of control", that he is determined to "destroy this nation". As that is the case, her solution to the problem is to "vote like your life depended on it".

She has managed to state the facts correctly, while at the same time implying that the problem is Trump, and the solution to the problem lies in voting him out of office. Except that Trump is not the problem, the problem is one of capitalism, and a mere change of face will not change the fact that the capitalists, the bourgeoisie, are in charge. It is not a change of face that is required, but a change of class! It is up to the working class, the proletariat, to overthrow the capitalist class, the bourgeoisie, and to set up a new state apparatus, in order to crush the bourgeoisie, under the Dictatorship Of the Proletariat.

This is not to say that people should be discouraged from voting, as voting is very important. It is one of our democratic rights, and we can exercise that right, or we can risk losing it. Not that Trump will be removed from office as a result of a vote. He has a small army of lawyers who are determined to make sure that does not happen.

The flip side to the coin, or the other aspect to the contradiction, is the working class motion. That motion is becoming ever stronger, as the desperation of the working class increases dramatically. The ranks of the unemployed are rising daily, as the country slides into another Great Depression. The "economic stimulus checks" are running out, so that ever more people are relying upon food banks. Further, tens of millions of people are about to find themselves homeless, as the laws against eviction expire. The onset of winter can only serve to intensify the suffering.

Yet in the midst of all this turmoil, with the middle class, the petty bourgeois, being wiped out and the suffering of the working class, the proletariat, reaching ever greater heights, the press is reporting, quite gleefully, that the "billionaires", the bourgeoisie, are becoming ever more wealthy!

Now is the time for action. The ruling class is in a state of confusion, fighting among themselves. Their current method of rule, which has served them so well for so many years, is no longer effective. At the same time, the suffering of the common people, the working class, has reached intolerable proportions. In short, the situation is similar to the situation of Russia in 1917, on the eve of the revolution. At that time, as Lenin stated it, "different classes now stand on the one and the other side of the barricade".

In Russia, early November, (new style calendar), some of the members of the Russian Communist Party (although at the time it was using a different name) were of the opinion that the revolution, or at least the seizure of power, the insurrection, should be postponed, for one reason or another. There was talk of waiting until after the convocation of the Constituent Assembly, or after another meeting of the Central Committee, or for some other reason.

By contrast, Lenin was of the opinion that "The situation is critical in the extreme . . . everything now hangs by a thread; that we are confronted by problems which are not to be solved by conferences or congresses . . . but exclusively by peoples, by the masses, by the struggle of the armed people . . . The government is tottering. It must be given the death blow at all costs. To delay action is fatal." (italics by Lenin)

A similar situation now exists in America. The finest bourgeois intellectuals are of the opinion that the government is "tottering, hanging by a thread". Now is the time to "give the death blow", before the bourgeois can regroup. They are at their weakest, so now is the time to strike. Now is not the time to wait for the federal election!

An important difference between Russia in 1917, and America in 2020, is that there is currently no American Communist Party to provide the leadership. That is a serious matter, but one which can be overcome rather quickly and easily.

It was just a little under four years ago that the American women flexed their muscles. They gave a whole new meaning to the expression "fight like a woman"!

In protest against the presidency of Trump, marches took place across the country, in almost all cities and towns. These protests spread to numerous countries of the world, in a show of solidarity with American women. To say that this was most impressive, is an under statement. Now is the time for those same women to "aim higher", to "raise the bar", to mount an insurrection, to overthrow the capitalist system and establish a truly democratic government, a democracy for the working class, a socialist government, one which will crush the capitalists, the bourgeoisie, under the Dictatorship Of the Proletariat!

Bear in mind that America was founded on revolution! The American founding fathers have given Americans the right to "abolish any government which does not represent them"! This right is guaranteed in the Declaration of Independence. By taking part in this next, socialist revolution, against a government which crushes and exploits all working class Americans, you are proudly following in the footsteps of your ancestors!

There can be no doubt that the ladies who organized that protest knew precisely what they were doing. It is very likely that most of them were middle class, well educated, professional people. That was then and this is now. In such a short time, the situation has changed dramatically. The crisis in capitalism has devastated the middle class, so that most of them are no longer middle class. But now, they are still well educated, professional people, currently members of the working class, proletarians. They still have their skills and experience, and they know first hand the mind set of the bourgeois. Now is the time to put those skills to work, not in the service of the ungrateful bourgeois, but in the service of the common people, the proletariat.

To a large extent, the fate of the revolution is in the hands of these ladies. So I say there is a great deal of truth in the saying, "To whom much has been given, of her much shall be required".

The American people are counting upon you. I have no doubt you will rise to the occasion.

With that in mind, I will now appeal to those ladies directly. No doubt you are aware of the revolutionary theories of Marx and Lenin. Equally without doubt, you are highly skilled with computers. As that is the case, there is no need to gather in one setting and form a Communist Party. You can do that on the internet, taking reasonable precautions. May I suggest a political platform being based on the fundamental tenets of Marx and Lenin. That includes the Dictatorship Of the Proletariat. The mere mention of that tenet should serve to distinguish Communists from social chauvinists, as well as utopian socialists.

Bear in mind that the self proclaimed socialists, those who are of the opinion that socialism is a good idea, are not the enemy. On the contrary, they are valuable allies, and we want all the friends we can get! Do not antagonize them! They are not to be confused with the social chauvinists, those who are the loyal servants of the bourgeoisie, dead set opposed to revolution and especially the Dictatorship Of the Proletariat.

You can expect membership in the Party to be quite limited. It is not the size of the Party membership that is of great importance but the policy it pursues. You want to appeal to as many working people as possible, regardless of race, religion, culture, ethnic background or personal belief. Stress the fact that we want to create a society which is not based on profit, but on the well being of all. A society where one person has one vote. A society where the background of a person is not held against that person. We can all start with a clean slate after the revolution.

You can also make it clear that any criminal elements who choose to carry on in the old way will be dealt with harshly. They will not be mollycoddled. They will not be allowed to hide behind lawyers. They can expect to be judged by working people, and those judges are to be elected by the working class. If convicted, criminals can expect to be sent to work camps, not to "correctional" country clubs, currently known as prisons. In these work camps, they can and will perform useful, productive work, for perhaps the first time in their lives.

Under the current, bourgeois system of capitalism, thieves and killers have all the rights. It is well known, among the criminal elements, that America is a "thieves paradise". No where else in the world is it so easy to "make a dishonest buck". Those days are numbered!

Under socialism, under the Dictatorship Of the Proletariat, working people can and will take care of our own. We will make sure that people are properly fed, clothed and housed. We will protect our seniors, our children and our helpless. Anyone who tries to take advantage of them will live to regret this. Or perhaps they will not live to regret this!

We will also attempt to correct mistakes which were made under capitalism, in that many women were assaulted and then denied justice, if only due to the "statute of limitations". Under socialism, such a statute will not apply. Those who seek justice will be allowed to confront the human scum who assaulted them. It may help to think of this as a little reunion. The numerous ladies who were forced to engage in acts of intimacy with these creeps, will be allowed to spend a little "quality time" with them.

I can only hope that many ladies can take inspiration in these happy thoughts.

Now is the time for insurrection. As I have gone over this in previous articles, perhaps a quick summary is sufficient.

Possibly not everyone is aware that the transfer of power now means armed insurrection. This may seem obvious, but perhaps not everyone has given thought to this. To repudiate armed uprising now would mean to repudiate one of the key tenets of Marxism. If that is the case, then such an individual does not belong in the Communist Party.

Armed insurrection is merely another form of political struggle, but a special form, one subject to specific laws. It was Marx, no less, who stated, quite emphatically, that "insurrection is an art quite as much as war". He went on to stress:

1) Never play with insurrection, but when beginning it realize firmly that you must go all the way

2) Concentrate a great superiority of forces at the decisive point and at the decisive moment, otherwise the enemy, who has the advantage of better preparation and organization, will destroy the insurgents

3) Once the insurrection has begun, you must act with the greatest determination, and by all means, without fail, take the offensive. The defensive is the death of every armed uprising

4) You must try to take the enemy by surprise and seize the moment when his forces are scattered

5) You must strive for daily successes, however small (one might say hourly, if it is the case of one town), and at all costs retain moral superiority

Marx went on to sum up the the lessons of all revolutions, in respect to armed uprisings, in the words of Danton, "the greatest master of revolutionary policy yet known": Audacity!

Insurrection is the order of the day, and this is not the time, or the place, for a pilgrim. Such pacifist souls can seek refuge in the Peace Corp. They certainly do not belong in the Communist Party, as it is the Party which is about to lead the insurrection.

The transportation and communications centres must be occupied and held, at all costs. The internet must be disabled! The telephones must be shut down. All railway stations must be occupied. Major highways must be shut down, and above all, the bridges must be closed! As well as the air ports and sea ports.

The most determined troops, the "shock forces", which will very likely include the young people, must be formed into relatively small detachments to occupy all the more important points and to take part in all important operations. These include seizing and occupying the White House, the Pentagon, including the Joint Chiefs of Staff, the Senate and House of Representatives. The state capital buildings must also be occupied. Under no circumstances should any of them be allowed to communicate with each other or anybody else. Give them no opportunity to go on the offensive. Bear in mind the words of Marx, to the effect that the defensive is the death of every insurrection!

We can expect that those who are detained will fake sickness, such as heart attacks, in an attempt to force the guards to give them an opportunity to escape and mount an offensive. For that reason, only the most resolute must be assigned this all important task. Even if the heart attack is sincere, better to let one bourgeois die than to allow for the failure of the uprising.

It is vitally important that the attitude of all, especially the shock troops, should be—victory or death! Better to die at their posts, than allow the revolution to fail!

Most working people have firearms, or at least have access to firearms. Very soon, those weapons are going to come in very handy. The capitalists, the bourgeoisie, will go to any length to maintain their hold on power. That includes ordering their troops to fire upon women and children. Let there be no misunderstanding on that point!

We can only hope that at the time of the insurrection, the leaders will follow the advice of Marx. The success of the revolution depends upon this. It is very likely that two or three days fighting will prove decisive.

Ladies, the success of the revolution now lies in your hands.

CHAPTER 20

AN APPEAL TO CONSCIOUS PEOPLE

Oct 18, 2020

As I write this, there are as yet seventeen days to go before "election day", that of November 3, which is the day Americans get to "elect their next president". Even now, it is reported that twenty two million people have already cast their ballots. Many people are being forced to wait in line, some for as long as eleven hours, while others are showing up to the polling stations as early as four hours before the stations open, in order to ensure they are able to cast a vote. The press is reporting a "drastic increase" in the voter turn out, over double that of the last presidential election of two years ago, at this time. This despite the fact that the government, which serves the capitalists so well, has placed various obstacles in the way of people exercising their democratic right to vote. For example, in the state of Texas, the ballot boxes are limited to one per district, so that each voter is forced to drive possibly an hour each way, during working hours, in order to cast a ballot. In the state of California, numerous phoney ballot boxes are set up, so that any ballots placed in these boxes are not counted. Other states have different methods of limiting voter turn out, especially that of minority voters.

This is taking place against a background of almost two hundred twenty thousand Americans dead due to the Corona Virus, with the infection rate "climbing". It is anticipated that as soon as the "second wave" hits, along with the flu virus, the "fatality rate" will sky rocket.

Despite this, the working class movement continues to gain strength. The city of Portland continues to be a leader in the revolutionary motion. On Columbus Day, otherwise known as Indigenous Day, the people of Portland pulled down two statues, that of President Abraham Lincoln and that of President Theodore Roosevelt. This is being referred to as a "Day of Rage".

Those two individuals are commonly thought of as "heroes", hence the statues, in their honour. In fact, it was President Lincoln who ordered the execution of 38 Dakota warriors, in 1862, as a response to the Sioux uprising. This mass hanging was carried out in Mankato, Minnesota. As well, it was President Roosevelt who ordered the removal of Indigenous people from their traditional territory, in the interests of "conservation". The descendants of those people have not forgotten the actions of the presidential "heroes". Now all people are receiving a little reminder.

The reactionaries have also been very busy. A "right wing militia group" made a supreme effort to kidnap the governor of Michigan. Apparently they planned to place her on "trial", as she refuses to support Trump, an act which they consider to be nothing less than "treason". Their plan was unsuccessful, but at least one sheriff has expressed his support for the members of the militia. And now Trump is leading the call, in reference to the governor, to "lock her up!"

To put this in popular terms, the "battle lines are being drawn". The Right Wing reactionaries, also known as the various "militia groups", are literally preparing for war. They are determined to preserve the "status quo", in support of the capitalists, the billionaires, the bourgeoisie, whether they know it or not. The leaders of the "militia" are well aware of this, while the rank and file members, those who tend to be less advanced members of the working class, are merely following along. A clear distinction should be drawn between the two.

By contrast, the progressive forces, including the tens of millions of people who are determined to vote, are focused on change. Most of them quite reasonably assume that their vote means something, as indeed it does. This is not to say that their votes will change the rule of the capitalists. With or without Trump as president, the bourgeoisie are determined to continue to rule.

The importance of the record breaking number of people who have turned out to vote, lies in the fact that, as Marx stated, it is an indication of the measure of the maturity of the working class! He went on to state that under capitalism, it cannot be anything more than that! Yet that is enough.

For that reason, it is clear that the working class, the proletariat, is now quite mature. They are doing their part, and are now preparing for war. They can go no further. The conditions of life, of the proletariat, do not lead to class awareness. That awareness can come only from an outside source, and that outside source is conscious people, most of whom are middle class intellectuals. That places a largely unwelcome burden upon the shoulders of conscious people. It is what it is!

It was Lenin who stressed the fact that "Without a revolutionary theory there can be no revolutionary motion". He went on to state that the "role of vanguard fighter can be fulfilled only by a party that is guided by the most advanced theory". (italics by Lenin)

It is also true that the Marxist, or Communist movement, is by its very essence an international movement. Countless people, in numerous countries of the world, are watching the American revolution unfold. It is reasonable to expect that such people will draw inspiration from the American revolution.

There can be little doubt that we are on the eve of revolution. The forces of the two classes are "dug in", prepared for battle. Equally without doubt, the only question is one of the duration, the length of time of the approaching civil war. The Revolutionary War, which gave birth to the country, dragged out for seven years. The Civil War raged for four years, at the expense of many thousands of American lives. It remains to be seen just how many lives will be lost during this next revolution.

This largely depends upon the leaders, the members of the American Communist Party. As a comparison, in Russia, October of 1917, (old style calendar) the Marxists, led by Lenin, mounted an insurrection which was almost bloodless. It was carefully planned and executed. Even though the revolutionaries lacked the element of surprise, it was quite successful. Sadly, two members of the Central Committee betrayed the plans for the uprising, yet the revolutionary motion was so strong, even this act of treachery was overcome.

As yet, the American Communist Party does not exist. It must be formed, and it must then plan and execute an insurrection. Otherwise, it will very likely result in another long and drawn out civil war, with countless casualties.

Now in 2020 America, the vast majority of working people are demanding change. Those who were previously apathetic, are now politically active. Most are of the opinion that Trump can be removed from office, due to a popular vote. They are about to find out that such is not the case. In this way they will learn a valuable lesson in bourgeois democracy.

It is up to conscious people, Marxists, to use such examples, with which people are familiar, to raise the level of awareness of the working class. They watch the news. They are aware that the former Chief of Staff to Trump, recently stated that "the depths of his dishonesty is just outstanding to me". They are also aware that a thirty five year veteran of the Department of Justice, a distinguished prosecutor, recently resigned, due to the Attorney General. This fellow openly accused the Attorney General of having "slavish obedience" to Trump, of being his loyal "lapdog". He accuses Trump of trying to turn the country into an autocracy.

Neither one of these men can be accused of being "Leftists", as both are bourgeois, right to the core of their being. The two are merely concerned with bourgeois democracy. This stands as a testament to the confusion within the bourgeois government. That confusion is about to intensify.

These are merely a few examples of current events, those which should be used to raise the level of awareness of the working class. Another example is the nomination of a new Supreme Court Justice, one which is receiving a great deal of coverage by the press. Make no mistake, working people are closely watching these proceedings.

As most working people do not have access to higher education, by which I mean a university degree, they are unaware of the revolutionary theories of Marx and Lenin. That education is largely limited to the bourgeois. It follows that it is up to the bourgeois, or more accurately the petty bourgeois, the middle class, to bring this awareness to the proletariat.

It is perhaps ironic that the ruling class, the billionaires, the monopoly capitalists, the bourgeoisie, are determined to keep the working class, the proletariat, in the dark, blissfully unaware of the existence of classes. Yet at the same time, they are helping to raise the level of awareness of the proletariat, by ruining the middle class, forcing so many members of that class, into the ranks of the proletariat! These former members of the middle class, now members of the working class, proletarians, are nothing less than Conscious people, aware of the revolutionary theories of Marx and Lenin!

It is to these people that I am appealing. No doubt many of you feel bitter. In return for giving a company the "best years of your life", you expected a little gratitude. No chance. There is no room for sentiment in the world of "business", which is the polite word for capitalism. People are mere tools, whether they work in production or in the field of management. When these "tools" are no longer useful, they are discarded. You are one of the tools which has been discarded.

This is not to say that you can no longer be useful. On the contrary, you can be more useful than ever before. You can bring the class awareness to the proletariat. You are in a unique position to do this, as you can speak from experience. For that reason, working people will listen to you. Further, you will find yourself involved with people whom you can trust. It is the bourgeois who delight in "stabbing each other in the back". Working people are not of that nature. You may even be surprised to find that you are having fun! As a bonus, the act of overthrowing the bourgeoisie and crushing them under the Dictatorship Of the Proletariat, will provide you with a certain personal satisfaction.

After all, those are the same people who ruined you. One good turn deserves another!

Another point of propaganda, which can be used to raise the level of awareness of the working class, is the fact that Trump plans to destroy the bourgeois democratic system, that which is currently in place. His plan is to challenge any state laws which interferes with the votes of the members of the Electoral College, allowing each and every Elector to vote for any person of their choice, for the offices of the presidency as well as the vice presidency, not just the candidates of the Republican Party or of the Democratic Party. This means that the candidate for president does not get to choose a "running mate", a candidate for the vice presidency. That is the duty of the Electors.

In fact, if Trump has his way and the Supreme Court rules in his favour, each Elector will be able to vote for any American citizen who is qualified to hold the office of president!

This could happen, and very likely will happen, as it is guaranteed in the Constitution. At least, the lawyers for Trump are prepared to make that argument before the Supreme Court, and very likely the Supreme Court will agree with them. As a result of this, it is quite possible that the Electors will be unable to agree on a candidate for president, as they need to form a majority of 270 Elector votes, for one particular candidate. In other words, we can expect a state of mass confusion, as the Electors, faithful servants of the bourgeoisie, one and all, squabble among themselves. Trump no doubt considers that this will work in his favour, as the election will then go to the House of Representatives.

In that case, it will be up to the House of Representatives to decide, by a majority vote of 26 states, in which each state has one vote. That too may not happen, the House too may not be able to agree, as the country is so deeply divided. As the members of the House will by that time realize, as a result of the anticipated Supreme Court ruling, that they do not have to choose between the two presidential candidates, that of the Democratic Party or that of the Republican Party, but can choose any American who qualifies for the office, then it is very likely that they too will be dead locked.

In such a case, on January 20, 2021, a new president will be sworn in, as provided in the Constitution, and that new president will be the Speaker of the House, Nancy Pelosi, the woman whom Trump hates more than anyone else!

It is safe to say that Trump has no respect for women, just as it is equally safe to say that Trump flies into a rage when any woman dares to defy him. The Speaker of the House, Nancy Pelosi, defies Trump on a regular basis. For that reason, Trump entertains a particular hatred for her. Yet he has decided upon a course of action which could result in placing her in the office of the presidency! It is very likely that Trump has not properly thought this through. As he does not engage in a great deal of thinking, this is not too surprising.

It is such details which can be used to drive home to the working class the differences between the two classes, the bourgeois versus the proletariat. The bourgeois are constantly plotting and scheming, setting traps for each other, and as a result, frequently step into their own traps. By contrast, the working class tends to adhere to principle.

Trump has concocted a very elaborate scheme to stay in power, one which could backfire badly. He is determined to overturn the current bourgeois method of rule, and will very likely succeed. In the process, he will create mass confusion. As a result of this confusion, it is entirely possible that the Speaker of the House, Nancy Pelosi, will be sworn in as president. That is the last thing

Trump wants, as it is also quite possible that the first thing she will do, as president, is to order the arrest of Donald Trump!

This is the state of mass confusion which we can expect to encounter, immediately after the "presidential election" of November 3, that which is a mere formality.

As all current or former members of the middle class are well aware, but are perhaps reluctant to admit, the American Empire is on the verge of collapse. Capitalism is dying. It is in its death throes. Socialism is on the horizon. No less that three separate socialist republics have already taken shape. Others will soon appear. These facts are beyond dispute. Equally without doubt, the capitalists, the bourgeoisie, are not about to accept this. They are determined to fight this, "tooth and nail". As reactionaries, it is their nature. The only question is that of the response of the working class, the proletariat. Given proper leaders, in the form of a Communist Party, the transition will be relatively painless. Without that leadership, it could result in a long and drawn out civil war. A bloodbath.

That is where you people come in, Conscious people, Marxists. You are needed, your help will be appreciated, and it will be rewarded. Preparations must be made for the Dictatorship Of the Proletariat, and topping the list of those preparations is the formation of a proper Communist Party. There is great danger in this, so secrecy is required. Yet there are a great many people who have managed to communicate with each other, using the internet, for their own purposes. This proves that it can be done.

Once the Party is created, it can also use the internet to raise the level of awareness of working people. Articles must be written, using current events as examples, and sent to various email addresses. Those who are politically active can be targeted, using their membership in various organizations, and that propaganda can be written at a somewhat higher level of understanding.

Bear in mind that we want to raise the level of awareness of the vast majority of working people, so with that in mind, use the technical terms, followed by the more popular terms. We all learned the alphabet in this manner, that of repetition. Do not be condescending, and under no circumstances resort to vulgarity. Use the particular, followed by the general. Feel free to put aside your prejudice against professional sports and use sports metaphors, as most working people are avid sports fans. Also, do not concern yourself with the sentiments of middle class social centrists, as by their nature, they disapprove of references to classes, and especially revolution.

Much of this work can be thought of as "illegal", even though it is not. Yet the government authorities can be expected to treat it as such. In addition, marches and demonstrations must be organized. Posters and banners should be carried, complete with slogans which contain class content. The best of these marches are entertaining, as has happened in the recent past, targeting politicians and government officials in their homes, restaurants, banks and places of business. The best way to educate people is by entertaining them at the same time.

A great many women are now excited, concerning the latest Supreme Court nomination, a woman who is Catholic, and probably of strong religious beliefs. The protesters are concerned that her religious beliefs will influence her legal rulings, especially as it concerns abortion. As a result of this, the "pro choice" people are taking a clear stand, in opposition to the "pro life" people. This could lead to a huge mistake.

Lenin made it quite clear that it is supremely difficult to start a revolution in a "cultured" country, but far less difficult to carry it through! Without doubt, America certainly qualifies as a cultured country, as bourgeois culture permeates society. Equally without doubt, we are going to need all the help we can get in order to overthrow the bourgeoisie. The more we fight among ourselves, the less chance the revolution has of being successful.

With that in mind, I am suggesting that all working people put aside our differences, including personality conflicts, as well as personal beliefs, pro life and pro choice. We can agree to disagree. We can place principles before personalities.

There is no point in denying personalities, as they certainly exist. There is a place for them, but only after principle. We, as members of the working class, have a common enemy, the bourgeoisie. We can stand together, against this enemy, while going our separate ways, after the battle is over.

To state this in other words, perhaps more accurately, our goal is to overthrow the bourgeoisie and crush the vermin under the Dictatorship Of the Proletariat. Under that socialist republic, we can then hash out our differences, in a civilized manner. The key thing is to have respect for each other.

Too many people confuse personal animosity with class animosity. As an example, the social centrists are allies, not the enemy. We must learn to work with them. The social chauvinists are the allies of the bourgeoisie, and they are the enemy. The leaders of the various right wing militia groups are the enemies, while the rank and file members are merely misled. It is absolutely essential that we distinguish between the two. We must attack our enemies, while striving to at least neutralize those who are less than friendly towards us. With regards to the less advanced members of the working class, patience is required.

In the heat of battle, with passions flaring, actions can be taken which may later be considered to be regrettable. The same is true of words, and in fact those words may do even more damage than actions. It is best to be well prepared before hand.

To summarize, as briefly as possible:

Prepare For the Dictatorship Of the Proletariat

CHAPTER 21

TRUMP DESTROYING TWO PARTY SYSTEM

Oct 23, 2020

Several years ago, Trump surprised himself by winning the presidency. Now that he is president, he has found that he loves the power and has no intention of relinquishing it. Perhaps he was even more surprised by the fact that the key to remaining in power lies in abiding by the law. As someone who came to power by breaking every law which he found to be inconvenient, the idea of using the law probably never occurred to him. But then, there is a reason for the existence of lawyers. As Trump is not entirely stupid, he hired a small army of lawyers to work for him, at tax payer expense, of course.

His lawyers have advised him that the current method of rule, that of the two party system, is something other than legal. Even though it is simple and convenient, and has served the bourgeoisie well, since the days of the civil war, it is strictly unconstitutional. Not that Trump or any other members of his class are terribly concerned with such little details, unless it serves their purpose. Now it serves the purpose of Trump, and he is paying strict attention. In order to stay in power, the only thing he has to do is destroy the two party system. His team has been working on this for the last few months.

As countless people are closely watching the presidential election, it is the duty of Conscious people, Marxists, Communists, to use the election as an opportunity to raise the level of awareness of the working class.

With that in mind, we can explain to working people that under the current "democratic" system, the people do not have the right to elect the President, or the Vice President. Those two are elected by the chosen few, the Electors, the members of the Electoral College.

The capitalists refer to this as the "Electoral College" system. Each Elector is appointed by a state legislature, and there are very few of them, a grand total of only 538. A simple majority of two hundred seventy is sufficient to determine both the President and the Vice President. This is spelled out in the Twelfth Amendment to the Constitution, and we can expect to hear a great deal more, concerning this Amendment, very soon, immediately after the "election", the popular vote of November 3.

Without doubt, many millions of people will be "glued to the tube" on that evening, as after the polls close, the votes cast in each state will be counted, starting with the East Coast states. The political pundits for the major television networks will be reporting the vote count for each state, and the percentage of votes for each candidate, and at some point the offscreen network executives will announce the candidate who "won" each state, along with the Electoral Votes for that state. At some point, the Electoral Votes for one candidate, either Trump or Biden, will reach the magic number of 270, and the networks will report a winner.

If Trump is reported to be the winner, and Biden concedes, that will be the end of it. But if Biden is reported to be the winner, then Trump can be expected to challenge the election results in the Supreme Court. It is very likely that the Supreme Court will agree with Trump that the popular election is meaningless, effectively abolishing the two party system.

This requires a little explanation. Under the current system, each state has a certain number of "Electoral Votes", as that is the technical term, which is to say the number of people who can be appointed as Electors. The more people in the state, the more Electors, the more Electoral Votes. The state of California, with perhaps forty million people, has the most Electoral Votes at 55, while the states with the fewest people have a mere 3 Electoral Votes, each. All states require their respective Electors, those who are appointed by the state legislatures, to vote for the candidates of either the Democratic Party or the Republican Party. Almost all states have a "winner take all" policy, in that the candidate who wins a majority of votes in the state, receives all of the Electoral Votes of that particular state. The lawyers who work for Trump are convinced that all of these state laws have one thing in common: they are unconstitutional.

In previous federal elections, numerous Electors have violated state laws and chosen to vote for a candidate of their choice, not the candidate chosen by the state they represent. None of these Electors has ever been charged, probably because the state prosecutors are aware that the law cannot be enforced.

The lawyers for Trump have been busy, earning their pay. For the last several months, they have been approaching the various state legislatures, encouraging them to appoint Electors who will vote for Trump, or at least vote for someone other than Biden! If Trump cannot secure 270 Electoral Votes, then he is at least determined to stop Biden from securing that many votes. If no candidate receives a majority of Electoral Votes, then the next step in the process, as spelled out in the Constitution, is to send the election to the House of Representatives, in which case each state has but one vote.

As so many people are focused on the election, it is important to let people know what is happening. With that in mind, I have decided to include the Twelfth Amendment:

"The electors shall meet in their respective states and vote by ballot for President and Vice President; they shall name in their ballots the person voted for as President, and in distinct ballots the person voted for as Vice President, one of whom at least, shall not be an inhabitant of the same state with themselves; which lists they shall sign and certify, and transmit sealed to the seat of the government of the United States, directed to the President of the Senate. The President of the Senate shall, in the presence of the Senate and the House of Representatives, open all the certificates and the votes shall then be counted; the person having the greatest number of votes for President, shall be the President, if such number be a majority of the whole number of electors appointed; and if no person have such majority, then from the persons having the highest numbers not exceeding three on the list of those voted for as President, the House of Representatives shall choose immediately by ballot, the President. But in choosing the President, the votes shall be taken by states, the representation from each state having one vote; a quorum for this purpose shall consist of a member or members from two thirds of the states, and a majority of all the states shall be necessary to a choice. And if the House of Representatives shall not choose a President when ever the right of choice shall devolve upon them, before the fourth day of March next following, then the Vice President shall act as President."

There are numerous experts on Constitutional law, and there are as many opinions on the meaning of this Amendment as there are experts. There are also other parts of the Constitution which deal with the federal election. The only opinion which really matters is that of the Supreme Court, and we can expect to hear from them soon.

If the vote of November 3, "election day", goes in the favour of Trump, then he will have no reason to challenge the results in court. It is only if Biden declares victory that we can expect Trump to "stand on principle" (Ha!) and challenge the election in court.

As concerns the democratic right of the citizens to vote, it is significant that the Amendment makes no mention of the popular vote! It is entirely possible that the Supreme court will soon rule that the popular vote is a mere formality.

The point to be driven home to the working class is that the ruling class, the capitalists, the bourgeois, have established two mainstream political parties, Democrats and Republicans, and that these two parties have "hijacked" the presidential election process. The Supreme Court will very likely rule, and soon, that the states have no right to interfere in such elections, that the Electors have the right to vote for the qualified candidate of their choice, for the offices of both President and Vice President.

Under the current bourgeois democratic method of rule, each of the two mainstream political parties selects a candidate for the office of President. This candidate in turn selects a "running mate", a Vice President. Voters are then allowed to choose between the two pairs, in a "general election". The candidates which receive the majority of "popular votes" in such an election, in each state, usually receives all, or at least most, of the Electoral Votes for that state. That is almost certainly about to change, as that is not spelled out in the Constitution.

That anticipated change will no doubt lead to a state of mass confusion, generally referred to as "throwing a monkey wrench", in the middle of a revolutionary uprising. In that case, it is up to Marxists to explain to the working class that democracy is not majority rule! It is a method of class rule! It is a state apparatus, an organization for the systematic use of violence by one class, against another class. In this case, under capitalism, it is the capitalists, the tiny minority, the bourgeoisie, who use the state apparatus to crush the working class, the vast majority, the proletariat.

After the revolution, after the proletariat seizes political power, the "shoe will be on the other foot". Then the proletariat, the vast majority of people, will be in power. Yet the tiny minority of capitalists, the bourgeois, will not resign themselves to their fate. In fact, they will fight "tooth and nail" to recover their "paradise lost". They will stoop to any level, resort to any subterfuge, as their hatred and fury rise to a red hot frenzy. We can expect them to send their agents into the Communist Party and try to subvert it from within.

For the benefit of the Marxists, it should be mentioned that we can expect the distortion of Marxism to be ever more subtle. As an example, there are "Marxists" who refer to our democratic rights under capitalism, under the bourgeois democratic republic, as "bourgeois democratic rights", rights which are "granted by the bourgeoisie".

This is incorrect, as our democratic rights are not bourgeois, just as they are not proletarian. They are democratic, pure and simple. Under capitalism, our democratic rights are "restricted, cramped, curtailed, mutilated by all the conditions of wage slavery", as Lenin phrased it. Further, they most certainly are not "granted" by the bourgeoisie, as the monopoly capitalists, the imperialists, are completely reactionary. To suggest that they "grant" the proletariat some democratic rights, is to imply that there is something progressive about the imperialists, the bourgeoisie. Such is hardly the case.

It is such subtle distortions of revolutionary Marxist theories, which we can expect. This is nothing other than revisionist, an attempt to subvert Marxism. It is up to Marxists to oppose these revisionist theories, especially within the Communist Party.

Without doubt, after the revolution, the bourgeois class will have to be crushed, and that will require a state apparatus, but a different sort of state apparatus, one set up to deal with their desperate and determined resistance. That state apparatus will be in the form of a different sort of democracy, a democracy of the vast majority, of the working class, referred to as the Dictatorship Of the Proletariat.

In preparation for the revolution and the subsequent Dictatorship Of the Proletariat, in the interest of raising the level of awareness of the proletariat, a few slogans are perhaps appropriate. With that in mind, may I suggest signs and banners which read: Capitalism is not Democracy; Down With Democracy For the Capitalists; Democracy For the Proletariat.

No doubt many middle class people will consider such slogans to be too basic. We are concerned with raising the level of awareness of countless millions of working class people, and we have to start somewhere. The less advanced workers (I prefer to avoid the word "backward" as it may be considered derogatory) must not be neglected, just as I try to avoid the use of the word "masses", as it seems much too impersonal. Such terms as "common people" or "members of the public" are preferred, as working people refer to themselves in those terms.

The fact is that many working class people are now expressing an interest in politics, if only at the level of being determined to vote. Of course many others are active on a higher level, such as taking part in marches and demonstrations, and in opposition to violent repression, especially of minorities. This is indeed class consciousness, but only in an embryonic form! It is, as yet, not true Marxist, or Communist, consciousness, nor can it be.

The working people are doing their part, and can go no further. The conditions of life among the working class does not lead to the awareness of itself as a class. This consciousness can come only from an outside source, and that source is middle class intellectuals, members of the bourgeois intelligentsia. The "good news" is that there is now no shortage of middle class intellectuals within the working class, through no "fault" of their own. The current crises in capitalism has led to the decimation of the middle class. The remaining members of the middle class are "living on borrowed time". Their "days are numbered", as ever more members are becoming impoverished, forced into the ranks of the proletariat. These "newly minted" proletarians are bringing with them the awareness of classes, as well as the awareness of the revolutionary theories of Marx and Lenin. As well, many of them are highly skilled as organizers, and that is precisely the skills which are so desperately needed at present.

It may be objected that the revolutionary motion is now very strong, with no less than three distinct republics in the process of formation. No doubt others will soon take shape. The American empire is collapsing, and the idea that it could break into a number of republics which could embrace capitalism, may sound absurd, but it could happen. Socialism will not happen by itself. It has to be created.

The fact of the matter is that it is up to Conscious people, Marxists, Communists, to imbue the proletariat with the consciousness of its position, and of its tasks. That task now is to create a socialist society, as opposed to a capitalist society. The trouble being that working people have lived all their lives under capitalism, and are saturated with the bourgeois ideology. This is referred to as the "ideological enslavement" of the workers, to the bourgeoisie. It is up to Communists to "break the invisible chains" of enslavement, as otherwise the revolution could merely give rise to smaller, capitalist republics. This is referred to as going "from the frying pan, into the fire".

As Lenin phrased it, "The fact that the working class participates in the political struggle and even in political revolution does not in itself make its politics Social Democratic (Marxist) politics." Without doubt, the political revolution is approaching. The only question is whether it will lead to socialism, under the Dictatorship Of the Proletariat, or to a continuation of capitalism.

The fact of the matter is that, as a result of the revolutionary motion, tens of millions of people are now in motion, determined to enact change. From among these huge crowds, leaders will emerge, the more advanced members of the proletariat. It is up to Marxists to bring to these people the class awareness, to bring their level of consciousness to that of Marxists, at least in regards to Party business. They have to become working class intellectuals, dedicated to the revolution and the subsequent Dictatorship Of the Proletariat.

Such workers can be counted upon to raise the level of awareness of other workers, as such advanced workers are highly respected, and they "speak the same language" as the less advanced workers. They are able to speak and even write articles in a manner which the less advanced can understand, concerning current events which have caught the attention of those workers, using metaphors which workers understand.

This is not to say that middle class intellectuals are incapable of communicating with such workers. It is to say that many of them are simply not up to the task, for whatever reason. No doubt they are capable of learning, given the time and motivation. Old habits are so hard to break.

As I write this, there are a mere ten days left before the "election". Almost everyone is agreed that the country is a "powder keg", in that tensions are very high, and any "spark" could cause an explosion. The political pundits are also agreed that Biden is heavily favoured to "win" the election. By this they mean that he is expected to win the majority of Electoral Votes, to be determined on "election night". That is not about to happen.

Assuming Biden "wins" the election, then the lawyers for Trump will challenge the election in the Supreme Court. They will argue that the Electors have to vote for President and Vice President "on the first Monday after the second Wednesday in December", as per the Constitution, that all state laws restricting the votes of the Electors are unconstitutional, and that the popular vote is a mere formality.

Do not be surprised if the Supreme Court agrees with that argument. That could be the "spark" which sets off the uprising, the revolution.

If nothing else, it would give the Electors the right to vote for the people of their choice, so it is still possible that Senator Bernie

Sanders could be elected as President. Or Senator Kamala Harris, or anyone else whom the Electors decide.

Now is not the time to "rest on our laurels", to "let nature take its course", as that course leads straight to capitalism. Now is the time to make a supreme effort, to redouble our efforts, to create a proper non revisionist Communist Party, to raise the level of awareness of the working class, to guide the approaching revolution onto a path of scientific socialism, in the form of the Dictatorship Of the Proletariat.

CHAPTER 22

CORRECTION TO OUR ATTITUDE TOWARDS THE PEASANTS

Nov 16, 2020

It has been pointed out to me that in my book, Occupy Movement and the Dictatorship Of the Proletariat, I was mistaken in saying that "the peasants are not the enemy". While this is largely true, it is not quite that simple.

As I pointed out in the book, the peasants are divided into three categories, the poor, rich and middle peasants. The poor peasants are the natural and desirable ally of the working class, the proletariat, under all circumstances. The middle peasants are also natural allies, although they tend to vacillate. Our attitude towards the middle peasant must be one of patience. The rich peasant can be an ally, although he can just as easily be the enemy. It all depends upon the situation.

Perhaps a well known historical example will help to clarify matters.

Consider the country of Russia in 1917. At the time of the February revolution, in which the Czar was overthrown, all of the peasants, without exception, were in an alliance with the proletariat, against the monarchy. That alliance remained in place for the following few months, until the "October Revolution", in which the capitalists, the bourgeoisie, as well as the landlords, were overthrown and crushed under the Dictatorship Of the Proletariat. This took place on October 25, old style calendar, or November 7, new style calendar. Immediately after the revolution, in fact the next day, the situation changed dramatically. On that day, not all the peasants were united behind the proletariat. In fact, the rich peasants, the kulaks, or "tight fists", became the enemy of the proletariat and poor peasants.

By way of explanation, all of the peasants were united in their hatred of the landlords, the human blood suckers who exploited all peasants, without exception. The October Revolution overthrew the capitalists, as well as the landlords. In fact, one of the first decrees of the new socialist government was that the land now belonged to the tiller. Under this "new reality", the rich peasants, the kulaks, were then able to focus entirely upon getting rich. As the landlords were no longer a concern, it was just a simple matter of hoarding their surplus grain, so that the starving of the working people and poor peasants forced up the price of grain, allowing the kulaks to sell their grain at a huge profit. Literally overnight, the kulaks went from being allies of the proletariat and poor peasants, to being the enemy. The kulaks became the new "rural bourgeoisie".

The lesson here is that in a revolutionary situation, alliances can change immediately and dramatically. The friends of today can become the enemies of tomorrow, and the enemies of today can become the friends of tomorrow. It all depends upon the conditions then prevailing.

As mentioned in the book, this particular situation is not one which the people of North America can be expected to face. The bourgeoisie have "graciously" simplified the class struggle, so that the peasants have been all but wiped out. For that matter, the middle class, the petty bourgeois, has been severely depleted. The remainder are "living on borrowed time", to use a popular expression. That is a fact, just as it is a fact that the working class movement is international in scope. This clarification may prove to be helpful to working people in less developed countries, where there may be a significant percentage of peasants.

If nothing else, it may serve as a fine example of the fact that class alliances can change immediately. It is best to be prepared for these changes, because they happen as the situation changes.

The current situation is explosive. Any spark could set off a revolution. Very soon, the working people will rise up and overthrow the capitalists. It is best to be prepared for all possibilities.

CHAPTER 23

REACTION IS TAKING TO ARMS

Nov 18, 2020

As I write this, the current death toll in America, due to the Corona Virus, is approaching 250,000, a quarter million! The press is reporting that in the previous week, an additional one million Americans were infected with the virus. The medical professionals anticipate the death toll to sky rocket, as soon as the flu season arrives and people are infected with the virus as well as the flu. It is further anticipated that most hospitals in the country, which are currently working at near capacity, will be overwhelmed at that time.

In response to this humanitarian disaster, the Trump administration has remained almost entirely silent. The suffering and death of so many Americans is a subject upon which they are completely indifferent. They clearly have other priorities, such as preparing the American public for a second four year term of Trump as president.

By contrast, the press is mainly concerned with the presidential election. They are determined that Trump "lost the election", and that he refuses to admit defeat. They refer to Biden as the President Elect, and are counting down the days until he will be sworn in as president. It is a subject upon which various journalists are deeply passionate. Perhaps someone should break it to these people that passion does not elect a president. The Electors elect the president.

In all fairness to the journalists, it is clear that they are aware of the Twelfth Amendment to the Constitution. On occasion, they refer to it, almost in whispers, so to speak. No doubt they are as yet, not prepared to face the fact that the Twelfth makes no mention of the popular vote. They desperately want to believe that the states have the authority to force the majority of Electors to vote for Biden.

All states have laws which require the Electors from any particular state to vote for either the Democratic candidate or the Republican candidate. None of these state laws has ever been challenged in court, at least not before now. Very soon, that will change. The lawyers who work for Trump will see to that. They have already prepared the arguments for the Supreme Court, to the effect that the states do not have the authority to interfere in a federal election. In the mean time, they are advising the Electors that they have the legal authority to vote for any qualified American, for the office of president, as they see fit.

The idea is not so much to ensure that Trump will win 270 Electoral Votes, but to make sure that Biden does not win that same amount of Votes. If no candidate wins the majority of votes, then the presidential election goes to the House of Representatives, in which case, each state has one vote. Trump is sure he can get twenty six states to vote for him, thus ensuring another four years in office. That remains to be seen.

In the mean time, the people who work for Trump are busy, creating as much trouble and confusion as possible. They are disputing the popular vote count in various states, and in each case the courts are ruling against them. They are also organizing demonstrations, particularly in the capital of Washington, D.C. The slogan they are using is "Stop the Steal", and a great many Trump supporters are taking part in these marches.

Without doubt, someone very clever is behind this, a "Propaganda Minister", so to speak, a modern day Joseph Goebbels. The plan is to create confusion, get people worked up, persuade them they have been cheated and to use the courts for this purpose. That "clever someone" rules out Trump, as he has the attention span of a hyper active two year old. That also narrows it down, to possibly his "personal lawyer" or even his "close associate", individuals who are very bright and equally devoid of principle.

The press is also focused on a few key dates. They assure us that all court challenges, at least concerning the election, have to be settled by December 8. Try telling that to the Supreme Court! They also say that the Electors have to vote on December 14, and that the ballots have to be in Washington by December 23. Then on January 6, the full Senate and House of Representatives, otherwise known as "both Houses of Congress", will meet. On that day, the President of the Senate, who is also the Vice President, Mike Pence, will open each and every sealed ballot, in their presence, and announce the candidates for office of President and Vice President. The press is hoping and praying that Biden, whom they rather optimistically refer to as the President Elect, will receive 270 Electoral Votes. We will see.

As the ballots are sealed, it is very likely that we will not know the election results until January 6. By that time, the "propaganda minister" for Trump may have his supporters worked up into a proper frenzy.

It is perhaps worth mentioning that the one date they are not mentioning is December 11, the day the federal government runs out of money, unless the national debt is raised, once again. Then again, concerning the manner in which the politicians are squabbling, it may be difficult to get them to agree on this. Another government shut down can only add to the tension.

It is clear that the reactionaries are aware of the strength of the working class movement and are determined to divert it. Their goal is to divide working people, to create a pro Trump faction and a pro Biden faction. Ideally, they would love to see the two factions involved in "physical altercations", which is to say, to fight each other. As the Trump supporters are now demonstrating, there is a distinct possibility that they may collide with Biden supporters. It is up to Marxists to make sure that does not happen.

It is necessary to organize demonstrations to further the socialist cause, to raise the level of awareness of the working class, complete with banners to that effect. As well, such banners should read "Neither Trump Nor Biden". This is to let the rank and file, among the Trump supporters, know that we do not regard them as the enemy. We have a common enemy, the monopoly capitalists, the bourgeoisie, and we want them to join with us, against our enemy.

It may help to consider the pro Trump supporters, or at least the rank and file members, as less advanced members of the working class. Many of them are quite passionate in their beliefs, just as many Biden supporters are equally passionate in their beliefs. The Biden supporters may perhaps be a little more advanced, but the supporters for both camps are mistaken. Both Trump and Biden serve the same class.

With that in mind, it bears repeating the words of Engels: "Without a revolutionary theory, there can be no revolutionary motion!" As well, it was Lenin who stated, quite clearly, that "the role of vanguard can be fulfilled only by a party that is guided by an advanced theory!"

As yet there is no true American Communist Party, one which calls for the Dictatorship Of the Proletariat, but no doubt it will soon be created. As the crises in capitalism continues to intensify, ever more members of the middle class are becoming financially ruined, forced into the ranks of the proletariat. Many of these freshly minted proletarians are intellectuals, aware of the revolutionary theories of Marx and Lenin. It is up to them, in fact it is their duty, their moral obligation, to take part in the creation of a Communist Party.

To such people, I can only say that I have complete confidence in you. Your past will not be held against you. March proudly in the footsteps of previous great revolutionaries, most of whom were middle class intellectuals. That includes Marx and Lenin. If they can do it, you can do it!

Bear in mind that "the stakes are high", to use a popular expression. American imperialism is among the most powerful in the world. It has to be destroyed. The American proletariat is now among the vanguard of the international revolutionary proletariat. Further, it is being led by women, for possibly the first time in history. I have no doubt you ladies will rise to the occasion and lead the American revolution to a successful conclusion, to the Dictatorship Of the Proletariat.

CHAPTER 24

DEMOCRACY AS A METHOD OF CLASS RULE

Nov 24, 2020

Of late, the "personal lawyer" of Donald Trump has performed a great service to all working people. He, the former mayor of New York City, along with several other lawyers, recently had a rather lengthy press conference, one which lasted an hour and a half. These people refer to themselves as an "Elite Strike Force Team", working on behalf of President Trump.

The value of this press conference lies in the fact that these lawyers, those who are staunch supporters of the bourgeois democratic system, chose to document the various ways in which the democratic system is being subverted. They claim the system is "corrupt in major cities", all across the country. They also claim that the corruption has spread to the judicial system, in that the judges, those who are supposed to be impartial, are really in the service of the bosses of the political parties, either Democrats or Republicans.

To say that these are serious accusations is an understatement. At best, these lawyers, or attorneys, as that is their technical title, could face disbarment, unable to practice law. At worst, they could face very serious charges, which could result in lengthy prison sentences.

With that in mind, they were careful to produce numerous "affidavits" from various citizens, those who worked at the polling stations. For the benefit of those who are not "legal eagles", I should mention that an affidavit is a legal term for a declaration that is voluntarily given, under oath, with a possible penalty of perjury, in case the statement is proven to be a lie.

The people who signed those affidavits had no reason to lie, and every reason to tell the truth. To come forward with these statements required a great deal of courage. No doubt they consider the democratic system to be of great importance. It is not by chance that they have chosen to come forward now. It is an indication of the strength of the revolutionary motion. These people deserve a great deal of credit.

Those workers say that while they were serving at the polling stations, they were told to not ask for voter identification, as is required by law. They can testify to the fact that various individuals were told for whom to vote, and then those same individuals voted for that particular candidate, on numerous occasions. Many people cast ballots by mail, and then voted in person. Some of those voters were illegal immigrants. Mail in ballots were especially fraudulent, with the post marks on the envelopes largely ignored. Workers were told to ignore or even change the date of the postmark, if necessary. Boxes and trash cans filled with ballots were brought into the polling stations, to be counted in turn.

In addition, in certain districts, the voter turn out was two or even three time greater than the number of registered voters within the district! To have more votes than there are voters is blatantly ridiculous.

The lawyers also documented the fact that certain districts used voting machines. These machines are easily programmed, even by remote control. (One of the marvels of modern technology!) That is certainly a fact, although it is a stretch to blame voter fraud on foreign countries. There is no shortage of home grown electrical engineers who are quite capable of programming these machines to spit out fraudulent results.

In all fairness, these lawyers are in the service of their client, Donald Trump, and their goal is to ensure that he is sworn in for a second, four year term. No one can fault those people for performing their duty. With that in mind, they have mounted numerous court challenges, questioning the validity of the vote in various states. All of these cases have been thrown out of court. The presiding judges have chosen to ignore all evidence of election fraud. In response to this bias shown on behalf of the judicial system, the lawyers are now appealing directly to the people, the American citizens.

We can learn something from the Elite Strike Force Team! It is absolutely correct to use the existing state apparatus, including the courts, to further our goals. It is also correct to appeal to the public, when appropriate. Now is the appropriate time.

No doubt a great many people are focused on the federal election, with good reason. Equally without doubt, they are deeply divided. Some are passionately against Trump, while others are equally passionate in their support of Trump. Very few people find the subject to be a matter of indifference.

From a Marxist perspective, the important thing is that this has the attention of people, so that it can be used to raise the level of consciousness of the working class. The fact is that the courts, which are supposed to be impartial, have refused to examine the evidence of voter fraud, as presented by the Elite Strike Force Team!

This can be explained by the fact that the courts are part of the state apparatus, and for that reason, cannot possibly be impartial.

That calls for a little explanation, as the subject of the state has been confused, sometimes deliberately, by representatives of bourgeois science. They would have us believe that it is a sacred institution, almost a commandment, one which should have been carved in stone. Such is hardly the case, but as it affects the interests of the ruling class so intimately, their passion is understandable.

In fact, the state apparatus did not always exist. In primitive society, at a time which is commonly referred to as the stone age, there were no classes, and consequently no state apparatus. Each and every member of that society had to "pull their own weight", as they lived constantly on the edge of starvation. All food had to be either gathered or killed. There was never a surplus. The survival of the group required all to do their part.

That situation changed dramatically at the onset of civilization. The cultivation of crops created a surplus, so that people had some free time on their hands. Some of these fortunate individuals used this free time to separate their neighbours from their property and even their freedom. This gave rise to the first classes, that of slaves and slave owners.

It is perhaps not too surprising that the slave owners were faced with a little problem, in that the slaves were reluctant to accept their lot in life. In fact, they had a rather annoying habit of rebelling. It is for this reason that the class of people, whom we refer to as slave owners, came up with a new invention. It is called a state apparatus, a method of keeping the class of slaves in check. At first, it was rather simple, perhaps men on horse back with whips and chains, to be used against "ungrateful" slaves.

Over the years, this state apparatus has evolved, as classes have evolved. In fact, Engels has done a fine job of explaining this in his book, The Origin of the Family, Private Property and the State. The state apparatus is now more elaborate, but it still exists in order to keep the "lower classes" subjugated. In modern times, this means the working class must be suppressed. All working people should be encouraged to read this book.

The current state apparatus includes the police, military, jails and prisons, as well as the courts. As the current system is one of capitalism, it is the duty of the state to serve and protect the ruling class, in this case the bourgeoisie, from the lower classes, in this case the working class, the proletariat. As the courts are part of the state, it is simply not reasonable to expect the courts to be impartial!

This is not to imply that the federal election was fraudulent and the results should be thrown out. Both Trump and Biden serve the same class. Our one and only goal is to raise the level of awareness of the working class, and we can do this by using the federal election as an example.

In fact, the election was fraudulent, which the Elite Strike Force Team has documented, and such fraud is common place. This has been going on for many years, in possibly all federal elections.

The ruling class, the bourgeoisie, determines the individual to be placed in power, and the popular vote is a mere formality.

There is a striking contrast between the working people who came forward, to testify in the matter of this election fraud, and the lawyers, those who work for Trump. On the one hand, the working people spoke up, in the interests of democracy, while the lawyers are merely working in the best interests of their client.

Remarkably enough, the situation can be compared to the situation, many years ago, in which the mafia found themselves. At that time, one of their own, a "made man", by the name of Joe Valachi, "turned rat", as is the common expression, and became an informer for the government. He revealed the inner workings of the "mob", including the induction ceremony. All of his former buddies were shocked and horrified, as Valachi broke the cardinal rule, the rule of silence.

It is safe to say that the current members of the bourgeoisie, the class of people to whom Trump belongs, the billionaires, now know precisely how those mobsters felt. One of their own has betrayed them. They decided that it was time for Trump to go, but instead of bowing out gracefully, as is customary, he has decided to tear down the state apparatus, as it now exists. The current democratic republic, in the form of the two party system, is about to be destroyed.

This brings us to the democratic republic, which is the ideal political shell for capitalism. It is indeed democratic, in that working people have certain democratic rights. As Lenin phrased it, "truncated, twisted, distorted democratic rights". That in no way changes the fact that it remains a state apparatus, a method of rule, a means by which one class, in this case the bourgeoisie, crushes another class, in this case the working class, the proletariat. It is not, and cannot be, "majority rule", still less can it be "pure democracy", as it is a method of rule, and there is nothing "pure" in one class ruling it over another class.

This is the point which must be driven home to the working class. We live in a class society, so that it is class rule. Either the capitalists are in charge, in which case we live under the dictatorship of the bourgeoisie, or the working class seizes power, demolishes the existing state apparatus, and sets up a new state apparatus, in order to crush the resistance of the capitalists, in the form of the Dictatorship Of the Proletariat. There is no third possibility.

We can perhaps stress that the admissions of the Elite Strike Force Team are most valuable, as they cannot be accused of being "leftist". On the contrary, they are among the most devoted followers of the bourgeoisie, loyal servants, one and all. It would never occur to them to offer assistance to the working class, in their struggle against the capitalists. They are merely working in the best interests of their client.

It is up to Marxists to take advantage of these valuable admissions, possibly even going so far as to support the lawyers in their struggle to prove that the election was fraudulent. It must be stressed that such a show of support in no way indicates our support for Trump. It can only indicate our support of the democratic process, as a means of raising the level of consciousness of the working class.

This is not to say that we can ever become "buddies" with these lawyers, as we serve different classes. It just means that for a certain time, for entirely different reasons, we may have a common goal.

CHAPTER 25

"DAY OF RECKONING" IN WASHINGTON

Jan 8, 2021

On January 6 of this year, the "lawmakers", which is to say the members of the House of Representatives and of the Senate, met in the nations capital of Washington, as per the Constitution, in order to ratify the Electoral Votes of the recent federal election, concerning the next president and vice president. Normally this is conducted in a most solemn, ceremonial manner, a "sacred undertaking", within the building of the "citadel of American democracy". This day has proven to be something other than "normal".

As all court appeals have accomplished nothing, Trump appealed to his "base", to his supporters, to go to Washington, on the "day of appointment", presumably in order to "express their disapproval". Trump has consistently maintained that the "election was stolen". A great many people believe him, and responded to his request.

It is estimated that thirty thousand people responded to this appeal. Many were waving American flags and carrying banners which proclaimed Stop the Steal. They were chanting U-S-A, marched up the steps of the Capital building and through the doors. The police who were guarding the building fled in terror, although it is reported that a few of them had their pictures taken with the protesters. Other members of the police blockaded the doors of the room in which the Members of Congress were meeting. The Members of Congress in turn lied down on the floor, hiding behind the chairs, terrified of the very citizens they had sworn to serve. Cowards! They showed their "true colours".

The Secret Service quickly escorted the Vice President, the "master of ceremonies", so to speak, out of the building, to the safety of an "undisclosed location". In turn, the VP, as the man of action that he is, immediately called out the National Guard, as a means of assisting the Capitol police, in their efforts to restore "law and order".

As the protesters were largely peaceful, it is not clear just what "law and order" the National Guard was expected to restore. Unless they were called out because a window was broken and a few people crawled through the openings, into the building. The vast majority merely walked through the doorway, as the Capitol police had politely stepped aside. None of the protesters was armed, although it is possible that a few criminal elements were carrying concealed firearms. But then no gun shots were reported, so that the reports of "four people being killed" is probably a fabrication of the authorities. As well, similar reports of two "pipe bombs" is also very likely bogus.

The revolutionary motion in now very broad and deep. The protesters, working class people, are convinced that the "election was stolen", and they are almost certainly correct. The election was stolen. The "powers that be", which is to say the capitalists, the ruling class, has decided that Trump has to go, and arranged to have him lose the election.

The working people, or at least the most advanced stratum of the working class, knows this for a fact because two of the most highly respected lawyers, members of the capitalist class, have gone public, have explained the methods the bourgeois use, in order to falsify elections! They have "spilled the beans". The cat is now "out of the bag". They explained, in simple, common everyday terms, the precise manner in which elections are falsified, "rigged" or "fixed", as most people refer to it.

These two attorneys, or lawyers, are among the highest paid in the country. One of them is the former mayor of New York City. Both are among the most devoted followers of Trump. Neither has ever been accused of being a "Closet Communist". Yet they explained that the simplest, "time honoured", method of rigging an election is by having individuals vote on numerous occasions. It was in this manner that the presidential election of 1960 was fixed, so that John Kennedy was elected, as opposed to Richard Nixon. As those were the days of black and white television, most of the younger generation cannot imagine this. As well, there were no computers, no internet. That same generation considers such a time as little different from the Stone Age.

Since those "olden days", times have changed, and thieves have changed with the times. More accurately, they have become better educated, if not smarter. Many have learned to use the latest technology. This has opened up whole new vistas of fraud and deception. A "brave new world" of most profitable corruption has appeared to the more enlightened mobsters. The modern day "geniuses of crime" have embraced the opportunities presented by the internet. Stealing from countries is far more profitable than robbing banks!

While the tried and tested method of multiple voting is still wide spread, as is the fraudulent use of mail in ballots, the modern mobsters have "broadened their horizons". Those who are skilled computer programmers now take great delight in falsifying elections, from the comfort of their own homes. Using the internet, they can send orders to machines which "count ballots". In this way the machine records the "correct" number of votes, cast for the selected candidate. The marvels of modern technology!

It is important to give credit where credit is due, and the American working class is eternally grateful to two of the finest, highest paid lawyers in the country. Remarkable but true. But then in times of revolution, very strange, very temporary alliances make their appearance. This is one of those strange alliances.

This was explained by Marx in the Communist Manifesto: "In times when the class struggle nears the decisive hour, the process of dissolution going on within the ruling class, in fact within the whole range of old society, assumes such a violent, glaring character, that a small section of the ruling class cuts itself adrift and joins the revolutionary class, the class that holds the future in its hands.

"Just as, therefore, at an earlier period, a section of the nobility went over to the bourgeoisie, so now a portion of the bourgeoisie goes over to the proletariat, and in particular, a portion of the bourgeois ideologists, who have raised themselves to the level of comprehending theoretically the historical movement as a whole."

It is clear that the class struggle is nearing the "decisive hour", that the revolution is very near. In fact, it could break out any day. As a result of this, a "small section of the ruling class", in this case two lawyers, have "cut themselves adrift", and effectively joined the working class, the proletariat, the "class that holds the future in its hands".

As yet, these two have perhaps not "completely comprehended theoretically the historical movement as a whole", but they have performed a valuable service to the working class. It is very likely that they "speak from experience", and have, in the past, probably "made a career" of "fixing" elections! By their actions, they have joined the working class, in opposition to the capitalist class. It is entirely possible that their practice leads their theory.

Either way, it is up to the working class to welcome them into their midst. Under no circumstances should their past be held against them! On the contrary, most workers will listen to them as they explain the "inner workings" of the capitalists. This in turn will no doubt help to raise the level of awareness of the working class. This is, of course, referred to as class consciousness.

The response of the capitalists to this "Day of Reckoning" is quite revealing. The journalists expressed the outrage of the capitalists, as they work for the capitalists, and to do otherwise is to face termination. In simple English, they would be fired.

With that in mind, they referred to this "Day of Reckoning" as an "attempted coup, an armed insurrection" (even though the protesters had no weapons), an "act of treason", "disgraceful violence". They accused the protesters of being "domestic terrorists", of engaging in acts of "insurrection", that such "disorder is borderline sedition". The protesters were referred to as a "mob", "anarchists", "thugs and punks". "They have undermined the rule of law through the use of force" (a window was broken!). "This was an assault on the rule of law . . . an attack on a most sacred ritual to affirm democracy, in the Citadel of democracy" (so now the Capital building is a religious site?) The protesters have "desecrated the chair of the Vice President" (one of the protesters sat in it!) just as another protester sat in the chair of the Speaker of the House. No doubt that chair too was "desecrated"! That same protester left a note for the Speaker: "We Will Not Back Down!"

The capitalists are not about to take this lying down! Even though they "have never seen anything like this", as it is "unprecedented", "not seen since the days of the Viet Nam war", (so how can it be unprecedented?), "similar to the revolution of 1776" (so now the Revolutionary War was waged by anarchists and domestic terrorists?). Yet the "guard rails of democracy have held", the "longest standing democracy is reeling" (Democracy for which class?), the "leader of the free world was under attack" (by free world you mean capitalist world!), and now it is time to show "respect for the upset voters by telling the truth". (Since when do capitalists know how to tell the truth?)

President Elect Biden has announced that "democracy is under assault, in the Capitol, no less". If by democracy, he means democracy of the capitalists, then he is correct. The protesters are determined to enact democracy of the proletariat!

A journalist announced that this "assault on rule of law does not represent who we are". Further, the "American people do not like anarchy, they want law and order". Speak for yourself and your class! The American people have just spoken, loud and clear! Your idea of "anarchy", of "law and order", is nothing other than working class democracy!

The authorities, those who guard the capitalist, swiftly took action. They announced a 6pm curfew. The DC National

Guard was mobilized. Various internet accounts have "locked out" Trump. No more tweeting for that boy! The "darkest day in American history" is now a thing of the past! Now it is time to hold people accountable!

With that in mind, the authorities have decided that Trump is entirely to blame, and must be punished. In fact, he must be removed from office! He must not be allowed to serve his final few days as president. The only question is one of impeachment (which has been tried before) or of invoking the twenty fifth, which is to say the twenty fifth amendment to the Constitution.

To say that this makes no sense, is an under statement. In fact, it is a complete muddle. It is also a fact that this muddle, on the part of the bourgeois, is sure to work in the favour of the working class.

This Day of Reckoning was an open conflict with the capitalists. It stopped short of being an armed insurrection, as the workers were not armed. It can be thought of as a skirmish, a "probing offensive", one which determined the strength of the defences of the Capitol. No doubt the information gained will prove to be most valuable, to be used at the day of the insurrection.

The working people who took part in that Day of Reckoning performed a most valuable service. They went to Washington in order to defend their democratic rights, in this case the right to a free and fair election. The fact that they are devoted to Trump is of secondary importance.

Perhaps this will help to drive home the point, to conscious people, those who are aware of the revolutionary theories of Marx and Lenin, that the proletariat need leaders. They are doing their part, active to the best of their ability. It is not their fault that they are not class conscious. That consciousness can only come from an outside source, middle class intellectuals. That is where you take centre stage.

In other words, there is an urgent need for a proper Communist Party, one which advocates for the Dictatorship Of the Proletariat. The ball is in your court.

CHAPTER 26

POSSIBLE ARMED INSURRECTION IMMINENT

Jan 10, 2021

The events of January 6, which took place at the Capitol Building, has been variously referred to as a "riot", the "Trump insurrection", an "act of domestic terrorism", a "Day of Reckoning", an "attempted coup", an "act of treason", a "mob of anarchists", "thugs and punks engaged in disgraceful violence". By whatever name it goes by, it has the ruling class, the capitalists, the bourgeois, deeply worried. With good reason, I might add.

It is clear from the videos that most of those protesters were Caucasian working people, none of whom appeared to be terribly young. As that is the case, it follows that the revolutionary motion is now very broad and deep. It is no longer confined to minorities, young people and women. The vast majority of working people have now been swept up in the revolution. Indeed, an armed insurrection is imminent.

The protester who had the audacity to sit in the chair of the Speaker of the House left the Speaker a message: We Will Not Back Down! That protester was not joking. It is quite possible that the Day of Reckoning was the opening salvo of this, the Second American Revolution.

There are unconfirmed reports that one of the closest relatives of Donald Trump has issued a statement: "Many of us will return on January 19, carrying our weapons in support of our nations resolve, to which the world will never forget. We will come in numbers that no standing army or police agency can match."

Those are very strong words. If true, the individual who gave voice to them, could face charges of sedition or even treason. It stands to reason that he is supremely confident, possibly at the head of a vast army. We can only assume that the reference to "return on January 19" is a threat to return to the Capital, on the eve of the inauguration, this time with weapons, and take over the government. In this way, they will make sure that Biden is not sworn in as president. Trump will continue to remain in charge, possibly as the self proclaimed president or any other title he may choose to give himself.

True or not, many people are taking this statement very seriously. A highly respected journalist, a producer of documentaries, one who is considered to be ultra liberal, says that there is, on the internet, a "call for an armed march on Washington." Further, that same call is for the "patriots to march on all state capitals and take back the country, on inauguration week."

The journalist went on to say that the "terrorist attack is not over". He is convinced that Trump was behind the "insurrection", and that it was well planned. He maintains that for this reason, security was "scaled down", that members of the security service "helped the mob", showed them the location of the various offices, which were well hidden. It also helps to explain the slow response of the other police agencies.

It follows that this "Day of Reckoning" was merely a "dress rehearsal", a probing offensive, on the part of the extreme Right wing, in preparation for the main offensive, on the week of the inauguration. This is not to suggest that Trump carefully planned this out, as he is seventeen times too stupid. It is far more likely that someone, a far more devious and cunning someone, came up with this plot, and left nothing to chance. Hence the "dress rehearsal".

As the capitalists are aware of the plot of one of their own to seize power, they have taken steps to prevent this. They closed down the "right wing alternative social media platform" that Trump has been using to plot his seizure of power. As if that is about to do a world of good!

This could well set off the Second American Revolution, as no doubt Americans are not about to put up with such a coup. It may well mean full scale civil war, which no one wants. The rank and file followers of Trump are not the enemy. They have merely been misled.

Most Americans are familiar with people of the "old west", such as Billy the Kid, Jesse James, Cole Younger and Wes Hardin. Later, during the Great Depression, such people as Machine Gun Kelly, Baby Face Nelson, Dutch Schultz, Scarface Al Capone, Ma Barker and Bonnie Parker became household names. More recently, Teflon Don John Gotti and Sammy the Bull Gravano distinguished themselves. All of these people had one thing in common: They were leaders! Countless people followed them, to prison, to the gallows and to the grave.

This is to drive home the point that Trump is a leader! Countless people are following him, onto a trail of death and destruction!

This is my way of appealing to fellow conscious people, intellectuals who are aware of the revolutionary theories of Marx and Lenin. Time to get active! The only way to stop that maniac is with working class leaders, those who can give the proper proletarian leadership. That means, first and foremost, a Communist Party, Dictatorship Of the Proletariat.

By all means, create such a Party and come out with literature for the less advanced members of the working class. Raise their level of consciousness. Write in a very popular manner, using metaphors with which working people are aware. Put aside your prejudice against professional sports—I feel your pain!—and use expressions with which such workers are familiar. These could include such terms as "strike out", "home run", "grand slam", "hit one out of the park" and "hat trick", among others. The workers who support Trump are not the enemy! They have merely been misled. They need your leadership.

CHAPTER 27

"STOP THE STEAL" PROTESTS

Jan 13, 2021

The protests of January 6, in the capitol of Washington, D.C., is being referred to as a "Day of Reckoning", an "Insurrection", an Unprecedented Attack On Democracy", an "Attempted Coup", an "Instigated Riot", an "Act of Treason" by a "Mob of Anarchists". Yet those protesters were not armed!

The people who took part in that protest, speak of it in different terms. They refer to it as a peaceful protest! They prefer to think of themselves as patriots, American citizens who are performing their patriotic duty to "take back the country", to "stop the steal", as they are convinced that the election was stolen! They maintain that there was no violence during the protest! That which they are saying is far different from the "tale of destruction" being put forward by the media! They cannot both be right! They are describing two entirely different events! What is going on?

We can start by facing one fact, which is a fundamental tenet of Marxism. That is the fact that the state apparatus has been set up, by the ruling class, with the express purpose of crushing the "lower classes". In this case, we have a very clear cut example of the capitalist class, the bourgeoisie, using the state apparatus to crush the working class, the proletariat. It is also a fact that the state apparatus consists of the police, military, prisons and courts, among other things. It would appear that the capitalists are using the media as an extension of the state apparatus. As Lenin pointed out, "the bourgeoisie maintains itself in power not only by force but also by virtue of the lack of class consciousness and organization" (italics by Lenin)

As the working class is not aware of itself as a class, the capitalists are using this lack of awareness of the working class, to the advantage of the capitalists. It is of course the capitalists who own the news outlets, and they pay the journalists to "slant" the news, to present the news in a manner which favours the capitalists. There is a fine line between "slanting" the news and spreading outright lies. The journalists have crossed that line.

The journalists, who work for the capitalists, are presenting the peaceful protests as acts of a "mob", in an attempt to overthrow a democratic republic. They now say that the problem is one of "putting the genie back in the bottle". This is their way of saying that the working class revolutionary movement must be stopped, or at least diverted. As that is the case, they are presenting the peaceful protest as that of a "mob", engaged in acts of looting and destruction. Such is hardly the case.

The working people are aware that the election has been "stolen", to put it in popular terms, or falsified, to put it in technical terms. They know this for a fact because two high priced lawyers, those who work for Trump, have explained this, quite clearly, in detail. All court challenges have proven to be unsuccessful, if only because the courts are part of the state apparatus which has been set up to serve the interests of the capitalists. As the capitalists have decided that it is in their best interests to "give the boot" to Trump, the courts are not about to "rock the boat".

It is possible that those two lawyers spoke up out of a sense of democracy, because it was the "right thing to do". This is referred to as "moving to the Left". Or it could be that it was part of an elaborate plot to "git people worked up", to set the stage for an armed uprising, a possible "coup", in order to ensure that Trump remains in power. This is known as moving to the Right.

In either event, the lawyers have performed a valuable service to the working class, in the sense that they documented the manner in which all elections, or at least those of any importance, are falsified. Regardless of their intentions, the lawyers have helped to raise the level of awareness of the working class, so that they no longer have such unquestioning faith in the election process.

The concern of the capitalists is well grounded, as the working class motion is now very broad and deep. It has touched upon the the broadest strata of the workers. It has extended beyond the minorities, youth and women. The videos from that protest prove that, beyond any shadow of a doubt. That is the "genie" which the journalists are determined to "put back in the bottle". Reality check: it cannot be done!

The working class is in motion, and it is going to take something more than a pack of lies from the journalists, in order to quell the movement. In fact, it is reported that the FBI expects a major uprising, momentarily. They report that they have heard "chatter", on various "Right Wing" internet web sites, to the effect that "rioters and anarchists" have plans to occupy the capitol of Washington, D.C., as well as all the state capitols, on or before the "Day of Inauguration".

This could well be the case, and if true, amount to a full scale revolution!

The FBI further reports that it is being led and coordinated by a close family member of the president, Donald Trump. As most members of that family are not overly blessed with brains, those reports are questionable. It is more likely that such a family member is being put forward as a "figurehead". The "power behind the throne" has yet to be revealed. Not that it matters.

The important thing is that an insurrection is being planned. It may happen within the next few days. The people organizing this may be "Right Wing" or "Left Wing". If Right wing, then their goal is to seize power and install Trump as president, probably for life. If Left wing, then their goal is to seize power and establish a democratic socialist republic.

Remarkably enough, the immediate goals of the Right and the Left are identical! Both are determined to abolish the bourgeois democratic republic, that which has been set up to serve the capitalists.

For that reason, the anticipated uprising should be supported by all Leftist people. This is to say that all those who consider themselves to be socialists, democratic socialists, anarchists, Marxists, Bolsheviks, Communists or merely concerned citizens, should take part in the uprising. We should support the working class in their struggle to "Stop the Steal", to install the democratically elected president into office. That man is none other than Donald Trump, the poster child for reaction. Yet that is the goal of the working people, so we should support them!

In this way, we show respect for the working class. That is of the utmost importance. We cannot expect them to respect us, unless we in turn show them respect. At the same time, we can make it clear that we consider the problem to be one of capitalism! Trump is merely a figure head, the most visible presence. Until capitalism is overthrown, nothing of substance will change. The solution lies under socialism, in the form of the Dictatorship Of the Proletariat. This Dictatorship is required, as the capitalists are not about to resign themselves to a life of manual labour. Such a life, to which working people are accustomed, is beneath their dignity!

The use of posters and banners may help to drive home this point. As this is the time of insurrection, all means of raising the level of awareness of the working class must be used. That of course means the spoken word, as well as the printed word. Literature, of a very popular nature, must be prepared, printed out and distributed. Under no circumstances resort to vulgarity!

It is clear that a section of the bourgeoisie has determined to take advantage of the revolutionary motion of the proletariat, and to use this to their advantage! No doubt their plan is to use the workers to seize power and then to disarm the workers! At the time of the insurrection, the workers will no doubt be armed with rifles and hand guns. Then the armouries of the military must be raided, and those personal weapons must be set aside for automatic weapons. As countless working people have been well trained in the use of such weapons, thanks to the military, they will then be well equipped. Then after the seizure of power, at the time when the capitalists order the workers to throw down their weapons, the workers can respond: Come and Get Them!

At that point, we can expect the Right wing leaders to "show their true colours", as they encourage the workers to disarm, to abandon their democratic right to bear arms, as is guaranteed in the Constitution! That is not about to happen!

In this way the insurrection, instigated by the Right, can and will be used against them.

With that in mind, may I suggest putting forward a few slogans:

Scientific Socialism!

Jobs For All!

Thirty For Forty!

Dictatorship Of the Proletariat!

CHAPTER 28

TERRORISTS, ANARCHISTS AND SOCIALISTS

Jan 18, 2021

The recent revolutionary events, and in particular those of January 6, have left the capitalists dumbfounded. They, or at least the journalists, are having a terrible time. Those who are paid to "spin" the news, which is to say, to present the news in a manner which is in the best interests of the capitalists, are at their "wits end". They do not know "which way to jump".

At first, they referred to this protest as an act of "sedition", by a "mob", an "attempted coup", an "insurrection", an "act of treason", "unacceptable lawlessness", an "attack on democracy". They even compared this to the Revolution of 1776, that which gave birth to the country, but quickly "walked that back", because it is accurate! In fact, the events of 1776, those which gave rise to the American Revolutionary War, were very similar.

In those days, the protesters were referred to as the "rag tag and bob tail". Now they are being referred to as "domestic terrorists" and "anarchists". Such is hardly the case. Just as in 1776, the people who are "rising up", demanding that their democratic rights be respected, are revolutionaries!

Perhaps the most ridiculous accusation, with regard to the events of January 6, is that the protesters are being accused of an "armed insurrection". None of the protesters were carrying any weapons, unless a pole for carrying a flag can be considered a weapon. Then too, on one occasion, a fire extinguisher was thrown. If that is their idea of an armed insurrection, then they are due for a rude awakening. Very soon, they will find themselves faced with something more than flag poles and fire extinguishers! The capitalists are about to learn the true meaning of the term "armed insurrection"!

Just as the American colonials achieved independence, through an armed rebellion against British rule, so too the American working class, the proletariat, will soon achieve independence from the capitalists, the bourgeoisie, through another armed rebellion. The Americans who taking part in this rebellion, this Second American Revolution, are no more terrorists and anarchists, than were the American Colonials who took part in the First American Revolution. Both are revolutionaries.

However, as the journalists are determined to pin the label "terrorists and anarchists" on this "mob", these "right wing thugs" who dared to "desecrate" the "temple of democracy", (the capitol building) while it was in the process of conducting a "most sacred ritual", (counting Electoral Ballots) to "affirm democracy", (democracy for the capitalists), then perhaps it is best if we examine these serious charges. About the only thing these protesters have not been accused of is blasphemy!

All joking aside, these are indeed serious accusations, against the protesters. As that is the case, they require a serious response.

Let us start with the accusation that the protesters are terrorists. What are terrorists?

As Lenin explained, in What Is To Be Done?, "the terrorists bow to the spontaneity of the passionate indignation of the intellectuals, who are either incapable of linking up the revolutionary struggle with the labour movement, or lack the opportunity to do so". Can we say that the protesters were "passionate intellectuals"? From the videos, it is clear that such is hardly the case. They are working people who are convinced that the "election was stolen". They are merely defending their democratic right to a free and fair election. That is a far cry from terrorism!

The journalists are also accusing these protesters of being "anarchists". Yet anarchists are opposed to any government, any "state apparatus". As the protesters made it quite clear that, in their opinion, Trump won the election, that the election was falsified, that the "election was stolen", that Trump should be president, that he should remain the "head of state", then they cannot be anarchists, as anarchists are opposed to any state!

This brings us to socialism, in the sense that Marx and Engels expressed it. This is referred to as scientific socialism, or Marxism, or Communism, and includes the Dictatorship Of the Proletariat. This stands in stark contrast to the socialism of the idealists, those who consider socialism to be a good idea, one which can be achieved through a gradual accumulation of reforms. Good luck with that!

A similar situation developed in Russia, 1917, on the eve of the October socialist revolution. At that time, Lenin wrote State and Revolution, in preparation for the forthcoming uprising. The question of the state was of vital importance, as it is now. For that reason, if no other, all working people, or at least those taking part in the revolutionary movement, should carefully read this book.

As Lenin phrased it, "The state is the product and the manifestation of the irreconcilability of class antagonisms. The state arises when, where and to the extent that class antagonisms cannot be objectively reconciled. And, conversely, the existence of the state proves that the class antagonisms are irreconcilable . . . According to Marx, the state is an organ of class rule, an organ for the oppression of one class by another; it creates 'order', which legalizes and perpetuates this oppression by moderating the collision between the classes". (italics by Lenin)

Lenin went on to say: "if the state is a product of irreconcilable class antagonisms, if it is a power standing above society and 'increasingly alienating itself from it' (Lenin quotes Engels), it is clear that the liberation of the oppressed class is impossible, not only without violent revolution, but also without the destruction of the apparatus of state power which was created by the ruling class". (italics by Lenin)

All scientific socialists, Marxists, agree with the anarchists, to the extent that the state apparatus must be abolished! That is the one and only point upon which they are agreed. The anarchists are of the opinion that no state apparatus should take its place. The Marxists are of the opinion that the current state apparatus, which has been set up for the express purpose of crushing the working class, must be replaced with an altogether different form of state apparatus, one designed to crush the desperate and determined resistance of the capitalists.

Perhaps it is best to stress the fact, however unpleasant, that the state is a special organization of force. It is the organization of violence for the suppression of a class. After the revolution, after the proletariat seizes political power, a state apparatus will be required to keep the capitalists from returning to power! This new state apparatus, without a standing army, without a police opposed to the people, without an officialdom placed above the people, is referred to as the Dictatorship Of the Proletariat.

As for the starry eyed optimists who question the need for a state apparatus, after the revolution, after the working people seize political power, may I suggest that I respect your belief. May I also suggest that the capitalists do not have your mind set. I can further suggest that you speak to anyone who is even vaguely familiar with any billionaire. They will tell you that billionaires are all the same: they worship money! All billionaires would sooner crawl on their bellies over broken glass, rather than part with even one dime of their hard stolen wealth! Those lowlifes are not about to resign themselves to a life of "poverty", as they see it. On the contrary, they will go to any length, stoop to any depth, any subterfuge, to restore their "paradise lost". They will never give up! Nor will we ever tire of crushing them! The Dictatorship Of the Proletariat will remain in place until all classes are abolished!

Now is the time to raise the level of awareness of the working people. The events of that day, January 6, leave no room for any doubt. It may have been carefully planned, or it may have been spontaneous. Either way, it was quite surprising, to all concerned. The security at the Capitol Building was no where near as strong as it was assumed to be. Possibly no one was more surprised than the protesters, except perhaps the elected officials. The members of both houses of Congress, the Senate as well as the House of Representatives, were hiding under their chairs, afraid for their lives. True leaders of people do not hide from the people they are representing!

In response to this, in preparation for the swearing in of a new president, the capitalists have called in an additional twenty five thousand troops, members of the National Guard. The usual security forces, that of the Capitol Police, F.B.I., D.H.S. and Secret Service, among others, has proven to be a dismal failure, in regards to protecting the tender hides of the democratically elected politicians. As well, numerous Guards people are being mobilized to defend the capitals of various states.

From the videos of the "Day of Insurrection", it is clear that at least a few of the Capitol police were cooperating with the protesters, or at least remaining "neutral". This is an indication of the breadth and depth of the revolutionary motion. The capitalists have also noticed this, and are now "vetting" all members of the National Guard, or at least those who are being sent to the Capitol.

Happily, their concern is well grounded. The National Guard troops are not their finest, "crack" troops. On the contrary, they are referred to as "Citizen Soldiers". They spend most of their time as working people, only part time as "soldiers". All receive ten weeks of basic training, followed by one weekend a month, and two weeks a year, of military service. Yet they can be called up for "active duty" at any time, as they are now. All of these troops are being issued automatic weapons, in the interest of protecting the capitalists.

This could work to our advantage, as almost all of these "weekend warriors" are really working people. Well armed working people, I might add. It is doubtful that many of them will be prepared to turn their weapons upon fellow workers. If a great many people, such as hundreds of thousands, march on Washington, it is far more likely that they will turn their weapons upon their own officers. That remains to be seen.

One fact we do know for sure: class consciousness can only come from without. The working class is doing their part, rising up spontaneously. Yet without the leadership of Marxists, Communists, those who call for the Dictatorship Of the Proletariat, it will degenerate, possibly into a counter revolutionary movement. Remember the words of Engels: "Without a revolutionary theory, there can be no revolutionary movement!"(my italics) This is my somewhat less than subtle hint to all Communists. Time is not on our side. Get active. Prepare for the Dictatorship Of the Proletariat. Form a true Communist Party, DOP.

CHAPTER 29

ESCALATION OF REVOLUTION

Jan 22, 2021

On January 20 of this year, Biden was sworn in as the new American president. He immediately called upon all Americans to "put aside their differences", to "establish trust", that the "uncivil war" must end. To that end, he promised to "restore democracy", as well as the "rule of law", that it was time to "stop the madness". He is clearly a man of exceptional ambition! He neglected to mention just how he planned to achieve these noble goals.

The journalists are all agreed that the last time the country was this deeply divided, was in the days of the civil war. At that time, numerous members of Congress, both of the House of Representatives and of the Senate, were removed from office, by an act of Congress, due to "treasonable behaviour". Now calls are being heard to remove other members of Congress, also due to "treasonable behaviour", for the part they played in "instigating the insurrection" of January 6. This includes two high ranking members of the Senate. So much for "putting aside their differences"!

Very few journalists are taking seriously the speech Trump made as he left Washington, presumably for the last time. As he put it, "We will be back in some form". Yet it is very likely that he was completely serious. It was a threat that people should take to heart.

Even though Trump is no longer president, he still has a great many followers. Most of those people are convinced that the election was stolen. Among them, there are members of "citizens militias", those who are referred to as the "extreme Right wing", who are openly calling for "civil war". They are well armed, well equipped, and well trained. They are also deeply devoted to their "cause". As such, they should not be under estimated.

Their ideology is based upon something referred to as QAnon, in that Anon stands for Anonymous, and Q is a reference to an individual or possibly a group of people. Then again, it may be a reference to the peace symbol. No one is quite sure. The journalists suspect that there are a great many members, organized in hundreds of groups, all across the country.

Regardless, all of the members who identify with QAnon are firmly convinced that there is a "deep state cabul", composed of "pedophiles who worship Satan". Further, they are convinced that many high ranking members of the American government, as well as celebrities, are involved in this "deep state cabul". Without doubt, the capitalists, the bourgeoisie, are behind this nonsense.

This in no way changes the fact that a great many working people, those who are honest, hard working, law abiding, tax paying citizens, are convinced that the "election has been stolen". They are convinced that Trump won the election, and are prepared to "take action" to correct this theft. It is very likely that the capitalists plan is to use these workers, for their own purposes.

This is not to say that the rank and file members of the QAnon movement, the working people, are the enemy, as they most emphatically are not. No doubt, they compose a bloc of working people who have fallen under the influence of the capitalists. As they are members of the working class, they are honest people, tax paying citizens, who are not interested in the profits of the capitalists. They are deeply interested in defending their democratic rights, as is guaranteed in the Constitution, and in saving children from pedophiles, properly so. They have merely been misled.

There can be no doubt that capitalism is in a state of crisis. The current death toll, in America, as a result of the virus, is well over 400,000 and steadily rising. The medical system is in danger of collapse. Already, numerous hospitals are turning away patients. They have no choice in the matter, as they are filled to capacity. The unemployment rate is at a level not seen since the days of the Great Depression. The national debt is at unimaginable levels. As soon as the moratorium on evictions expires, it is expected that an additional forty million Americans will be homeless! Yet the stock market is soaring! The billionaires are amassing ever more billions! It is truly the "best of times, the worst of times".

Then again, the capitalists are aware that they can no longer rule in the old way, due to the various crises in capitalism, and have to change their method of rule. As that is the case, they have dreamed up this QAnon nonsense. The idea is to appeal to the less advanced members of the working class, and use them against the more advanced workers. It is very likely that the capitalists plan, in this way, to "mount a coup", to seize political power, to set up Trump as a figure head president, using the disillusioned bloc of workers.

A similar situation existed in Russia, in the spring of 1917. At that time, according to Lenin, the leaders of several political parties had "allowed themselves to be deceived by the capitalists, and in their turn, are deceiving the people". His solution to this problem was to fight with the weapon of "comradely persuasion", with regard to the working people, the rank and file, but not their leaders.

In much the same way, it is now up to Marxists, Communists, to approach the followers of QAnon, among the American working people, in a comradely manner. Our goal must be to raise their level of awareness, to persuade them that their grievances are legitimate, but that their approach is mistaken. As most of these working people are literate and many no doubt have computers, this may not be as difficult as it once was. May I suggest literature of a very popular nature, although certainly not vulgar, appealing to them to join our cause.

It is completely understandable that the American working people have lost all faith in the government officials, those who have been elected to political office. Who can blame them?

As for those who consider this QAnon movement to be of little importance, bear in mind the words of Lenin. He mentioned that such a deception of the working people could lead to the defeat of the revolution! As such is the case, it is hardly a joking matter.

This stands in stark contrast to the latest events in the city of Seattle. The workers in that city continue to be among the leaders of the American revolution. Many of them attacked the ICE building, in that ICE stands for Immigration and

Customs Enforcement. It is one of the most hated of all government agencies. As well, they attacked the Democratic Party headquarters, and the federal courthouse. No doubt this will serve as an inspiration to all working people.

It is significant that the "protesters", those who are really revolutionaries, have learned new and improved tactics. They are reported to have used pepper ball guns (what ever that is) and "electronic control weapons similar to tasers", wore helmets and gas masks, carried shields, and threw rocks and fireworks. This was clearly not a spontaneous event. The revolutionaries were well armed and equipped. No doubt, leaders have emerged from their midst, competent, well respected people. What is more, they are no longer content to occupy part of the city. The revolutionaries are now on the offensive. This amounts to a major escalation of the revolution.

These newly emerged leaders are certainly competent, and may, or may not, be Communists. It is possible that a proper Communist Party has taken shape, one which calls for the Dictatorship Of the Proletariat. If that is the case, it only stands to reason that the members should take reasonable precautions, such as using the "dark net". Either way, these actions should inspire conscious people, Marxists, to become active. The revolution has just taken a giant step forward. Take part in the formation of the Communist Party. Prepare for the Dictatorship Of the Proletariat.

CHAPTER 30

POSSIBLY TWO APEX PREDATORS IN OKANAGAN LAKE

Jan 29, 2021

Without doubt, there is a huge predator in Okanagan Lake, commonly referred to as Ogopogo. As I have previously documented, this animal is almost certainly an ichthyosaur, a prehistoric swimming animal, thought to be extinct. It is classified as a reptile, even though the evidence suggests that it is a mammal. Yet the latest information I have received, suggests the existence of a second species of apex predator, one which matches the description of an ancient species of whale, also thought to be extinct, that of basilosaurus.

Of course, apex predators kill each other at every opportunity, so the idea of two apex predators existing, in one fresh water lake, may sound rather unlikely. At least, that was my opinion. Now I am not so sure. There have been reports of sprays of water rising from the surface of the lake, similar to the spray released by whales, when they first come to the surface. Whalers used to watch for these sprays when hunting whales, and the crew would announce "thar she blows"! It was proven to be an effective hunting technique, so effective that the population of whales was severely depleted. Now that strict hunting regulations have been put into effect, the population of whales has steadily increased.

The second piece of information that has come to my attention, has been provided by scuba divers. They report the existence of "tracks" on the bottom of the lake. Clearly something has been "walking" underwater!

All scientists are agreed that there was a time, fifty million years ago, when all whales had legs and walked on land. Then as different species of whales took to the water, they gradually lost their legs, as they had no use for them. From an evolutionary viewpoint, this makes perfect sense. Nature has no use for appendages which serve no useful purpose.

The point being that if basilosaurus still exists, and if it still has legs, then it must use those legs! Otherwise, it would have lost them, many millions of years ago. Perhaps the best way to proceed is to compare them to species which still exist.

Possibly the closest living relative to basilosaurus is the hippopotamus, or hippos. These animals spend the day light hours in the water, coming out of the water to graze, only in the coolness of the night. They consume a great deal of vegetation, mainly in the form of grass, although they have also been known to eat meat.

It is entirely possible that basilosaurus still exists, and has adopted a similar life style. They are apex predators and consume a great deal of meat, but may also consume vegetation. Assuming that to be the case, then they may come out of the water only after dark. At that time they may walk on land, which would explain the continued existence of the legs on this whale. It would also explain the fact that they are rarely seen.

We can compare them to other apex predators, in other parts of the world, and in particular Africa. On the plains of that continent, we have lions and hyenas living together, sharing the same habitat, although certainly not peacefully. The scientists who study those animals are convinced that they hate each other! Nothing else can explain the enthusiasm with which members of one species torment the other! In fact, members of each species go to considerable length, and on a regular basis, to make the lives of the members of the other species, as miserable as possible. Yet they are so evenly matched, and the plains are so vast, that neither species has managed to eradicate the other.

It is entirely possible that a similar situation exists in Okanagan Lake. We may have two apex predators, each killing the other at every opportunity, as is characteristic of apex predators. Yet due to the size of the lake, one is unable to wipe out the other.

Then again, there may be only one apex predator in Okanagan Lake, and that predator may not be an ichthyosaur. I could be completely mistaken. Not for the first time, I might add. The important thing is that we prove the existence of this animal. With that in mind, it is important that we consider all possibilities.

CHAPTER 31

CAPITALISM IS IN ITS DEATH THROES

Jan 29, 2021

It is clear that the capitalists are at their "wits end", not sure "which way to jump", to put it in popular terms. In Washington, the top politicians are calling for unity, while at the same time demanding the impeachment of Trump, even though he is no longer president, (which makes no sense!) and the removal from office of various top politicians, from both the Senate and the House of Representatives. (which makes even less sense) In fact, a top Republican politician is telling other Republicans to stop attacking each other, or as he put it, in terms which were something less than eloquent, to "cut that crap out". (This is their idea of unity!)

This is merely an indication of just how confused the bourgeois politicians have become. As Lenin phrased it, in a similar situation, referring to the idiotic remarks of a bourgeois politician, "this argument shows in particular how muddled even the most intelligent members of the bourgeoisie have become and how they cannot help committing irreparable blunders. That, in fact, is what will bring about the downfall of the bourgeoisie".

The only difference between the time in which Lenin worked and the present, lies in the fact that the present situation is much simpler. We no longer have to deal with the class of people known as the nobility. As well, the peasantry and the petty bourgeois, the middle class, have been pretty well wiped out. The bourgeois have simplified the class struggle, in that they have largely succeeded in destroying those classes. Now it is a simple matter of workers versus capitalists, proletarians versus bourgeois. Yet the bourgeois is still as confused as ever!

In addition, the Speaker of the House, Nancy Pelosi, recently announced that "the enemy is within the House of Representatives". In this, she is correct, and that is an indication of the strength of the revolutionary movement. There are now members of Congress who are revolutionary!

As for those who find this to be shocking, may I suggest that people read the Communist Manifesto, written by Marx and Engels. They explain this quite clearly: "In times when the class struggle nears the decisive hour, the process of dissolution going on within the ruling class, in fact within the whole range of old society, assumes such a violent, glaring character, that a small section of the ruling class cuts itself adrift and joins the revolutionary class, the class that holds the future in its hands".

There can be no doubt that the class struggle is near the "decisive hour", that the "dissolution going on within the ruling class", in this case the capitalists, the billionaires, the bourgeoisie, has caused a "small section" of the bourgeoisie to "cut itself adrift", and that this small section has joined the "revolutionary class", in this case the workers, the proletariat, the class which "holds the future in its hands".

This is not to say that the bourgeois is entirely stupid, and in fact the sharper ones have noticed this revolutionary motion. In response, they recommend the building of another wall, this time a "permanent wall", (as opposed to a temporary wall?) around the Capitol Building. As if a flimsy wall is going to stop a million angry workers! They do not know much about workers! Yet the bourgeois certainly do love their walls! Such childish faith in flimsy walls is touching! We will see how strong their faith is, when the workers put that wall to the test!

The press, which serves the capitalists so well, is having a difficult time in presenting the news in a manner which is favourable to the bourgeois. Now the journalists have been forced to admit that even before the Capitol Building was "stormed" on January 6, another Capitol Building, in the state of Oregon, was also "stormed". As that is the case, it is reasonable to conclude that the working class, in the state of Oregon, and especially in the city of Seattle, is a leader of the American revolution.

In particular, there are scattered reports that the workers who have occupied part of Seattle, as well as other parts of Oregon, are now well organized and on the offensive. Videos show them with helmets and shields, and by now, they very likely have been armed with "night sticks" or clubs. As well, the press reports that they have "bullet proof vests", or body armour. (The journalists also think this is terrible!) That is in addition to the tasers, pepper ball guns and "fireworks". We should not lose sight of the fact that those fireworks are nothing less that gun powder!

As yet, there are no reports of those workers being armed with slings. With a little practice, and armed with the proper ammunition, such as marbles, slingers can become surprisingly accurate. The advantage of marbles, as ammunition, is that each is precisely the same size and weight. Such weapons, as well as tasers, can be quite effective when used against people mounted on horses. When a horse is struck with a taser or a marble, the horse will very likely give the rider flying lessons.

No doubt, the capitalists will continue with the tried and proven method of using water cannons against the revolutionaries. The water trucks get their water from fire hydrants, so that a simple way to neutralize the water cannons is with the use of pipe wrenches, in order to open up as many of the fire hydrants as possible. In that way, the water pressure will quickly drop to nil, so that there will be no water for the water cannons.

The journalists are unwilling, or unable, to refer to the people who are protesting as revolutionaries. Instead, they prefer to use the terms "rioters", "anarchists" or "domestic terrorists". Possibly the idea of another American revolution is too terrible for words. Or possibly it is not in their interests to mention the word. Either way, very soon they are about to learn the meaning of the word.

As an indication of the confusion surrounding the revolutionary uprising, a statement by the head of the Republican Party of Oregon is revealing: "Whereas there is growing evidence that the violence at the Capitol was a 'false flag' operation designed to discredit President Trump, his supporters, and all conservative Republicans; this provided the sham motivation to impeach President Trump in order to advance the Democratic goal of seizing total power, in a frightening parallel to the February 1933 burning of the German Reichstag".

I mention this merely as an example of the "process of dissolution" going on within the bourgeoisie. They are turning upon each other, much as mad dogs bite each other.

POLITICAL AND SCIENTIFIC ARTICLES, VOLUME 3

The DHS has also issued a bulletin to the effect that there is a "heightened threat from domestic violent extremists". That same bulletin also mentions the fact that "domestic terrorists" may be motivated by a range of issues, "including the virus".

If nothing else, this provides a very clear cut example of the difference of outlook of the two classes, workers and capitalists. Working people are concerned with the suffering and death of so many of their fellow workers, while the capitalists are concerned that it may give rise to a "threat from domestic violent extremists". In other words, in simple English, the capitalists are afraid that the working people, whom they refer to as "domestic violent extremists" and "domestic terrorists", may revolt!

It is also clear that the labels of "rioters", "anarchists" and "terrorists" has been replaced by "domestic violent extremists" and "domestic terrorists". Perhaps the working class revolutionaries have been given a promotion!

The death rate due to the virus is perhaps the highest in the world, because the one and only way to control the spread of the virus is through social isolation. The trouble is that people who are not moving, are also not spending their money. Americans are being encouraged to travel and enjoy themselves. Planes, bars and clubs are hot spots for the virus, yet that is precisely the places that people are being encouraged to frequent. Profits before people!

The bourgeois have clearly not learned the lessons of the first American revolution, or of the following French revolution, of 1789. For that matter, they have absolutely failed to grasp the significance of the February Revolution of Russia, 1917. That Revolution, which resulted in the overthrow of the Russian Czar, was completely spontaneous. There were no leaders! We know this for a fact, because all the leaders of the workers and peasants, by which I mean the Marxists, had been thrown in prison and either killed or exiled.

Lenin was one of the Marxists whom had been first thrown in prison and later exiled. At the time of the February revolution of 1917, he was living in Switzerland. It was not until April of that year, that he was able to return to Saint Petersburg, the capital of Russia. He was then able to complete the revolution, to lead the Russian common people to victory over the nobility, landlords and capitalists, on October 25 (old style calendar) or November 7 (new style calendar) of 1917. A Soviet Socialist Republic was established, under the Dictatorship Of the Proletariat.

The point is that working people spontaneously get into motion, and on occasion, manage some very impressive victories. The overthrow of the Russian Czar was one such victory. The occupation of the Capitol Building, on January 6 of this year, was also quite impressive.

Yet the fact remains that the Russian working people were not capable of carrying through the revolution to scientific socialism. Through no fault of their own, they were not class conscious. That consciousness was brought to them by the Russian Communist Party, with Lenin as the leader. Armed with that knowledge, the working people of Russia were then able to overthrow the capitalists and establish a proper socialist republic, under the Dictatorship Of the Proletariat.

A similar situation exists today in America. The American workers have managed to secure some impressive victories, and for this they deserve full credit. Yet it is safe to say that the American workers can carry the revolution no further. They too are not class conscious. They require knowledge, which can only be brought to them by Marxist intellectuals. Of necessity, most of these intellectuals will be middle class, or more likely former members of the middle class. The capitalists will see to that!

As for those who are prejudiced against middle class intellectuals, bear in mind the words of Lenin: "According to their social status, the founders of modern scientific socialism, Marx and Engels, themselves belonged to the bourgeois intelligentsia".

Now it is up to modern day bourgeois intellectuals to raise the level of awareness of the American proletariat, or at least that of the most advanced workers, to the level of conscious people, which is to say Marxists. They have to be made aware of the necessity of overthrowing the capitalists, the billionaires, the bourgeoisie, of smashing the existing state machine, and replacing it with a proletarian state apparatus, to be used to crush the desperate and determined resistance of the capitalists. This new state apparatus is referred to as the Dictatorship Of the Proletariat.

As Lenin went on to state, quite clearly, "Without a revolutionary theory, there can be no revolutionary movement". He further stated that "the role of vanguard can be fulfilled only by a party that is guided by an advanced theory. (italics by Lenin) He placed the preceding in italics as a means of stressing the importance of a truly scientific socialist Communist Party, one which calls for the Dictatorship Of the Proletariat. Without such a Party, the revolution is in danger of being diverted onto a Right Wing tangent.

Here too, the Communist Manifesto makes it quite clear that the purpose of the Communist Party is the "formation of the proletariat into a class, overthrow of the bourgeois supremacy, conquest of political power by the proletariat".

That is a fact, just as it is also a fact that the current crisis in capitalism has forced a great many middle class intellectuals into the ranks of the proletariat. They bring with them their knowledge of the revolutionary theories of Marx and Lenin. To such people, I can only say that now is the time to become active, to put those theories to good use, to form a true Communist Party, Dictatorship Of the Proletariat, and lead this, the Second American Revolution, to victory. The workers are doing their part. Now it is time for you intellectuals, scientific socialists, true Marxists, to do your part. The fate of the Second American Revolution depends on this.

www.ingramcontent.com/pod-product-compliance
Lightning Source LLC
Chambersburg PA
CBHW062117020426
42335CB00013B/1004